# OCCUPATIONAL DISORDERS

## A Treatment Guide for Therapists

## MARTIN KANTOR

Westport, Connecticut
London

**Library of Congress Cataloging-in-Publication Data**

Kantor, Martin.
    Occupational disorders : a treatment guide for therapists / Martin
Kantor.
        p.    cm.
    Includes bibliographical references and index.
    ISBN 0–275–95529–X (alk. paper)
    1. Industrial psychiatry.  2. Occupational diseases—Psychological
aspects.  3. Psychology, Industrial.  I. Title.
    [DNLM:  1. Occupational Diseases—therapy.  2. Occupational
Diseases—psychology.  3. Occupational Diseases—diagnosis.  WA 400
K160   1997]
RC967.5.K36   1997
616.89—dc20
DNLM/DLC
for Library of Congress            96–28536

British Library Cataloguing in Publication Data is available.

Library of Congress Catalog Card Number: 96–28536
ISBN: 0–275–95529–X

First published in 1997

Praeger Publishers, 88 Post Road West, Westport, CT 06881
An imprint of Greenwood Publishing Group, Inc.

Printed in the United States of America

∞™

The paper used in this book complies with the
Permanent Paper Standard issued by the National
Information Standards Organization (Z39.48–1984).

10 9 8 7 6 5 4 3 2 1

This book was designed and typeset by Letra Libre, 1705 Fourteenth Street,
Suite 391, Boulder, Colorado 80302.

*To M. E. C.*

There's no sort of work . . . that could ever be done well if you minded what fools say. You must have it inside you that your plan is right, and that plan you must follow (p. 399).

It always remains true that if we had been greater, circumstances would have been less strong against us (p. 568).

—*George Eliot,* Middlemarch

# Contents

*Acknowledgments*                                                      xiii

1   Introduction                                                          1

    About This Book and Its Author, 5


        **Part 1   Endogenous Occupational Disorders**

2   Somatoform Occupational Disorders                                   11

    General Principles, 11
    Classification, 13
    Developmental Factors, 14
    Cause, 14
    Making the Diagnosis, 15
    The Individual Disorders, 20

3   Depressive Occupational Disorder                                    37

    Diagnosing Depression, 37
    Exogenous Factors, 38
    Endogenous Depression, 47
    Treatment, 51
    An Overview, 55

4   Anxiety Occupational Disorder                                       59

    Manifestations, 59
    Causes, 62
    Cure, 67

5   Phobic Occupational Disorder                                        71

    Specific Phobias, 73
    Treatment, 78
    Summary, 85

6   Obsessive-Compulsive Occupational Disorder                    87
    Manifestations, 87
    Cause, 92
    Treatment, 93

7   Sexual Disorders Occupational Disorders                      101
    Manifestations, 101
    Cause, 102
    Treatment, 103

8   Personality Disorders Occupational Disorders                 105
    Schizophrenia and the Schizophrenic Spectrum, 106
    Other Personality Disorders, 109

9   Job Dissatisfaction                                          119
    Manifestations, 119
    Psychotherapy, 123

10  Non–*DSM-IV* Occupational Disorders                          125
    Workaholism, 125
    Overload, 125
    Depletion, 127
    Burnout, 128
    Flooding, 129

        **Part 2   Exogenous (Reactive) Occupational Disorders**

11  Exogenous (Reactive) Occupational Disorders                  133
    The Literature, 134
    Specific Sources of Stress and Trauma, 134
    Treatment, 152

                    **Part 3   Treatment**

12  An Overview of Treatment                                     159
    The Need to Make an Adequate Diagnosis, 160
    The Need to Use an Eclectic Treatment Approach, 161

13  Psychoanalytic/Psychodynamic Approach                        165
    The Role of Individual Contribution/Responsibility, 167
    The Role of the Past, 169
    The Role of Dreams/Dream Analysis, 178
    Slips of the Tongue, 188
    Summary, 188

14   Cognitive Therapy                                                    191
     Specific Cognitive Errors, 193
     Cause, 202
     Treatment, 204

15   Supportive Therapy                                                   207
     What It Does, 207
     What It Does Not Do, 208
     Specific Supportive Techniques, 209

16   A Step-by-Step Guide to Treating Occupational Disorders              213
     Step 1: Recognizing the Patient's Immediate Needs, 213
     Step 2: Recognizing Disorder When and Where It Exists, 214
     Step 3: Making a Proper Diagnosis, 215
     Step 4: Determining What Is Causing the Disorder, 219
     Step 5: Treating the Disorder, 221

17   Handling Low Self-Esteem and Guilt                                   229
     Low Self-Esteem, 229
     Guilt, 234
     Treatment, 236


*Bibliography*                                                            245
*Index*                                                                   249

# Acknowledgments

I would like to acknowledge the editorial assistance given to me by Virginia E. McCullough and thank her for her invaluable contribution to my book.

*Martin Kantor*

# 1

## Introduction

Occupational disorders do not take life, they merely ruin it. The victims of occupational disorders are rarely hospitalized or die by their own hand. Instead they are up and about, but constantly miserable and wishing they were dead. Every Monday morning, at work, they ache for Friday night to come. Then every Friday night, at home, they fear the coming of Monday morning. Their careers are either compromised or in a shambles, with some stuck in dead-end jobs, mired at the bottom of the corporate ladder, and others closer to the top of the ladder, but tottering and about to fall off.

The scientific literature offers very little in the way of assistance to those who need help with their occupational disorder. Just as some art critics see representational as inferior to abstract art, and just as some scientists see applied as inferior to abstract science, psychiatrists and other mental health professionals tend to view occupational disorders as inferior disorders, unworthy of serious consideration. As a result, the subject has not attracted much scientific interest. Instead it has remained a stepchild resolutely cloistered and neglected by the rest of the family. The *Diagnostic and Statistical Manual of Mental Disorders, 4th edition (DSM-IV)* focuses more on the interpersonal than the occupational manifestations of the disorders it studies. Borderline personality disorder, for example, is discussed almost exclusively in terms of problems with love, not problems with work. It is as if borderlines merge and emerge with (and idealize and devalue) others not 9 to 5 Monday through Friday, but nights and weekends only. There is a separate branch of the mental health professions devoted to occupational disorders, and this has its own, often autistic, terminology. What the *DSM-IV* calls conversion symptoms the occupational disorders branch of the mental health profession calls writer's cramp or repetitive strain injury. Often these professionals diagnose occupational disorders improperly.

They give their patients diagnostic labels more vague than the specific ones they merit, like burnout when they have a depression; more specific than their vague symptoms warrant, like Epstein-Barr chronic fatigue when they are suffering from general malaise or transient insomnia; or more wrong than right, as when a patient with hysterical paresis of a hand is said to have repetitive strain injury, or a patient with an inadequate personality disorder is said to be suffering from burnout. And they have a whole new set of dynamics. Some of their patients who in fact suffer from unconscious conflicts and introjected anger are said to suffer mainly from conscious stress and burnout. Others who in fact are under stress and are burned out are believed to be in conflict, so that all repetitive strain injury is called conversion even when it is due to a poorly designed computer keyboard; all headaches are viewed as psychosomatic, even when they are due to poor light; and all shortness of breath is believed to be a symptom of anxiety, even when it is the building that is making its inhabitants sick.

In the lay literature the occupational disorders are not overlooked so much as they are mishandled. The subject has a certain following or notoriety. However, the problem is one of questionable, and even disturbing, practices. Many of the more popular books and papers on the subject are by people without training in their field, who cannot bring much expertise to their subject. Often the author's main qualification is having suffered the disorder personally. Many books on writer's block are by writers who have themselves suffered from block, and while there are notable advantages to having been there, there are also limitations to the extent to which empathy is a substitute for science. These writers tend to view occupational disorders as trivial problems, and they expect everyone to have some difficulty working. They fail to address (1) both the serious psychological problems and the long-term suffering that professional disorders cause, and (2) the deep psychological causes of the disorders themselves; they overlook completely such factors as a fear of success, which can cause a CEO to masochistically turn an intended corporate expansion into what Peter Lynch (Lynch & Rothchild, 1989) calls a corporate "diworseification" (pp. 146–150). In particular, we are given one-size-fits-all formulations that do not recognize the importance of the differences between people. Yet only some workers respond to a given stress, because stress is only stress when it is allowed to cut deep into the psyche in a personal way. This is a particularly important consideration for treatment because while therapists cannot change the world, I know that they can change their patients' reactions to it. I have seen this happen regularly with my patients.

For example, Emil Pascarelli and Deborah Quilter's (1994) book *Repetitive Strain Injury: A Computer User's Guide* is coauthored by a worker

(Quilter) who herself developed a hand syndrome. I feel that her personal involvement makes a moving story more than a scientific presentation. Too often, in my opinion, she allows her emotions to obscure her judgment and thus she overlooks classical principles to make a point about the suffering of humankind in general and about her goals as a savior of humankind in particular. Both authors' causality is a simplistic one whose insights cover the same ground as what is generally known by a lay audience and are limited to such superficial external causes as overwork, poor physical working conditions, the stress of corporate downsizing, and the trauma of being in an uncertain business climate. There is too much emphasis on the stress corporations put on their workers and too little emphasis on what workers do to themselves and to their corporations. In the authors' view, important internal emotional factors are mostly the response to, not the cause of, occupational disability. Repetitive strain injury does not develop because a worker is angry with the company; the worker is angry with the company because repetitive strain injury has developed. Workers are depressed because they were downsized, never downsized because they are depressed. Workers are downsized because their corporation contracts, never because they are incompetent; they then flounder because there are no replacement jobs—it is not the case that they do not find replacement jobs because they are floundering. This not-me view of the world predictably leads to a not-me therapeutic approach. For example, the authors suggest improving posture at the work station to treat all hand syndromes even when these originate in a Reichian characterological armoring,[1] a tensing up that makes the worker vulnerable to an injury that might otherwise not be injurious. It is temporarily reassuring for workers to feel that they play no role in their disorder. But it hurts them in the long run because, since they do not understand the past, they do not bother looking to the future and making course corrections to spare themselves a repeat performance. It also leads to a problematic therapeutic approach that eschews sound therapeutic practices developed over the years. As if Sigmund Freud and Aaron Beck had never lived, these authors make up new treatment approaches as they go along and do not offer their patients psychodynamic, interpersonal, cognitive, or supportive treatment but instead shunt them off to social engineering groups, where they commiserate with each other about what the corporation is doing to

---

1. Wilhelm Reich (1959) says, "The character consists in a chronic rigidity [protecting] the ego against external and internal dangers [that] can rightly be called an armor" (p. 145).

them, without understanding what they might be doing to themselves and to their corporations.

A major reason many therapists are floundering is that there is not much written on the specifics of treating occupational disorders. Some texts are too general; they can do no better than emphasize the professional and personal challenges to the psychiatrist treating patients with occupational disorders. They offer only superficial exercises that are suitable and helpful for minor, transient, day-to-day work problems, such as anxiety over asking for a raise, but do not adequately address the serious disorders. Yet occupational disorder is often more severe than a few weeks of compromised productivity or the barren creative ground experienced by writers (or idea people in industry) in between projects; and the serious disorders are often the ones counselors, psychotherapists, and their patients have to face. The following case is from my patient files:[2]

> A therapist writing on how to treat the occupational disorders recommended that tense patients to relieve stress say the mantra "om" as they exhale. She treated writer's block by "unleashing the writer within," though writer's blocks, and their cure, like all the occupational disorders and their cure, are often due to inhibitions that are too fixed and deep to yield to a simple unleashing—that is, like a dog that stays by its master's side through thick and thin, the disorder stays put, even after the leash has been removed. She fed them one-size-fits-all platitudes like, "be loyal to yourself, not your company," which was just the wrong advice for certain patients, especially borderlines whose sense of self was too unstable to permit them to function adequately without the structure provided by their group and who should have been told instead, "Find yourself another corporation to identify with as soon as possible." Sometimes her platitidues came uncomfortably close to metaphorical or concrete thinking. For example, in treating writers with writer's block she in effect recommended sharpening pencils as a way to sharpen the mind. Child-like was the overoptimism inherent in her belief that positive thinking could inspire positive action and positive action was enough to create positive results. Most blocked writers thought of such advice as "think positively" or "keep at it" themselves, and would follow their own advice if they could, but they cannot. So they ended up feeling even more like a total failure. After all, they concluded, they must be really lazy or untalented if they cannot follow a few easy tips, and get over this "thing" that is holding them back.

---

2. Excerpts from my cases appear throughout the text. All excerpts without a source citation are from my personal notes and case studies.

## ABOUT THIS BOOK AND ITS AUTHOR

I am a psychiatrist with experience in evaluating patients suffering from occupational disorders and helping them take charge of their lives and careers by understanding and solving their occupational problems. Thus, although this book is primarily meant as a how-to guide for on-the-job counselors and office-based therapists, its relative absence of jargon and its patient-oriented approach make it useful for actual or potential patients. It will help them decide if they need therapy and what therapy they need. For those already in treatment, it will help them determine if they are getting what they need and the most out of their therapy.

This book emphasizes how most of the occupational disorders are little more than 9 to 5 manifestations of a larger physical or emotional (*DSM-IV*) disorder. For example, what is popularly called repetitive strain injury is probably either a tendonitis (or its equivalent) or a conversion disorder, while burnout is really just another word for adjustment disorder, posttraumatic stress disorder, or reactive depression. Many of the occupational disorders are personality disorders, so we must ask not only "What kind of disorder does this patient have?" but also "What kind of patient does this disorder have?" This book also discusses those occupational disorders that do not have a *DSM-IV* counterpart, such as the ones primarily due to flooding because of overstimulation (which makes the worker unable to master and integrate excitement) and the ones primarily due to depletion (in which the worker simply becomes exhausted, having done more than his or her share, or runs out of ideas, having spent all his or her resources).

This book delves deeply into the dynamic causes of occupational disorders. It emphasizes that most work disorders originate at least partly in the worker's early relationships. Often workers get sick because the boss reminds them of their hostile father, co-workers remind them of their competitive siblings, and underlings remind them of the new baby that displaced them from being their mother's favorite. Hand syndromes, when not due to repetitive strain, can be a symbolic fist made at a boss who disappoints and angers the patient, just like father did. Or, while some chronic fatigue syndromes are due to biochemical factors, others are due to feeling tired of and fed up with stubborn subordinates, who moreover remind the worker of a rigid, unyielding, uncooperative brother or sister. While some of the same psychodynamic features are present in all of the occupational disorders (for example, many patients suffer because they are masochistic or fear success), in many cases unique dynamic factors distinguish one occupational disorder from another, and these differences have both important diagnostic and therapeutic significance. In particular, this book stresses the importance of the differences between the endogenous, or internally caused, and the exogenous, or stress-related, disorders and emphasizes the different therapeutic approaches for each.

Regarding treatment, this book goes beyond such general statements as "stress that plays a role in the development of occupational disorders should be relieved," and instead specifies the different kinds of stress, shows how they affect the individual, and states what, if anything, can be done to relieve the stress.

This book describes in detail how much of what we call stress originates in a corporation's mishandling of its workers, creating a hostile climate that workers must contend with. This is an area not dealt with adequately in most studies, which maintain far too much silence about the way in which society as a whole and the corporations and bureaucracies that represent that society fail to nurture—or actually abuse—their most talented people. A certain amount of mishandling, or outright abuse, is probably unavoidable. Downsizing is going to occur in today's business world. Incompetent bosses will always exist (like the one that insisted a worker come back to run a test although he was sick and although he could have done the test before he became sick if only the boss had done the preparation she was supposed to do before the test could be run). There will always be hostile co-workers attacking from the sides and hostile underlings attacking from below, putting the worker in the middle, trying to make sense of it all and survive. But often corporations abuse their workers not gratuitously, without thinking about what they are doing, but deliberately and purposefully. For example, there are envious bureaucracies just as there are envious people, and they are out to prove Victor Hugo's (1982; originally published 1862) contention that genius invites hostility (p. 995) until, as one worker put it, "the smart ones become extinct, while the dodoes still survive." In these bureaucracies the more intelligent, creative, effective, and talented workers are not only the most exposed, the least protected, and the most vulnerable, but the ones deliberately targeted for extinction because they cross, offend, or threaten those in power. So they are the ones who fall ill and leave, and ultimately their corporation sinks to a lower level and functions marginally, or shuts its doors permanently.

> At a hospital where I worked, a brilliant lay analyst who subsequently wrote a number of original and effective psychology books on creativity was forced out in the belief that because she was unusual, . . . she was crazy. In contrast, a not-so-brilliant, and far less original, psychiatrist stayed on for years, though unable to do any better than to brood aloud on an almost daily basis about the difficulty of distinguishing, in any given

case, between the causal effects of nature and those of nurture. It seems as if in hospitals, as in literature, politics, and all of life, what is exceptional is what threatens, and what is unexceptional is what sells.

My treatment approach is an eclectic one—that is, it is a combination of those facets of psychodynamic, interpersonal, existential, cognitive/ behavioral, and supportive techniques that I have found particularly useful in overcoming occupational disorders. I adapt the method as a whole to the special needs of patients who have a disorder that primarily affects not their inner peace of mind or their interpersonal relationships, but their job performance and their careers.

Throughout I make two important points repeatedly. The first is that occupational disorder is neither so mysterious that it cannot be understood nor so entrenched and resistant that therapists and their patients should continue to feel that it is untreatable. The second is that treating occupational disorder is crucial not only for the individual affected but also because in any society individual disorders coalesce to create a social problem. While I do not exactly point the way out of what we might call today's age of iron into a new golden Elizabethan era, I do recognize that we seem to be in the middle of an epidemic of anticreativity that is bringing many of us down, and I suggest that we study this raging epidemic from a patient-centered viewpoint to see if we can arrive at at least a partial answer to pressing and still unanswered questions about creativity, ranging from Edward Gibbon's (1776–1788) question about why Rome declined and fell to a question we hear more and more today: When are we going to have a new Beethoven?

PART ONE

# Endogenous
# Occupational Disorders

# 2

## Somatoform Occupational Disorders

### GENERAL PRINCIPLES

#### Description

The somatoform disorders, according to the *Diagnostic and Statistical Manual of Mental Disorders*, 3rd edition, revised (*DSM-III-R*) as quoted by G. Alan Stoudemire in the *American Psychiatric Press Textbook of Psychiatry* (1988), consist of "physical symptoms suggesting physical disorder for which there are no demonstrable organic findings or known physiologic mechanisms, and for which there is positive evidence, or a strong presumption, that the symptoms are linked to psychological factors or conflicts" (p. 533). A patient's emotional problems are expressed not as such but in physical terms, as a medical disorder, like gastritis, or as a neurological disorder, like a weakness of the muscles of the hand. Typically, the symptoms are accompanied by an emotional overlay that appears to be the result of, when it is in fact the cause of, the physical condition.

Although somatoform symptoms are extremely common in the workplace and create much unnecessary suffering for workers and unnecessary expense for their employers, the workers themselves, the companies that employ them, and the therapists that treat them tend either to overlook them entirely or to misdiagnose them and then mistreat them accordingly. All three close ranks to make what I call a pathognomonic "somatoform scenario," in which

- Workers, although they have an emotional disorder, think they have a physical illness and say that "they would work, if it weren't for that."

- Workers' companies think otherwise, and correctly diagnose the illness as emotional, but incorrectly argue that the patients are malingering because it is all in their head, criticize them for misbehaving, and demand that they recant and return to work.
- Therapists, although they recognize that the patients are ill and not malingering their illness, misdiagnose and mistreat an emotional as a physical disorder, offering ineffective treatment that does no good or dangerous treatment that leaves the patient even more disabled than before.

A pianist could not move his right hand due to conversion disorder, so he had to retire from performing and become a conductor. His doctors diagnosed psoriatic arthritis without the psoriasis and offered him first physical medicine/rehabilitation and acupuncture, and then surgery on his hand to release his tendons, believed frozen due to inflammation.

His case contrasts to that of another patient who developed RSI (repetitive strain injury) due to a tendonitis of the hand associated with "tennis elbow," and then was misdiagnosed as having a conversion disorder and given psychotherapy when rest, painkillers, and special exercises, accompanied by a change of work habits, were indicated. Not only was needed treatment withheld, but the patient felt that he was being called "emotional," "neurotic," or "crazy." While there is no crime in having an emotional disorder, he felt there was, and he gave up his job to deny any possibility that he was a "psychiatric case"—really, a criminal.

Somatoform disorder can be the result of endogenous or exogenous psychological factors. A somatoform disorder may be the result of conflict over sexual or angry feelings. In this case the somatoform disorder is a symbolic expression, in body language, of the patient's conflicts and their attempted resolution. Or it may be the result of stress, in which case the somatoform disorder is in effect a primitive reaction, like developing gooseflesh or passing out when danger looms. In both cases there is what Felix Deutsch (1959) called in the title of his book a "mysterious leap from the mind to the body." This leap, in turn, has the effect of hiding what patients are really thinking and feeling both from themselves and others, with two main consequences, one for the patient and one for the patient's therapist. For the patient, insight is compromised, so the patient cannot connect emotional cause with physical effect and then disavows a personal contribution to the disorder, which ultimately gives the disorder a not-me quality. For the therapist, the therapist's ability to understand and treat the patient is limited, or seriously impaired, both because of the patient's generally compromised insight and because of the patient's disavowal of involvement in and personal contribution to his or her disorder.

## CLASSIFICATION

The following are *DSM-IV* somatoform disorders (the examples are mine).

1. *Somatization disorder*, such as gastric reflux and hyperacidity from job-induced tension, and some cases of job-related low back pain
2. *Conversion disorder*, such as emotionally induced paresis of the hand that is part of carpal tunnel syndrome, RSI, or writer's cramp; or pseudoneurological attention deficit disorder, in which the inability to concentrate is due to an emotional conflict about concentrating
3. *Pain disorder*, such as some cases of emotionally induced low back pain and some cases of emotionally induced painful RSI
4. *Hypochondriasis*, such as constant worrying about health, which keeps workers away from their desks and in their doctors' offices

I include the following *DSM-IV* disorders with the somatoform disorders:

5. *Factitious disorder*, a *DSM-IV* disorder in which, according to the *DSM-IV*, "physical symptoms . . . are intentionally produced or feigned in order to assure the sick role" (p. 471)
6. *Malingering*, a *DSM-IV* V-code, a condition that is the focus of attention or treatment though it is not attributable to a mental disorder, in which physical symptoms are "produced or exaggerated motivated by external incentives such as avoiding military duty, avoiding work, obtaining financial compensation, evading criminal prosecution, or obtaining drugs" (p. 683)

I also include two non–*DSM-IV* "disorders" in my list:

7. *Psychosomatic disorder* (psychophysiological conversion), a non–*DSM-IV* disorder, exemplified by emotionally induced "splitting" headaches or asthma
8. *Somatic manifestations of nonsomatoform disorders*, such as
   a. Somatic delusions in schizophrenia, as when a patient develops a headache due to imagining he or she smells bad odors believed deliberately put there to harm
   b. Somatic delusions in major depression, as when a patient believes abdominal pain is due to his or her insides having rotted away
   c. Somatic equivalents in dysthymic disorder, such as depressive headaches

    d. Anxiety equivalents in anxiety disorder, such as palpitations
    e. Flashbacks in posttraumatic stress disorder, in which the flash-
backs are physical symptoms either because the original trauma
was a physical one or because what was an original emotional
trauma elicited a physical response such as palpitations

## DEVELOPMENTAL FACTORS

According to Stoudemire (1988), developmentally speaking an infant originally expresses ideation and affect nonverbally, for example in autonomic responses. These nonverbal cues can become the exclusive basis of communication when the environment suppresses more direct expression of ideas and feelings. This leaves the "individual developmentally fixated at a predominately somatic level of experience, conceptualizing . . . communicating" (p. 534) and resolving conflicts, leading to a "reliance on somatic complaints to express oneself and to get attention and support" (p. 534).

## CAUSE

According to Stoudemire (1988), most somatoform disorders are multifactorily determined and have to be evaluated from several theoretical perspectives. While psychodynamic perspectives are valuable, to provide a complete causal picture we must also study "linguistic development, family dynamics, cultural factors, and behavioral conditioning" (p. 534).

### Exogenous Factors

Stoudemire (1988) emphasizes how the somatoform disorders are reinforced by the attitudes and reactions of others. For example, caretakers who meet dependency needs which have never been met can encourage the patient to relish the sick role the disorder provides. Parents who "respond more readily to physical complaints than [to] signs of emotional distress in their children" (p. 534) fix the somatic mode of expression as do cultural attitudes and educational limitations which can account for whether or not the individual "welcome[s] the sick role" (p. 535) and uses it for gain. Educational limitations and low IQ can also lead to compromised psychological insight and ability to express oneself verbally.

### Endogenous Factors

According to Stoudemire, masked expression of forbidden impulses, punishment for guilty wishes, a desire for removal from an overwhelming threatening life situation at times of stress, a need to assume the sick role, and a "communica[tion] of helplessness [which facilitates] an environment in which attention and support are gained and aggression impulses avoided" (p. 537) are dynamic aspects of many, and probably all, the somatoform symptoms/somatoform occupational disorders.

## MAKING THE DIAGNOSIS

### Physical or Mental?

There are three possible causes for a given so-called physical disorder in the workplace: a somatoform disorder, a physical disorder, or a combination of physical and emotional disorder. For example, in writer's cramp, a given cramp may be a conversion disorder, a physical dystonia, or a true dystonia made worse when the patient tenses for emotional reasons. Although causally distinct, these symptoms look alike clinically—that is, they present in rather similar ways, but the structural and dynamic differences between them are not always immediately apparent.

Today's clinicians, however, usually do not see it that way. Instead they take a one-or-the-other view, lining up in two camps. Some are antipsychiatric and will not admit that disorders like RSI can be emotionally caused; that emotions can contribute to symptoms that are physically caused, as when a hand tensed for emotional reasons becomes more vulnerable to physical injury because of the position in which it is held; or that a preexisting physical disorder can be used by an emotional disorder seeking expression, so that workers do not construct a new physical symptom for their purposes but instead say, "Why bother, I already have a battering ram to use against myself," and use a symptom they already have to express their work conflicts somatically. They do not have to have new headaches. The old ones they already have will, unfortunately, do. Other clinicians are excessively propsychiatric. They see emotional causation everywhere; overlook the possibility that "somatoform" physical symptoms can actually be physically caused; and buttress their view by denying that physical disorder can occur in the absence of actual physical evidence, such as X-ray changes or abnormal laboratory tests. Such clinicians forget that it is not very difficult to produce wrist pain experimentally (say, by flexing the wrist and spreading, then moving, the fingers—the kind of thing that can actually occur when typing at a nonergonomic computer keyboard).

The first school, as exemplified by those who view repetitive physical strain injury as the chief and only cause of carpal tunnel/repetitive strain syndrome, is my present and main focus of attention and concern. This school is typified by Emil Pascarelli and Deborah Quilter's book *Repetitive Strain Injury: A Computer User's Guide* (1994).

Quilter's (Pascarelli & Quilter, 1994) description of RSI is partly derived from her observations of her own repetitive strain injury and forearm tendonitis, which she blames exclusively on physical factors. She says that she developed her disorder due to the physical distress associated with her overworking 50 to 60 hours a week (p. xi), but she does not mention that such a schedule is as likely to produce emotional as physical distress. Yet the description she gives of her repetitive strain injury is strangely reminiscent of the classic descriptions of conversion symptoms familiar to many of us from patients who are certified conversion hysterics. She says, my "arms were so heavy and tired I could hardly hold them to the keyboard" (p. xi), and there was a "strange electrical charge [that] buzzed though my gut" (p. xi). Her apparent suggestibility is another familiar characteristic of conversion hysteria and so is suggestive of a hysterical rather than a physical cause of her symptoms. For example, she states that as she interviewed RSI patients, she noted that "when they massaged their sore spots, my sore spots would hurt" (p. xii). These considerations make it difficult for her to claim, as she does, that, as far as RSI goes, "conversion hysteria, which originates to a great extent in suggestibility, has nothing to do with it." It also undercuts her strong disagreement with Yolande Lucire, who saw RSI as "a form of conversion hysteria" (p. 11). Finally, when she disagrees with those who cite epidemic hysteria as a cause for RSI by saying it could not account for RSI in self-employed people who work in isolation, she overlooks that emotional illnesses do not require contiguity with an "infected human being" to spread because, unlike viral epidemics, they can be transmitted in other ways (for example, by an article in the daily press).

Grudgingly, Pascarelli and Quilter (1994) do mention some causative emotional factors, but they are mainly superficial conscious ones generally known to the layperson, like overwork in those who are driven; shyness so that people who do not "assert themselves" do not "have the nerve to state their needs about work pace or ask for a new chair" (p. 35); job dissatisfaction, which leads to an "unhappy, injured, and *angry* workforce" (p. 7); or factors related to the corporate culture, such as fast pace and high pressure, bred by a bad economy (pp. 35–36). Primarily, the emotional factors that are mentioned are assigned a secondary, consequential role. For example, a disorder makes the patient angry, not the other way around. (But anger is a formative factor in many somatoform disorders, either producing muscle tension, which promotes injury, or being converted directly into somatoform conversion symptoms.) And the interplay between external and personal factors is mainly ignored.

All workers who work for "62 hours a week for six months" (p. 36) are presumed equally troubled by hard work, fast pace, and high pressure, although some like it and get sick in its absence. Not all, as Quilter (Pascarelli & Quilter, 1994) suggests, do not speak up because they are afraid of losing their jobs (p. 36). Some do not speak up because they have no complaints.

The authors' therapeutic solutions are equally superficial. They start off well, quoting Robert Karasek and Torres Theorell, who note that "'most of the solutions currently advanced to reduce stress—relaxation therapies, for example—address only its symptoms'" (p. 37) and complain that "little is done to change the source of the problem" (p. 37). Predictably, however, like Karasek and Theorell, the only "problem" they identify as needing change is "the work organization itself" (p. 37). This overlooks what individuals bring to the work organization and how they create their own problems by reacting more catastrophically than even a bad situation might warrant. Not surprisingly, given their lack of insight into individual dynamics, Pascarelli and Quilter (1994) can advise their patients that "the best stress reducer, then, may be quitting your job" (p. 37). But even when that is a viable option practically, emotionally speaking not working—even not working in a stressful environment—can be more stressful than continuing to work even under the most difficult conditions because patients are sitting at home not relaxing but getting depressed—as one patient forced to retire early put it, "pacing the floor, and just waiting to die."

### Ruling in the Diagnosis

In making the diagnosis of a somatoform disorder, it is not enough to rule out physical disorder; one must also rule in emotional disorder. To do this, the clinician must first carefully study and evaluate the symptom itself. The clinician must ask which, if any, of the classical patterns described in the textbooks the symptom most closely resembles. For example, a disorder of the fine movements of the hand may be RSI and not conversion because conversion typically affects the proximal part of the extremity more than the distal, the arm more than the hand.

Next the clinician should do a careful mental status evaluation. The mental status evaluation is the equivalent of the physical examination of psychiatry. For example, both Stoudemire (1988) and Wilfred Abse (1959) stress that in evaluating possible somatoform symptoms, we have to evaluate the patient's concurrent mood and degree of anxiety. Conversions, in particular, are associated with a specific affective state called *la belle indifference*, a grand or striking indifference, in which the predominant affect is detached and there is a certain removed attitude about even the most serious paralyses or sensory loss, without the overconcern (anxious affect) we would expect given the degree of impairment.

The mental status evaluation should include specific questions of proven diagnostic value, like "What do you think is causing your problem?"; "Do you think your problem is physical or mental?"; and "What do you think will happen to your job because of your problem?" For example, a train conductor's chronic fatigue syndrome diagnosis looked questionable after he was asked, "What do you think is causing your problem?" and answered that he was actually an insomniac who in effect kept himself awake deliberately to make himself too tired to do his work effectively (he hoped to be discharged from work on disability due to chronic fatigue syndrome).

A diagnostic rule I have found useful is this: If the patient consciously hopes the disorder is physical, then it may very well be emotional; while if the patient consciously hopes that the disorder is emotional, then it may very well be physical. Patients with nerve damage want to have emotionally caused writer's cramp or RSI because to them that means that their illness is potentially curable. On the other hand, patients with conversion hysteria often prefer to see themselves, and want their therapists to see them, as suffering from nerve damage, because to them that means that they are not "a psychiatric case."

The clinician should do a careful dynamic and developmental evaluation. Abse (1959) stresses that our evaluation of a conversion symptom must not rely on descriptive clinical presentation alone (p. 279) but should be based as well on dynamic and developmental features. Similarly, Stoudemire (1988) notes that evaluating a conversion symptom completely requires that we do an analysis of the precipitating event; take a family history; determine the interpersonal conflicts and communications problems; and take a history of sexual trauma, incest, or molestation.

One goal of understanding a patient's individual dynamics is to understand the interplay between the patient's psychological problems and his or her on-the-job stress. Stress is itself traumatic, but it is more likely to cause symptoms when today's stress reminds the patient of yesterday's trauma. For example, a noisy workplace, while annoying in itself, did not cause headaches in most of the people who worked there. It was only intolerable for two groups of workers: ex-combat veterans, who once lay in the trenches, bullets whistling by and shells exploding over their heads; and patients with parents who kept intruding on their lives, when the patients wanted to be left alone and in peace.

Another goal is to understand the psychodynamics of a given somatoform symptom. Depressive equivalents, such as depressive headaches or back pain, are often physical expressions of feeling abused and rejected. For example, in one case the patient's associations revealed how his depressive headaches represented feeling "kicked in the head" by rejecting co-workers, and his depressive back pain represented being "stabbed in the back" by competitive underlings.

Hand syndromes often dramatize a fear of success paradoxically associated with a fear of failure, and they express both in what amounts to a symbolism of thwarted ambition. Hand syndromes also express conflicts over inappropriate anger and aggressiveness (which often do and should make the patient guilty) and over appropriate anger and aggressiveness (which should not, but usually do, make the patient guilty).

A patient's dynamics often explain a patient's symptomatic behavior as well as his or her actual symptoms.

> For example, a man who was humiliated almost sexually by a boss who constantly demeaned him and his manhood felt defective, developed a conversion hand syndrome, and began to act out sexually to deal with his not feeling like a man.
>
> This patient first developed a weakness (a flaccid paralysis) of his hand to express the humiliation he felt at work at the hands of the boss, who in effect castrated him by constantly telling him of his defects. Then he began an office affair meant both to impress co-workers with how masculine and desirable he really was and to "get a little love" as an antidote to the hatred he felt from the humbling environment in which he worked.

The patient's real problems and existential plight at the time of the original and ongoing presentation of the symptoms must not be neglected in making a dynamic formulation. Patients may not be suffering from childhood fixations as much as from on-the-job predicaments which make them feel helpless. This was the driving force in the pain syndrome of a man harassed personally by a paranoid boss, who got the patient into his delusional system, and in the headaches of a man who was the romantic target of a borderline co-worker, who overvalued and tried to merge with him without considering his unwillingness to overvalue and merge with her.

A transference and countertransference diagnosis is a part of dynamic evaluation of the patient. A therapist made a transference diagnosis by noting that a patient with stomach pains at work developed the same pains in the therapist's office when the therapist seemed to be criticizing him for failing and/or depriving him of money by telling him that he could not get disability compensation. Another therapist made a transference diagnosis by noting that a patient with pounding headaches at work developed the same pounding headaches in the therapist's office when the therapist pressed the patient for information, which the patient interpreted as being nagged. He was in effect telling the therapist, "You are giving me a pain." As for a countertransference diagnosis, the therapist's reaction to these patients is often a good source of needed diagnostic material (but this is only true when the therapist's reaction to the patient reveals more about the patient than it does about the therapist). Does the therapist sympathize with the patient or condemn the patient for taking advantage of the system? Depressives elicit sympathy while patients with a hysterical disorder tend to find themselves accused of malingering or "faking it"—not unconsciously, but consciously, and not unwittingly, but criminally.

Certain diagnostic tricks can be helpful in distinguishing somatoform from physical disorders, and some clinicians perform them as part of the mental status examination. For example, with the patient not looking, the examiner touches an area of supposed sensory loss and then asks the patient, "Do you feel that?" Patients who say no may be suffering from a conversion hypesthesia. Or patients who claim to be completely blind are asked to look at a revolving drum, with the clinician observing to see if their eyes follow the drum reflexively. Gion Condrau (1988) cites how patients with emotionally caused writer's cramp, unlike patients with true dystonia, can write comfortably if given pens that make no marks (possibly because they think that if the pen makes no marks, then they are not really writing).

A therapeutic trial might also be a part of the mental status evaluation. Conversion can be diagnosed by the response of the symptom to therapeutic intervention. Induced regression of a symptom due to suggestion, like spontaneous regression of the symptom due to autosuggestion, is characteristic of conversion disorder. For example, hysterical stocking and glove anesthesia has been known to disappear when the doctor runs a pin from the upper demarcation line of the anesthesia down along the arm, while telling the patient that the upper level of anesthesia will follow the pin down the arm until the anesthesia "vanishes off the tip of your fingers."

Finally, therapists should take a careful medical history as part of any diagnostic work-up. In particular, the diagnosis of somatization disorder requires the presence of more than one somatization symptom. Therapists must do follow-ups as well, because what can look like conversion disorder today can turn out to be myasthenia gravis or multiple sclerosis tomorrow.

## THE INDIVIDUAL DISORDERS

### Somatization Disorder

Somatization disorder is characterized by multiple persistent somatic complaints that express general emotional distress more than specific psychological conflict. As a result, somatization symptoms seem empty of idea, and the patients themselves seem nonverbal. They tend to express their dysphoria not conceptually but in "body English"—in dress, posture, or muscle tone. A chronic sufferer of back pain stooped not only to protect the sore area but also to express the suffering she felt at the hands of the cruel world, while another patient mopped his brow not only because he felt feverish but as a way to say "whew," to tell the world of how his life was perpetually a close call with death. Such patients produce few associations to their symptoms beyond noting when they come and go in relationship to external stress. They cannot say much about the specific relationship between their symptoms and their thoughts and emotions.

According to Martin Kantor (1988) patients with somatization symptoms tend to present their symptoms in dramatic terms, underscoring what they say with charade or pantomime to catch their audience's eye, keep their interest, and impress them with how much they are suffering. Often they soon become annoying. They seem insensitive to the reactions their listeners are having to them. They do not care how others feel—others are supposed to care how *they* feel. They are deliberately intrusive with their timing, which is calculated to spoil occasions with news of new illnesses and updates of old. When we ask "How are you today?" they invariably give both a general answer and a medical answer, although "fine" is all we want to hear. On the job, such people put their co-workers in a difficult position. They force them to listen to their medical complaints when they are supposed to be working, and if their co-workers do not listen they are either criticized for being unsympathetic or condemned for being rejecting. Such patients stand in contrast to patients with a physical illness, who tend to be secretive about their symptoms. Recognizing that they are really sick, they try to minimize how bad they feel in specific and avoid talking about their health in general. At most they give a general nod in the direction of the problem and do not dwell on it. When they do talk of their aches and pains, they tend to do so not voluntarily but because they have been asked (pp. 310–323).

Individual personality disorders color the specific way somatization disorders present, as follows.

The more paranoid somatization patients are not worrisome, as are obsessives, or overtly demonstrative, as are hysterics, but are mean and vindictive people who, having made symptoms out of their anger, express their anger, in turn, with their symptoms. Feeling victimized by their company, they victimize the company in turn with their imaginary illnesses. They demand special treatment at work, extra time off, and so on. The boss feels abandoned and becomes angry. Co-workers feel used and retaliate. Then the patient feels first less loved, and second persecuted, so the symptoms increase. Most of these patients are as vindictive and paranoid with their doctors as they are with their co-workers. For example, when their medical evaluation is negative, they accuse the doctor (1) of misdiagnosing them, and (2) of using unnecessary medical procedures to make the misdiagnosis.

The more passive-aggressive somatization patients go on the attack, and they do so indirectly and discreetly. Instead of angry outbursts and wild accusations, they simmer with pregnant pauses that often imply, "My illness is the company's fault," without stating this. When asked, "How are you?" they raise provocative questions that are really disguised assaults, such as "How could I be all right, given that you make me sit all day hunched over at a tiny computer screen typing on a nonergonomic keyboard?" Although their questions are clearly disguised complaints, when confronted they deny being hostile and blame others for imagining hostility that they say is not there or, if there, is not intended.

Passive-dependent somatization patients develop and maintain their symptoms primarily to get love and attention. For example, one patient's hand syndrome became an excuse to quit her job and go to live with her mother, both guilt free. Others might routinely call co-workers at home after business hours, to present medical complaints they feel will not wait until morning. In contrast to the hypochondriac, who feels that each symptom is a matter of eventual importance, somatization disorder patients who are dependent tend to feel that each symptom is a matter of immediate importance. They engage others on nights and weekends, not in spite of the inappropriate hour, but because of it. They wish to complain outside of, not during, regular hours, for if others respond at such inconvenient times, that means they love them; for they love them enough to help them not only 9 to 5, but at all hours of the night.

Because obsessive somatization patients cannot tolerate any degree of imperfection in themselves, they desire immediate relief from their symptoms, which they perceive as flaws. One result is that they try to avoid any job stress that they anticipate will make them sick. Another is that they dislike doctors who are correct but dilatory because they take their time and make a proper diagnosis before initiating treatment. Instead they prefer doctors who (1) respond to their complaints with an immediate diagnosis, and (2) prescribe without further ado. As a result they often seek, accept, and actually prefer the opinions of careless practitioners. Eventually they accumulate a list of incorrect or controversial diagnoses (like physical RSI due to strain, diabetes, rheumatoid or psoriatic arthritis) and the questionable or inappropriate treatments that go with them, ranging from drugs for a nonexistent yeast infection to acupuncture for emotional pain. Many treat themselves with proprietary medications. Then, in an attempt to create the illusion that they approach their problems in a scientific fashion, they research their illness on their own. They read the instructions on their medications carefully and check with medical texts (their "Bibles" are the *Physician's Desk Reference, Prevention* magazine, and medical columns in the *New York Times*) so that they can institute treatment based on what they consider to be precise diagnosis. However, because they are not qualified to diagnose medical illness, any diagnosis they make will likely be imprecise.

The more depressed somatization patients want to look worse than they feel. They want to convey in actions and words that they are severely ill, in great distress, and without hope. They often imply that they feel guilty about having caused their illness in some way. While somatization symptoms in an obsessional worker respond positively to medical reassurances, somatization symptoms in a depressed worker are more likely to get worse with reassurance, because such people hear what is intended positively as dismissive and misinterpret statements like "You are not sick" or "You will get better" as a rejection like "I won't give you the love you want from me." Such patients respond more positively to personal support and sympathy (although ultimately this can fixate them in the sick role).

There is a *DSM-IV* category of undifferentiated somatoform disorder, in which one or a few somatization symptoms are present and last for more than 6 months. An example from the *DSM-IV*, which is of special relevance to the occupational disorders, is chronic fatigue of emotional origin.

### Conversion Disorder

#### General Principles

Conversion disorder is responsible for many (although not all) of such emotionally caused physical blocks as conversion writer's cramp (depression is another significant culprit here). Descriptively, in conversion normal body function may be quantitatively diminished, as in numbness; quantitatively increased, as in tremor; or qualitatively altered, as in paresthesias.

Conversion symptoms, unlike somatization symptoms, are more likely to be single than multiple. They may be acute and transient, or may persist and become chronic. In the acute stage, organic end-stage pathology, such as contractures, is unusual. But it is common in the chronic stage and can become irreversible if the symptoms persist for too long.

In contrast to somatization symptoms, which tend to prefer an autonomic over a sensorimotor pathway for expression and discharge, conversion symptoms tend to prefer a sensorimotor pathway for expression and discharge. This choice of pathway, in turn, reflects how somatization symptoms are meant to express gut feelings in a general way ("I ache"), while conversion symptoms are meant to express mental conflict and its resolution in a specific way, as in pantomime ("I freeze in place to keep myself from killing").

Dynamically, conversions can develop de novo. When they do, they are put into place to resolve a conflict between wish and fear by the process of compromise formation. Numbness, for example, can be a compromise between "I feel angry" and "because I feel guilty, I feel nothing at all," much as a paralyzed arm can be a compromise between "I feel I wish to kill" and "because I feel guilty and don't intend to do it, I can't make any move at all."

In cases of conversion disorder we often find typical, or textbook, fantasies and conflicts, which some say are oedipal fantasies and conflicts. We also often find evidence that the patient is translating these fantasies into body symptoms by the process of conversion. In some cases we can truly appreciate, listening to the patient's associations and watching the symptoms evolve, how the patient first represses an idea or emotion and then follows that by converting the repressed material into a somatic symptom. Often the patients make the connection themselves between fantasy and the presenting symptom, revealing at least an unconscious awareness that they are translating psychic concept into bodily expression, making what Deutsch (1959) called in the title of his book "the mysterious leap from the mind to the body." As a result, some physical conversion symptoms virtually beg to be translated back into the emotions that underlie them. They seem pregnant with meaning. Who, for example, seeing a hysterical hand contracture, does not think "fist" and wonder about the patient's anger; or seeing clonic followed by tonic contractures of hysterical seizures does not ask, "Is something sexual going on here?"

Conversion symptoms can also develop de novo via autosuggestion, which plays a significant role as patients unconsciously convince themselves that a muscle cannot move or that paresthesias exist. Autosuggestion, in turn, explains much of what clinicians too glibly call malingering, in which patients are less deliberately faking than they are unconsciously convincing themselves that they are sick.

Conversion symptoms do not always develop de novo. At times they are the product of an identification with similar symptoms in others. This can account not only for epidemics of group hysteria, in which one individual gets sick and all the others follow, but also for the development of individual symptoms, as happened to a typist who, while typing, thought, "I hope I don't get occupational cramp just like those cases

I read about," and then promptly felt her hands tightening at the keyboard. The paresis of the hands that can occur in repetitive strain injury or carpal tunnel syndrome is frequently imitative. The person imitated may be someone the patient knows, or it may be someone the patient read about. It is rumored that Vladimir Horowitz, the pianist, spawned at least two pupils with a paralyzed hand in some ways like the one he himself is rumored to have had.

Developmentally, persistent childhood wishes and fears contribute to the pool out of which conversion symptoms arise. In turn, conversion symptoms tend to replicate earlier childhood experiences, which resurface in adulthood when the time is ripe, as when workers are frustrated or criticized by a frightening authority figure (like the boss, who reminds them of a frightening authority figure from their past, such as a mean parent or teacher).

> For example, a typist's hand pain began when, and recurred each time that, the boss complained about her typing skills and pointed out the errors she made, and did so in a highly personal and critical fashion. This experience reproduced how her first piano teacher hit her with a ruler each time she made a mistake at the keyboard. And a pianist's right hand went numb after a bad review because he was attempting to protect and cover his hand from his father, who "might cut it off" as a punishment for gratifying his wish to play the piano, his wish to become a musician, and other "unmentionable dirty desires and doings."

Conversion symptoms can also be explained phylogenetically, according to the developmental dynamics of the race, as well as ontogenetically, according to the developmental dynamics of the individual. Just as all of us seem to develop the same jaunty gait when we are happy, or the same slow gait when we are sad (much as our ancestors did), all of us have the potential to freeze and be unable to move when we are afraid, and can only relax and move freely when we feel comfortable again (much as our ancestors did). Along these lines, conversion symptoms are profitably viewed as a primitive expression of such ancestral defensive activities as reflexive rolling into a ball to protect the sensitive underbelly and becoming immobile to become invisible. In this view a hysterical paralysis is less a compromise between a sexual wish and a guilty fear than it is a kind of regression to the primitive, defensive freezing in place in abject terror when the individual feels in danger.

It bears repeating that a careful diagnosis or differential diagnosis of conversion disorder is necessary to avoid unneeded diagnostic procedures, such as a CAT scan for hysterical blindness; relatively ineffective therapeutic procedures, such as acupuncture for conversion pain; or harmful therapeutic procedures, such as immobilization of the neck for conversion whiplash when the physical injury might be best treated by not by immobilization but by mobilization (i.e., not by urging the patient to rest, which can fix dependency, but by urging the patient to get back to work as soon as possible, in order to stop the tendency to regress).

### Specific Conversions

*Conversion Writer's Cramp.*    Conversion Writer's Cramp is a cramping of the hands when attempting to perform a manual occupational activity, like writing, playing an instrument, or word processing, in which at least certain aspects of the disorder cannot be explained as the result of any known medical or neurological problem. As with other conversions, the underlying conflicts are often obvious to those who observe the patient even casually.

> Recently I attended a performance by a pianist who could play with his left hand but not with his right. (He laid his right hand carefully on the piano's top while he played.) According to legend, his right hand was unusable due to repetitive strain injury. But I had to question this purely physical explanation of the hand problem when I noted that at the end of the performance he turned not to the audience for approval, as would be expected, but away from the audience and to the orchestra. This not only surprised me but suggested to me that he had conflicts about success, completion, and exposure. I wondered if these figured in the formation of his hand problem in the first place, and if his behavior suggested that conversion pianist's cramp was a more likely diagnosis than dystonia.

*Carpal tunnel syndrome/RSI.*    Patients with carpal tunnel syndrome/ RSI, according to Tammy Crouch and Michael Madden (1992, pp. 2–4) develop the following:

- Sensory deficit, such as numbness, especially at night, associated with tingling, burning, and coldness, and sometimes accompanied by stiff swollen painful joints; and
- Motor deficit, including loss of hand strength, weakness of the thumb, clumsiness, and an aching that goes from hand to shoulder. (While sometimes the paresthesias, stiffness, pain, and immobility seem to start at the wrist and hand and extend up the arm and into the neck, at other times the problem seems to originate in the neck, and move down).

There are many possible causes for carpal tunnel syndrome/RSI. Some carpal tunnel syndromes/RSIs are physically caused by a compressed, inflamed nerve; others are emotionally caused by conversion; and still others are due to a combination of emotional and physical factors, as can happen when an injury causes the syndrome but an emotional problem causes the injury. For example, many patients develop hand syndromes from using the computer because they tense up at the keyboard so much that they hurt their muscles and tendons. Others develop hand syndromes because they are too relaxed and do not tense up enough when typing at the computer keyboard or when doing another form of repetitive work. Workers whose muscles are flaccid can sustain just as much injury to their hands as those whose muscles are too tense. So the therapeutic goal is not relaxation, but maintaining a proper balance between relaxation and tension/contraction.

Proper diagnosis of carpal tunnel syndrome/RSI is founded in a careful description of the symptom itself. For example, the numbness associated with a carpal tunnel syndrome/RSI is likely to be due to pressure on the nerve when it is partial and diffuse (i.e., poorly demarcated) so that there is gradual transition between the normal and the abnormal areas, accounted for by the overlapping innervation supplying the area in question. In contrast, the numbness associated with conversion disorder tends to be complete and confined, with a sharp line of demarcation between the affected and the normal area, giving what the literature variously calls a "stocking and glove" or "sock and glove" effect. This is because the distribution of the anesthesia is determined not by neurological innervation of the extremity but by the fantasies involving the area in question.

In physical carpal tunnel syndrome/RSI, the paralysis is more distal than proximal. The reverse is seen in conversion carpal tunnel syndrome/RSI, in which the gross movements are affected more than the small ones. Hysterics, invested less in re-creating a physical illness than in producing a grand and meaningful gesture, may develop, in addition to an inability to fan and separate their fingers, an inability to lift and swing their whole arm, because the latter is much better theater than the former. The most diagnostic confusion seems to be caused by the paresthesias of carpal tunnel syndrome—abnormal sensations like itching, crawling, pins and needles, pain-causalgia, and hyperesthesia—because these symptoms are consistent either with traumatic nerve injury and nerve injury due to diabetic or alcoholic polyneuropathy, or with conversion hysteria.

*Conversion attention deficit/hyperactivity disorder of adulthood.* Some cases of so-called attention deficit disorder (ADD), in which occupational deficit is mainly due to inattention, are really pseudoneurological conversions, a kind of hysterical organicity, like hysterical amnesia. Dynamically, some of these patients are hostile to authority, so that their learning disability is a subtle sabotaging of those who want them to learn as a way to get back at them for expecting cooperation, which they see as submission. Sometimes there is a significant sexual element, and the individual is unconsciously soft-pedaling the intellect as part of a plan to emphasize the body.

*Conversion burnout and chronic fatigue.*    The validity of burnout and chronic fatigue as diagnostic entities is controversial. Some see them as hard-edged diagnostic entities, while others believe they are catch-all terms, really just new words for *tired, bored, fed up,* and *unwilling to take it any more.* The literature sometimes uses the terms *burnout* and *chronic fatigue* to refer to a number of withdrawal behaviors whose various manifestations include stubbornness, simple exhaustion, and pathological depression. Some of the patients described do not so much feel bad as they are lazy. Others do feel bad because they are fed up and seriously demoralized. Some are stuck in a boring or stressful job, while others have a good job but for personal reasons cannot handle it. Some are hypersensitive people who cannot stand much stress. Others, either long suffering or insensitive, depending on one's viewpoint, tolerate situations in which the stress would be too much for most anyone, until they collapse under the weight of it all.

Dr. Herbert J. Freudenberger and Geraldine Richelson's description of the burnout syndrome (1980) is as follows. Freudenberger says his own disorder consisted of feeling overworked, too busy to do routine things, bored, and incompatible with his job. There were also inappropriate eruptions of anger, depletion and exhaustion of physical and mental resources, fatigue, cynicism, sadness, forgetfulness, irritability, silence, and distancing (p. 18). There were associated physical complaints like aches, pains, headaches, a lingering cold, disorientation, and decreased sexual interest. He attributes his problem to his being a workaholic, doing his job frantically (almost fanatically), until the inevitable let-down occurred. He was overinvolved with his patients, felt that they needed him (p. xix), and held himself to impossibly high standards (p. 10) only to find that meeting the standards did not produce the expected reward (p. 13), at which time he felt betrayed and a failure. There was a schism between the real self and the image of the self, as well as a tendency to put everything into the one particular situation he considered be the focal point of his life (p. 53). (In his case the unrealistic expectations were self-expectations, self-imposed. In other cases the job imposes them, as when it says, "The work has to be done, even though there are not enough people to do it," and demands that workers stay overtime, with no pay, because "part of your job is to get your job done, period." In still other cases it is society that makes impossible demands on individuals, asking them to be moral in an immoral environment, not to lie, cheat, and steal when every one else is doing just that.)

One possibility is that Freudenberger was depressed. Another is that he was suffering from a conversion disorder, or at least a disorder with notable conversion elements. The aches, pains, headaches, lingering cold, exhaustion, fatigue, disorientation, and decreased sexual interest may not have been depressive equivalents but classical conversion symptoms. Burnout and chronic fatigue are discussed further in Chapter 10.

*Psychophysiological conversions.*    Psychophysiological conversions, or psychosomatic disorders, such as headaches or gastrointestinal symptoms, are more a factor in the absenteeism associated with occupational disorder than is generally appreciated.

> A patient with pain supposedly due to a hiatus hernia could hardly do any work at all after lunch. After he ate he developed excruciating pain that got worse if he bent over. So he could do no better than spend the rest of the afternoon standing or siting bolt upright at his desk. As a result, he could not type or even answer the telephone all afternoon. Eventually he underwent unnecessary surgery, and then was out of work for weeks, undergoing what to his doctors seemed to be a prolonged recovery—when in fact he was really still sick, having gotten no benefit at all from his operation.

A differential diagnostic point is that physicians react differently countertransferentially to patients with somatization symptoms, conversion symptoms, and psychophysiological conversions. General practitioners, for example, sometimes view somatization patients as complainers (i.e., as "belly-achers"), conversion disorder patients as fakers or malingerers, and psychosomatic patients as neurotics.

## Pain Disorder

Somatoform pain disorder is characterized by severe or prolonged pain in excess of what would be expected from an underlying physical condition, if present, so that psychological factors are judged to play an important causal role. An example is a dull ache in the back, attributed to arthritis, in the absence of significant arthritic changes, as demonstrated by X-ray findings. Another is chronic pain in the teeth, leading to multiple extractions, which are done because the patient is pressuring the dentist to do them although there is no demonstrable dental pathology.

The following discussion may help to differentiate conversion pain from somatoform pain disorder. As previously mentioned, because conversion symptoms are concept symptoms, conversion pain is concept pain—specifically, the pain is an expression of conflict. For example, a patient converted her forbidden sexual wishes into intense throbbing pain located over her uterus and bilaterally over each ovary. Her associations to the symptom were richly sexual in nature and revealed both her need to be gratified sexually (and have a baby) and her reactive guilty need to be punished for her desires and suffer for her actions. In contrast, in somatization symptoms (to which pain disorder is closely related structurally), the concepts associated with the pain tend to be rudimentary and undeveloped. The physical pain may be a distillate of emotional pain due to grief, inexpressible angry disappointment in others, loss, or helplessness. In turn, symptoms of pain disorder will tend to be bereft of emotional or ideological association. The pain seems to be buried deep in the body, away from idea and feeling, and as such seems independent both of internal conflicts and of external stress. As a result, the individual says, "I hurt," but little more. At most the pain seems to be accompanied by depression—usually one that looks like it is the consequence of the suffering, however much it may be its cause. We can nevertheless usually find an interpersonal context for the pain if we look hard enough. A study of relationships at work with management and between co-workers is a good place to look for pain triggers and often reveals why the problem began and what is sustaining it.

Clinicians have long sought guidelines for making the distinction between organic and psychological pain, but these remain elusive.

> The reason for this is well illustrated by the problem of making a differential diagnosis of pain in a patient's cocker spaniel. The dog would not walk in the morning, and her veterinarian said it was because of pain due to arthritis. The owner accepted the diagnosis until he realized that when he tossed a ball before her to get her to move, she ran after the ball without seeming to suffer any distress at all. Perhaps her "pain" was not pain at all but emotional stubbornness. Or was it the high-pitched whine of the ATM her master headed for as a matter of course each morning that bothered her? Perhaps there was another possibility—she was in pain, but she wanted to catch the tossed ball so badly that she put up with the pain just so that she could run after it.

### Factitious Disorders

Factitious disorders are self-induced to maintain the sick role.

> A hospitalized patient with a fever of unknown etiology was "exposed as a fake" when it was discovered that when she was left alone when her tem-

perature was being taken, she put the thermometer under the light bulb next to her bed so that her doctors could think she had a fever and give her the sympathy she craved.

They contrast with malingered disorders, which are self-induced for specific external gain, such as avoiding military service or getting a doctor's note to use to stay home from work.

More job-related disorders than we think are factitious, although most are not as serious as the following:

A veteran developed symptoms of a posttraumatic stress disorder due to his battlefield experiences in Grenada and Beirut, but he got inferior compensation, he said, because neither "skirmish" was officially classified as a "war."

After discharge from the service he went to work for a company that, in spite of his disability, put him in the field working near whirring machines, machines that reminded him of wartime sounds heard in Grenada and Beirut.

One day on the job he thought he was back in battle and began play-acting being in combat. He ducked repeatedly, tried to shoot his co-workers with an imaginary gun, and so forth.

The boss took no pity on him. Completely disregarding his personal disability and the Americans with Disabilities Act,[1] he fired him, giving him only a few days notice.

In reply, the next day the patient injured himself on the job with a deep puncture wound to the arm. This led to osteomyelitis. The osteomyelitis never healed properly, in spite of adequate treatment, and the surgeons did not know why.

The reason was that the patient was manipulating his wound to keep it from healing. When confronted, he denied this but admitted the possibility that he was doing it in his sleep. If so, he said, "My reason would be to get revenge on the boss, and to feel less rejected and more loved by my company."

A patient hated her job so badly and wanted to get love from her family so much that she tore open the skin of her leg to make a raw, bleeding ulcer that confined her to bed. Many skin grafts did not take, because she tore them off, too. Finally, in desperation the surgeons hospitalized her and covered the ulcer with a plaster cast—in those days called an Unna's boot. That did not work either because, when no one was looking, she went to the coat closet in her room, opened up a wire hanger, inserted the hanger

1. This 1990 act prohibits discrimination against people with mental and other disabilities.

under the Unna's boot, and used it to once again scrape off the skin graft covering her ulcer.

Doctors and allied health workers are often appalled at the mere idea of patients producing factitious disorders like the ones just described and criticize their patients instead of evaluating and treating them. Yet the factitious disorders (as well as malingering, which is discussed next) can be true illnesses when they are not, strictly speaking, consciously planned but have unconscious roots and the patient is (like most patients with a mental disorder) a desperate person who does not know how else to express himdelf or herself and get what he or she needs and wants. In addition, like many mental disorders, factitious symptoms developmentally and dynamically (1) reproduce a positive or negative early childhood experience (for example, they re-create an illness to bring back the old days when the patient was in bed as a child, with a similar illness, taken care of by mother); (2) enable the patient to live out a general sense of dysphoria or more specific guilty sexual and aggressive fantasies (for example, they express both sexual heat and sexual regret in the feigned "high temperature" of illness, just as patients with a conversion disorder express sexual heat and sexual regret in pudendal pain or a claw hand); (3) allow the patient to identify with someone loved (or identify with a hated aggressor); and (4) express the patient's evolutionary inheritance, as when being sick represents a throw-back phenomenon (for example, to the hibernating animal within).

As many clinicians wonder, who but patients with severe emotional problems would do such a thing to themselves?

## Malingering

In contrast to the factitious disorders, in which the primary goal is to play the sick role, the primary goal in malingering is to gain a real advantage from the world. Sometimes, as the *DSM-IV* states, the patient wants money—an insurance settlement or a pension. At other times the goal is relief from onerous work conditions, or release from military responsibility or jury duty.

There are two kinds of malingering. In opportunistic malingering the patient acts deliberately and consciously, often taking advantage of an on-the-job accident or injury to maximize the financial compensation by exaggerating the symptoms (for example, the familiar exaggerated whiplash).

One veteran was overt about his malingering. He said he was faking symptoms of PTSD (posttraumatic stress disorder) to increase his disability benefits, and then he presented a list of faked symptoms to back up his assertion. He admitted he got his list from the library, where he had looked up the disorder just before the interview. Another who claimed disabling painful arthritis referred constantly to his need for money and his anger that his disability benefits had been reduced, and spoke mainly of the several appeals he set in motion after his benefits were reduced and his application for reinstating them was denied. When I saw him in the clinic, he was limping. When I ran across him by accident outside of the clinic, he was walking without any deficit.

In contrast, in unconscious malingering there are significant unconscious reasons for what at first looks entirely like conscious and intentional behavior.

Most cases are both opportunistic and unconscious. For example, the veterans I studied who were, by their own admission, faking posttraumatic stress disorder or a pain syndrome to get compensation had significant emotional problems, ranging from schizophrenia to severe personality problems like passivity and psychopathy. To some extent their malingering was merely one expression of their underlying emotional difficulties. These patients, while certainly somewhat naive, were not merely larcenous at heart, for in many cases extraordinary combat experiences seemed to have left them with a sense of narcissistic entitlement so that they saw themselves as being in a category apart—those entitled to special consideration in life—and left them so depressed and dependent that being cared for was the only thing that they felt could improve their self-esteem. Another unconscious issue is one that particularly figures in the epidemics of PTSD often seen in veterans' clinics: the herd phenomenon, in which passive and suggestible individuals got carried away and did what others were doing, in spite of themselves, just to avoid defying the group leader and just so that they could continue to belong to the group.

## Hypochondriasis

According to Kantor (1988) hypochondriacs are obsessive worriers. They dress too warmly or carry an umbrella and wear heavy galoshes even on sunny days because they are afraid that they will get a cold from a chill or get rained on and get pneumonia. They hold onto the railing as they walk because they are afraid they will fall and break a brittle, decalcified bone. They hold handkerchiefs over their nose and flee smoke-filled board rooms to avoid getting emphysema or lung cancer. On the job they may be observed avoiding the onslaught of germs by carefully checking the rim of their water glass for smudges or lipstick prints, taking pills from a bottle, or sipping sugar fluids from a vial. Some even dress in a stark blue suit, as if they are preparing to attend their own funeral, while simultaneously holding themselves in a fixed cadaverous posture (one reason for muscle strain), as if funeral time has actually arrived (pp. 342–357).

Hypochondriacs worry about illness until they convince themselves that they are sick. Being sick is actually what they have wanted all along, for it enables them to get love and attention, as well as masochistic gratification.

> A successophobic older employee who could not remember a name even though he had not thought about the person for years declared that his memory was gone and he was getting senile. Each time he forgot what he wanted to say, he would loudly proclaim, "Call the nursing home and make me an appointment." In fact he was really talking about senility not as an organic disorder but as a metaphor for punishment. He hoped against hope to be punished because he felt guilty about having more than he believed he deserved, and more than others of the same age and social status had. Ultimately he quit his job, saying he wanted to enjoy the years remaining to him, although he actually left not to enjoy himself but to suffer from being idle, as a way to even the score.

For hypochondriacs, being sick is often a way to get sadistic pleasure. A worker regularly took sick leave as "preventive medicine," less to avoid work than to make his co-workers suffer, because they had to do his work and were kept guessing about when he would come back to work to resume carrying his share of the load.

Hypochondriacs seem to get sick in reality more than nonhypochondriacs. They usually say, "I told you so," but in fact they get sick more often than others for two reasons that are not proof that their prophecies of doom are correct. First, they get depressed when others catch on to them, accuse them of faking, and reject their complaints and them as well. Second, they are too enamored of imaginary illnesses to pay attention to the real ones, and as a result they neglect their health. For example, one elderly patient constantly worried about getting cancer, which she did not have, but dismissed the dizziness that she did have and that was a side-effect of the excessive doses of antianxiety agents she took for her cancerophobia. One day she fell, broke her hip, and became permanently bed-ridden.

## Physical Manifestations of Other Disorders

Somatoform symptoms are often little more than the well-known physical manifestations of familiar disorders, such as anxiety and depression. Somatoform symptoms, like emotionally induced faintness, palpitations, and chest pains, are an integral part of the anxiety syndrome. As previously mentioned, pain can be a depressive equivalent, expressing a visceral sense of emptiness, or a depressive somatic delusion, as was the case for the aforementioned patient who felt that worms were eating her gut, and the aforementioned patient who, convinced her gums hurt, sought to have all her teeth pulled to relieve the pain.

More disabled workers than we think are schizophrenics unable to work because of somatic delusions and hallucinations. Some feel that computers are putting out penetrating rays and suffer accordingly. Others complain of job-related tinnitus when they are really hearing "funny sounds" in their heads, like burbling sounds, sounds that are in turn modified or actual voices. Sometimes their "physical symptoms" are a concretization of a psychotic thought process disorder, as when the sensation of rushing in the head is a concretization of disorganized thinking. Sometimes the "physical symptoms" are a concretization of their decompensation, as when the feeling that their body is falling apart is a concretization of ego flooding and massive psychotic regression.

Rarely do such patients give the real reason for their complaints. Instead, generally aware of the serious implication of their symptoms, they censor them for presentation. They often rebottle a somatic delusion into a somatoform symptom to avoid appearing as mentally disturbed as they suspect they are and as they are afraid others will find them. A schizophrenic delusional about computer rays complained not of rays, but of the pain believed to be the consequence of the rays. He did this to make his problem seem as physical as possible and to avoid giving the illusion that he was mentally unstable. He also qualified other true delusions with an "as if." He was able to convince others that his schizophrenia was a carpal tunnel syndrome by qualifying his conviction that his paresthesias were due to worms crawling under the skin of his hands with, "It is as if worms were crawling there."

Some patients who appear to have a somatization or other somatoform disorder are really suffering from a posttraumatic stress disorder. As mentioned previously, when original traumata (which may be emotional or physical) produce a physical response, later flashbacks that reproduce the effects of the original trauma will reproduce that physical response, and so the patient will appear to have a somatoform disorder or an actual physical illness. I have seen many cases in which pseudoneurological symptoms arise in the here and now because veterans flash back to a time when they sustained a concussion (or worse) during combat.

# 3

## Depressive Occupational Disorder

Depression is perhaps the greatest single problem workers face. Depression keeps workers from being sufficiently motivated to start on a project because they feel the world will not appreciate what they do, so they should not bother putting in the effort. It keeps them from working on a project already started because they feel inadequate to the task, or because their minds go blank as they withdraw what is theirs in the belief that if it is theirs it must be worthless. It keeps them from finishing a project already started because they believe that what they do not finish cannot be held against them. It keeps them from promoting a project once they have finished it because they feel guilty and ashamed about what they have done, so that they either hide it or destroy it.

### DIAGNOSING DEPRESSION

Many individuals, especially sensitive and creative individuals, have one or more depressive symptoms. But therapists should not diagnose major depressive disorder and treat for depression unless a certain number of these symptoms are present (the *DSM-IV* criteria for diagnosing depression should be reviewed thoroughly and followed carefully). Therapists also have to distinguish depressive symptoms from symptoms of another disorder whose features are similar to the symptoms of depression (for example, depressive marasmus has to be distinguished from phobic avoidance, and schizophrenic anhedonia, all of which contain a component of withdrawal). It is particularly important to distinguish schizophrenic from depressive symptoms to avoid treating schizophrenics as if they are depressives, because that can excite them and cause them to decompensate in a paranoid fashion and even become violent.

## EXOGENOUS FACTORS

### General Considerations

Some workers are innately depressed. Even when things are going well, they worry constantly about failing and being fired from work. But others become depressed because of their work. In part, depression is a predictable outcome of working. First, work is hard and depleting; and often the more creative the work, the more depleting it is because most people cannot be creative effortlessly, like Mozart, moving forward without a snag. They have to go back again and again to revise what they have done, and then revise it once more. That takes effort, and they get tired and feel defeated. Second, usually there is an inverse relationship between level of pay and degree of job satisfaction, so that individuals satisfied on their jobs are dissatisfied with their pay, and vice versa.

Depression is a predictable complication of certain professions. For example, many writers get depressed, partly because they constantly have to deal with rejections from publishers and from hostile critics. Many workers in a government bureaucracy get depressed because they get the equivalent of authors' rejections in the form of unalloyed negative feedback from an establishment that has a built-in mechanism for criticism but not one for praise. They do not mind working hard, but they do mind doing a good job only to have it go unnoticed and unremarked, whereas when they do a bad job, it is immediately noticed and frequently mentioned. I once worked in a government clinic. I remember being criticized for any one of a number of things. Yet at the same time, in spite of all my training and years of experience, almost no one on the staff (for reasons never explained to me), in all the years I was there, ever asked me a single question about psychiatry.

Some depression is a function of conditions that prevail in the world today. There are more creative people in a particular field than the world has room for, so the world picks and chooses what creativity it wants and needs. As a result, the odds are that, however brilliant and talented an individual is, he or she will go unpicked and unchosen by chance alone; thus blind luck is more often the reason for success than quality of product. It is depressing when one inventor's superior mousetrap languishes, while the world beats a path to the door of the person who invents the inferior one.

Depression is a complication of excellence. This is because creative people do things better than most, and disappointment looms because most jobs give points not for quality but for quantity—what the government clinic I used to work in called "keeping one's numbers up." Creative people are also more likely than uncreative people to try something new and then make beginner's mistakes and be ridiculed for having made them. As one pianist put it, "Being creative exposes you like performing a Mozart piano concerto exposes you. You can't hide in one of those like you can with a Rachmaninoff concerto, blurring your mistakes beneath the loud pedal." Creative workers are vulnerable to coworkers and underlings who are envious and jealous of people who are bright and successful and defeat them by criticizing and undermining them. Intrafamily jealousy is the main reason why family businesses are often run so poorly and why the employees are tense, angry, and depressed: Family hostility on the job is particularly hard to take because it reminds of family hostility off the job.

> One father who ran a business with his two sons viewed both of them as his rivals and envied each his youth, good looks, and intelligence. He made up and then passed on bad things one son supposedly said about the other son to cripple each of them. The two brothers realized what he was doing and, even though they were arch rivals themselves, learned to put aside their differences long enough to follow one rule slavishly together: When Dad says you said this about me, don't believe it until you ask me first if I actually said it. Nonetheless, the entire experience was draining and depressing to all concerned.

Friends and family can be especially hard on the creative person when the friends and family are not creative workers themselves. Misunderstanding those who are, they either deprive them of the support they need or selfishly abuse them, demoralizing and depressing them in the process. Typically they complain that they bring work home with them and disrupt family life or retreat into the privacy of their office at home, thus abandoning the family.

The following case, of a Jewish homosexual psychologist, illustrates both how people abuse creative people on the job and how abuse from others can so easily become the self-abuse that is characteristic of depressives.

> An extremely bright Jewish gay psychologist worked in a clinic alongside homophobic associates and with homophobic patients. Because of the civil rights laws, no one dared actually come out and tell him that they disliked him, and certainly no one dared openly abuse him because he was gay. Instead they claimed their dislike, which was apparent, was for other reasons. One patient, who had severe brain damage from an old head injury, was a hostile bigot who hated Jews, gays, and blacks—the three most common victims hate-filled people use and abuse to express angry feelings already in place. As far as this patient was concerned, this doctor had three strikes against him. The patient would follow the doctor around the

clinic, talking in stage whispers, saying, "kike, fag, shrink," loud enough for the psychologist to hear. There was nothing to be done, for the man was abusing his position as a patient (i.e., he was using it effectively to protect himself from any negative consequences of his bad behavior).

A colleague of the psychologist decided this patient was a gift from heaven, for he found that he, the colleague, could express his own hatred toward the psychologist (one he apparently shared with the patient, and for the same reasons) by quoting the patient to the psychologist. He sidled over to the psychologist day in and day out and told him, over and over again, at every chance he got, "This man hates you," and then he quoted the patient's list of reasons why.

The doctor could not stand much more of it, and telling his colleague to stop did not work. So he went to the administration and complained. But he only got the following unhelpful response: "He does it because he thinks it's funny."

The psychologist went home each night angry and depressed. On the job, nothing he did seemed right. And off the job, as soon as he got home, he began to abuse and second-guess himself, all evening and all night long. He got little sleep, had nightmares about his lover rejecting him, and woke up tired and even more depressed the next morning.

The patient had turned the tables. He, and those who quoted him, were evaluating the psychologist—not, as it should be, the other way around.

Worse, the psychologist was basically in agreement with his negative evaluators. He concluded not that his tormentors were misinformed, but that he was miscast in his role as a doctor. He thought, "What did I do to this patient?" "How can I make it up to him?" "What should I do to improve my technique—and myself—so that it doesn't happen again?"

He took what others said about him to heart, all without considering the source. In effect, by agreeing with them, he was lowering himself, getting down to their level. As depressives do, he was lying down with dogs and getting up with fleas. Then he was blaming his having fleas not on the dogs, or on the fleas, but on himself.

## Specific Stressors

Some specific sources of on-the-job stress are as follows:

*Being double-binded.* A woman experiences a typical double bind when she is sexually harassed at work and then told that she will be fired if she complains.

*Criticism.* Criticism, which may be either in the form of a lack of positive response or an actual negative response, is an occupational hazard for every one, but especially for depressives, who are highly sensitive to criticism because their low self-esteem makes them dependent on what others think. But oversensitivity to criticism is not the depressive's only problem, for depressives also tend to be criticized more than individuals who are not depressed, mostly because they are creative people and have the aforementioned problems creative people experience in working with others.

*Rejection.* Depressives are people who get more deeply, and more intensely, involved in their relationships with others, partly because as creative people they find others interesting and challenging, and partly because as needy people they require more human contact and warmth than many. One result is that a depressive's relationships are like a violin string: taut and likely to snap—often when least expected, and usually with the most disastrous of consequences. Depressives may snap when the boss or their co-workers reject them on the job. Or they may snap when they are rejected at home. In one case a depressive was rejected by a mate who envied her her triumphs and reacted to each by asking, "What does this mean for me?" and answered her own question by concluding that it made her a lesser person comparatively and meant that she would languish at home as her lover got more and more involved with her work. In another case a depressive was rejected by selfish children who responded to their father's latest triumph with, "Does your having to work late and bringing work home mean we can't have my friends over for dinner?" Writers are often the victims of envious friends and relatives, who reject them by puncturing their balloons with sadistic comments about what they think they should be doing that they are not already doing—for example, not writing poetry for self-expression but Harlequin romances for financial gain—and then cleverly hiding their humiliations as supportive (hiding their "What you are doing is not worthwhile" beneath an unsolicited, and often inappropriate, "I have some worthwhile suggestions to help you do better").

*Losses.* Losses due to a relationship ending or due to death often produce depressive occupational disorder.

> When a famous composer died suddenly, one of his students, who was also one of his assistants, became depressed and had to be hospitalized. The student, a hostile, competitive person by nature, thought he had killed the composer simply by wishing him dead so that he could take over his job as head of the music department at the university.

Curing depressive occupational disorder that follows the death of a boss, teacher, parent, or mate requires an especially gentle, supportive approach. Insight into the meaning of the loss is not enough to reverse the disorder. The cure requires less talk than action. It requires support, given without the therapist being intrusive or crossing boundaries. Supportive therapists can be compared to a swimming buddy who hovers in the background, ready to move in in case of trouble. Supportive helpers do not harass depressives, insisting that they "cut it out." They are happy to be there, no questions asked, and make no demands for themselves. They do not intrude abrasively on workers' memories, demanding they live for now and pushing them to substitute a new for an old relationship immediately. Instead they allow the worker to replace the lost object gradually as a way to avoid raising the question of disloyalty. On the other hand, they are not distant and remote, like strict cognitive-behavioral revisionists or psychoanalysts, whose theoretical precision is a way to avoid any semblance of hand-holding. They do not play into the worker's need to pick distant and remote therapists deliberately because of a pathological lack of desire for a new relationship, because of an excessive focus on the enormity of the loss, because of the feeling that replacing lost objects means being unfaithful to their memory and to the person lost, and because of the guilt associated with grief so that "what I did wrong" becomes the cry. In such cases the patient wants to continue to suffer and accomplishes this by refusing any offered hand that promises to be a helping hand.

Therapists can, however, overdo supporting their patients. They can overprotect them. They can treat them with kid gloves, avoiding even constructive criticism because they are afraid that because of low self-esteem the depressive will see all criticism as destructive. Afraid of saying even the slightest unflattering thing, they confine their treatment to befriending the patient and giving sympathy (saying something like, "I see how you must be suffering; I myself suffered in exactly the same way") and commiserating ("bad things so often happen to good people"). One therapist was so fearful of criticizing her depressed patients that she could not even tell them to read about their illness, to study the lives of the great company people, or to practice their word processing so that they did a better job, because she feared accusing the patients of being unknowledgeable, ineffectual, and incompetent, respectively. Yet many of her depressives would have welcomed the advice. They disliked being complimented when they themselves knew they needed to be criticized. Depressives know that constructive criticism is necessary if they are to change, and when it is not forthcoming they get more depressed, thinking they have put something over on their therapists, do not deserve real therapy, do not deserve to get better, or do not deserve to have a therapist who knows what he or she is doing. Writer's workshops are notorious for providing support that should be withheld until it is more deserved. Group therapy at work too often follows the same pattern. The patient is given indiscriminate emotional support that deflects from the need to change and that is not supportive (1) because the patient knows it is the wrong thing for him or her to have, and (2) because the patient knows the support is insincere.

One depressive said he hated to be criticized, so he was given only cheerful support. But he got not less depressed, thinking, "My therapist likes me the way I am," but more depressed, thinking, "I have put one over on that fool." Eventually the therapist began to criticize the patient constructively, and he welcomed and allowed it, without getting paranoid about the therapist's intent. He knew he deserved it and that the criticism was necessary if he were to improve to the point that he no longer deserved it. Ultimately he even thanked his therapist for "being tough with me."

Along similar lines, the grieving worker has to work. A year and a half of grief is a year and a half out of one's life, and this is a big chunk out of a potentially productive career. Few workers can afford to lose so much time, particularly since many griefs affect any one life. So they must do their job as they work through their grief, and they must not coddle themselves, waiting until the work of grieving is done before they go back to work. Instead of brutalizing themselves by not working, they should tell themselves, or be told by their therapists, "If you must brutalize yourself, try to do it symbolically, by suffering for your work, instead of actually, by not doing any work at all in order to suffer."

Some people who are depressed after suffering a loss do best with a conservative therapeutic approach. For them the tincture of time is the best cure. Grief and depression often remit, as if spontaneously, after a period of time (which can be up to a year or two). This happens because their depression is a self-limited disorder, and the individual works the depression through implicitly. Or it happens because given enough time, the world changes for the better. Which depressions should be treated conservatively is beyond the scope of this text. In the meantime, the greatest favor workers can do for themselves is to avoid doing harm to themselves, particularly by burning personal and professional bridges, by becoming remote from, or angry and paranoid with, friends and colleagues they need now or will need later.

Gay workers who are in ambivalent relationships and suffer a loss are, after that loss, in particular danger of developing chronic, unremitting, unresolvable, grief and the addictions that can go with it and make it worse. I feel most gay workers must, if they are to survive without disaster after significant loss, get into supportive psychotherapy. I suggest individual rather than group therapy because group therapy, when poorly run, tends to put too much distance between the individual and the therapist, creating yet another loss.

Although many books recommend self-help as a way to get over grief, self-help alone may be no help at all, or even contraindicated at times of intense grief, for two reasons: First, when it is simplistic, it is ineffective, and that sets the stage for further disappointment as the individual sees no change and then feels, "It's my fault that I can't get over this silly problem." Second, self-help can mean being alone, which can reinforce the loss.

*Getting older.* Getting older (which I include here for convenience although it is as much an internal as it is an external event) may cure or cause occupational depression. Occupational depression can improve with advancing age if increasing maturity leads to sensitivity to nuance, clarity of vision, or increased personal depth. It can also improve if individuals become better able to shake off negative opinions of others because after a while they have become philosophical and inured to what others think or because they are self-reliant and need less in the way of external sources of gratification and love than they did before.

But getting older can create occupational depression as well. The older some workers get, the more tired, testy, ornery, and impatient they can become. Their views can become fixed and frozen, and they themselves can become hypersensitive and irrational. They can react catastrophically to very little, and with hardly any provocation at all. Ordinary events become disasters when they stand as evidence that the individual is getting older and feels life is close to being over. The more successful workers get depressed when there is the slightest hint of trouble because they have so much to lose. The more unsuccessful ones get depressed because they have more trouble than most in life. They find that job applications go unanswered. Having depleted some or all of their store of material, they begin to become repetitive. They are no longer the bright helpless youngster that other, often older, individuals want to take under their wing. For workers who are used to being taken care of, it is disconcerting to have others look to them as a source of intellectual or emotional support. At the same time, the worker becomes less personally desirable because less sexually desirable. Others may not try so hard to form overt or covert sexual relationships with older people. So, feeling less of a sex object, older workers feel (and sometimes become) less of a romantic, and so less of a creative, presence.

In addition, older people sometimes call up others' sadism. Sadists move in for the kill when they smell blood, and most of them view all older people as bleeding. Sadists are basically cowards who like to pick on those they can identify as too weak to fight back effectively. Older people buy into the sadism when they do not protest abuse because they accept it as better than being ignored completely and because, ashamed of being old, they chime in with self-abuse of their own. They apologize for themselves. In effect, they excuse ageism as a rational stand (for example, by saying "I can see why companies don't hire older people; after all, they *do* get sick and use their major medical policies more often than younger ones"). Often, after accepting abuse they retire from work to get away from being abused, using a rationalization like "It's time for me to move on and make room for someone younger," as if younger is better.

> An author used to write three books a year but now writes only one every three years because she thinks she is "over the hill." Feeling weak and vulnerable because of her age, she tolerates criticism less and needs congratulations more—yet behaves in a way that assures that criticism will be likely and congratulations will be unlikely to be forthcoming. She becomes so personally difficult that she loses all her friends. Now she has no one to support her through the rough times, to encourage her to continue her good work when her inspiration dies, to say, "You, and only you, can do it." Because she feels unloved and unwanted, her thrust is diminished, her ideas faint. This she blames not on her being personally difficult, but on what she calls the "depletion of old age."

In conclusion, older depressives see old age as a time of infirmity, and they retire, without regard for what they as individuals can do. They are often the victims of their own circular reasoning: They feel over the hill because they are depressed, and they feel depressed because they feel they are over the hill. In reality, their old age is not the accumulation of exhaustions and depletion of the finite pool that they think it is, but is instead a giving up. To paraphrase George Eliot (1964), they have not been great enough to make circumstances less strong against them (p. 568). If they have an occupational disorder, it is not due to age but to the perception that their age is a weakness without compensating strengths. For them old age is less an actual physical or mental deterioration than it is a depressed state of mind.

Therapists should help their older workers become hardened to and refuse to accept the inevitable putdowns they will get for being older. In this it helps to consider the source, a technique advocated throughout this book and one especially useful for challenging ageists, as well as bigots of all kinds (including sexists, racists, and homophobes). Ageists are not right; they are sadistic, and their sadism originates in envy and jealousy. They see older people as having it all, so they attack them as "greedy-geezers." Sadism also originates in fear, and sadists fear older people because they fear becoming "defective" like them; thus they attack them to reassure themselves that "what happened to you won't happen to me." Their own fears about becoming menopausal or impotent cause younger sadists to stereotype older workers and put them in their place, "over the hill," because over the hill is out of sight and out of mind. Thus they can postpone the inevitable realization and deny the inescapable conclusion that "I am next."

Another useful technique involves identifying with the aggressor. It is not difficult for older people assertively to counter the more sadistically inclined ageists in their midst. All they have to do is seize control by letting the ageists know that they know what they are thinking and why they are thinking it, and by not desperately appealing for love but instead making it a matter of whom the older person chooses to love and permits to love them. Instead of trying to please the younger generation, older people should ask or demand that the younger generation try to please them.

At the same time, older workers should rein in any excessive need for love. If they must care at all about what people think, they should settle for respect when necessary. They should do their work without fretting unduly about their reviews. They should focus on enhancing their performance, not on enhancing their image. There are worse things than being creatively lonely, but there are few worse things than destroying oneself just to force recognition at whatever cost.

Self-acceptance is another good way to thwart sadists as well as to get what love is absolutely necessary. The cause of self-acceptance is not well served by continuous references to age, which should be avoided as far as possible (for age is a nonissue when it does not negatively affect behavior). Nor is it served well by acting older than one's age (say, by discussing aches and pains in a complaining fashion or otherwise getting into the bent-over-walking-with-a-cane rut, whereby people constantly complain of their emotional and physical aches and pains, perhaps hoping to be reassured that their looks are still acceptable and their health still good). Instead of looking for false reassurance, which is the only possible kind they can get, they should straighten up as much as they can and never, if they have been crying, let others see the red of their eyes. If they keep everything on a light and positive note, soon they will feel that there is plenty to be light and positive about.

Particularly to be avoided are restitutive behaviors meant to make the patient appear younger than his or her actual age. Acting one's age is better than trying to hide it. Too often older people make themselves into an inferior version of the young, instead of someone special in their own right. Women wear excessive makeup and men ineffective toupees, and both dress in inappropriately youthful ways. This does not work, and it often makes things worse.

Older people should also be as active as possible. Whenever possible, they should not retire. For energy comes from activity, and vice versa. So many older people retire because they cannot face the inevitable changes in their reputation that come with the passage of time. But society changes, and companies grow, and both want new standard bearers. Any worker, but especially one in a fast-changing field, will likely quickly become the older generation, defined as "out of date." Even the most talented should not expect to be "in" forever. Instead of taking it personally and seriously, older workers should keep up when indicated; ignore the winds of fashion when it is the wind and the fashion, not the field itself, that is changing; or face facts when one must inevitably be the older generation that the new generation wants to lead, not follow. If they cannot face facts and accept changes of fashion, at least they can ignore them and wait out the generation gap, expecting that the next gap will be in their favor. For when tastes change again, "bad old romanticism" becomes "good new neoromanticism." In the meantime, older workers should recognize that no generation is a monolith. There are always the neophobics, who hate anything new, to save them from the neophiles, who dislike anything old. Finally, it is often reassuring for the worker to hear not only, "Wait, your time will come again, don't force it or beg," but also, "Remember, too, that if they *really* hate you, and everything you supposedly stand for, that's not necessarily a bad thing. It is a good thing if it means you have gotten, and are keeping, their attention."

## ENDOGENOUS DEPRESSION

Endogenous depressions can appear in the absence of external stress. Sometimes they appear to begin without an identifiable stressor, although in fact there is one that cannot be identified. Most times there is apparent stress, but it is minor and by itself insufficient to cause depression. Depression only results because the stress cannot be handled in a healthy way. Most people can handle the big things in life. It is the little things in life that give them the most difficulty.

> An accountant became depressed during her last weeks on a job that she had voluntarily quit. She hated the job and could not wait to leave it, until a seemingly minor incident occurred. She had an old set of china her parents left her, and the cups were broken. She called some people who advertised that they did a search and replacement for china, but she was snubbed with mysterious, knowing, demeaning chortles when she told them the brand. Apparently it was cheap china. She began to think that if her parents had loved her more they would have left her better things. Next she began to feel unlovable and reacted negatively to leaving, thinking, "I need that job, I'll miss it, I am leaving the only family I have, and I'll never be able to replace them," and she became overtly depressed.

## Mental Manifestations

### *Affect*

Patients tend to call any bad feeling "depression," and their therapists in turn tend to take what their patients say at face value and diagnose accordingly. But depressive affect, especially the affect that is associated with endogenous depression, is unique. Depressives feel blue, and they feel blue specifically in the pit of their stomach or beneath their sternum. The feeling hurts and gnaws. While it comes from within, it often feels as if it comes from without. For example, one depressive described it "as if a vise has been placed on my chest and is being gradually, but inexorably, squeezed closed."

The more insightful patients associate feeling blue with feeling angry toward others. Depressives feel themselves getting angry but believe that they cannot express their anger. So they keep their anger inside and try to hide it, in part by taking it out on themselves. They do not get mad, and they do not get even. They get depressed. They say, "I hate myself," but they mean, "I hate you." They know, however, that they have not really hidden how angry they feel, and they are right. Their anger shows, and that makes others feel and get angry with them. In turn, they feel they deserve the anger that others feel toward them, so they accept it and even make it their own. They think, "They are right to be mad at me; I deserve it because I am an angry person, mean, and worthless as a consequence, and that others are angry with me just proves it." They then completely suspend their self-evaluation in favor of evaluations from others. The composer Anton Bruckner thought himself and his symphonies needed fixing because others hated them. The composer Samuel Barber thought his opera *Anthony and Cleopatra* needed revising and that he was a bad composer because his critics condemned the work. Herman Melville may have stopped writing for 35 years because he took what Zachary Leader (1991) called "American philistinism" (p. 28) as a deserved negative judgment of his work and of himself. Many workers, from Melville to clerks, develop low self-esteem (discussed in Chapter 17), do a poor job, leave the company, or quit work not because they really think that that is what they should do, but because they sense that others think that that is what they should be doing.

The process does not stop there, because patients can keep their anger inside for only so long. Eventually they have to express at least some of their anger. They do this directly, in temper tantrums, or indirectly, passive-aggressively, by torturing others (one of the few indulgences they allow themselves). They grouse and complain. Or they withhold what others need, often citing their depression as both reason and excuse. A depressed writer, to get back at an editor who blue-penciled his latest masterpiece, tortures him by missing deadlines. A depressed salesperson, to get back at customers who interrupt her "psychic siesta," replies to their requests in a desultory fashion, saying, "If you don't see it on the rack, then it isn't in the store," without actually checking the computer or the storeroom. A depressed bus driver, to retaliate for having to do the extra work involved when asked "How often does this bus run?", silently points to the schedule, as if to say, "Look it up yourself." Other people become angry with such behavior. Most people do not like depressed people, and the depressive manifestations of anger only justify their dislike further and give them a new reason to dislike and abandon the depressed person. With everyone seemingly angry with them, depressives can both justify a low self-esteem, lower their self-esteem even further, and proceed apace with a withdrawal from the world that is already in process.

> While it was true that in today's world it was difficult to produce a good product because most people did not recognize quality, or if they did, it was not what sold, for one corporate head this should have been a reason to try harder to win, not a reason to try harder to affix the blame—on the media that criticized his product, on the rating agencies that did not give it the highest approval, and on the customers who "are too stupid to know a good thing when they see it." But he reacted to what was in essence constructive criticism not by accepting it in the spirit in which it was offered and using it for purposes of self and product improvement, but by feeling abandoned and humiliated. Then he got angry, blamed the messenger, and took his anger out on others. This made him more comfortable inside, but at the expense of his personal relationships and professional success. For example, he became a critical contentious person who, instead of working with others the company dealt with, devoted much of his time, as Edmund Bergler (1959) might put it, to collecting injustices from them. Predictably his product languished unsold, and the company was threatened with bankruptcy.
>
> Fortunately he had a sensitive therapist, who recognized that underneath he was depressed and held off rubbing his nose in the problem and salt in his wounds. Instead of nagging him to understand himself and change on command based on this understanding, she recognized that his personal and professional behavioral problems were symptoms of his depression, and then she treated his depression supportively, by focusing on all the worthy things he did and on how he was a worthy person himself, who deserved to treat himself and be treated better. Thus personally fortified, he was able to accept that it was possible to have a flawed product without being a flawed person. Thus instead of merely blaming others for his failure, and himself for his having failed, he took steps to fix what was wrong and rescue his company from the brink of insolvency.

### Thought

Depressives get depressed because they make cognitive errors in thinking about themselves and the world. In a vicious cycle, self-esteem falls as a result of the cognitive errors they make, and they then let their low self-esteem further distort their cognitive thinking. Their self-esteem falls when, to paraphrase Hirschfeld and Shea (1985), they draw specific negative conclusions without sufficient evidence; pick out a single negative detail and ignore other more important positive aspects of an experience; overvalue the significance of that particular negative detail; and evaluate life and themselves in an all-or-none way so that they dislike themselves completely if they find anything about themselves to dislike at all (p. 817). As a result, they see only what they did wrong and not what they did right; think that because they have one bad day, every day will be bad from now on; and think that others hate them even though others are merely having a bad day themselves.

### Behavior

*Withdrawal.* Severely depressed people slow down and withdraw. Less severely depressed people still function—they feel bad but continue to work, though not up to par.

*Mania.* For some depressives, mania is the equivalent of a superiority complex, put into place to obliterate an inferiority complex and as a way to refuse to accept a bad review, either from the world or from oneself. Mania usually reverts to depression when denial no longer works and what was denied hits home, and twice as hard.

Some manics work effectively when they are manic, but others cannot work effectively, not because they say and do too little, but because they say and do too much. For example, in a blink of the eye a composer writes another 100 opus numbers, or in the same amount of time a CEO takes over another 100 companies, as part of the process of what Lynch and Rothchild (1989) calls "diworseification" (pp. 146–150).

*Diurnal variation.* Due to diurnal variation, depression is often worse in the early morning and then clears up as the day progresses. Depressives do not want to get up and out of bed to face the day, and they are often late to work, if they go at all. They feel better as the day goes on, and by quitting time they feel at peace with the world and may even like their job. The next morning, however, they cannot get up and out of bed to face the day.

*Vicious cycling.* Two vicious cycles often conspire to make a mild depression severe and an acute depression chronic. In the first, workers cannot work because they are depressed, and they are depressed because they cannot work. In the second, depressives are depressed because few want to take care of them, but few want to take care of them because they are depressed.

## Physical Manifestations

### *Depressive Equivalents*

These include such symptoms as depressive headaches, depressive fatigue, and depressive hand syndromes. Depressive hand syndromes start with the patient feeling unappreciated or unloved. There is a repetitive strain injury, but it is really due to a strain on and an injury to the ego. The hand tightens (say, at the computer keyboard) as a demonstration and concretization of feeling angry at being rejected (that is, such people are making a fist at the world); as a demonstration and concretization of their guilt (that is, they are keeping their hand, really themselves, from striking or stabbing others); and as a way to hurt themselves by hurting their career (this is also prompted by their guilt feelings about their anger). Such people must not be operated on thoughtlessly, lest they see surgical intervention as deserved punishment and become even more depressed.

Conversion disorder—not depression—should be considered when the hand syndrome is more the product of sexual conflict than the product of conflict about anger. Clinicians can tell the difference by listening to the patient's associations. For example, the dental hygienist described in Chapters 13, 16, and 17 said in one breath that she hated her boss because he mistreated her, and then said in the next breath that she had trouble moving her hand. The context in which the symptom occurs is equally important in making a differential diagnosis. Hysterics develop hand syndromes when they feel too close to someone they love. Depressives develop hand syndromes when they feel too distant from someone they feel does not love them.

Fatigue that is a product of depression has to be distinguished from fatigue due to chronic fatigue syndrome. Treatment of depressive fatigue requires treatment of the depression. This often means not vitamins or yeast extracts, but exercise, discipline, and more hard work—the goal of which is to change the unpleasant "sick" depressive fatigue into the pleasant healthy kind of fatigue, in which the patient is tired but happy, not tired because unhappy.

## TREATMENT

### Some Treatment Suggestions

Therapists can help depressives deal with abuse by learning to consider the source of the abuse—in the vernacular, by understanding where their abusers are coming from.

A doctor thinks a nurse who denigrates his abilities does so because of who he is and what he does. But she does so because of who she is and what she does. She hates him first because she is a chronic complainer who finds fault with every one, and second because she envies him, and she envies him because he is better trained in some areas than she is and makes more money than she does.

Therapists should help depressed patients take some responsibility for their depression, instead of blaming it entirely on their work or other not-me events like chemical imbalance (in effect, blaming allows patients to disown the need to manage both themselves and their careers).

A self-employed patient who made teddy bears became too depressed to work. He suggested that the reason he could not work was that he had a chemical imbalance he heard about on a talk show. He seemed delighted to at last discover what was causing his work inhibition. But the real problem was not his chemical imbalance. The real problem was that instead of working he was watching talk shows. He was just being lazy and then excusing his laziness by telling himself that he had a disease.

Therapists should help depressives learn to deal with their anger. Depressives should not simply be told to get their anger out. They should never get inappropriate anger out. Instead they should always keep inappropriate anger in and then resolve it implicitly, in their minds, so that they become less angry. Depressives *can* get appropriate anger out, although getting the appropriate anger out is not entirely risk free. Often it is dangerous, first because it creates guilt about abusing others, and second because it antagonizes people the patient needs. A better way is to work the anger out by resolving the problem that is causing the anger.

Treatment of low self-esteem and guilt, a central issue in depression, is discussed in Chapter 17.

### Some Psychotherapeutic Errors to Be Avoided

Some commonly used methods for treating depression are either unproductive or dangerous. Depressed workers need more than a mere cheering up. Therapists cannot improve a reactive depression simply by saying, "Smile, you are better off than you think, because things aren't as bad as you see them, because there are worse things in the world than what just happened to you." It may be true that serious physical illness, disability, or death is worse than having one's creative ideas rejected, but for the moment that is the worst thing in the world for the patient, and suggesting otherwise is dismissive and rejecting. Patients will feel that no one cares and takes them seriously. They will feel accused of being crybabies, whiners over nothing. A much better approach is to be honest about it. All professional life is hard. There are worse things in the world than financial, artistic, and popular failure. But for now those will do. But sometimes there is a bright side. Usually it does not mean the end of a career. Usually there is an opportunity to try again, make creative and personal course corrections, and even snatch success out of the jaws of failure.

It is cruel to tell workers not to react negatively to professional rejection because it is not meant personally. Bosses and other critics who want free reign to abuse their workers promote the myth of the distinction between the personal and the professional. But for good workers, every professional rejection is a personal rejection because good workers are their work. A better approach is to admit that rejection is meant personally and then talk about why a personal rejection should matter so much.

## Pharmacotherapy

There are two schools of thought about the use of antidepressants. Some therapists see psychotherapy as a last resort, to be used if antidepressants do not work, while others see antidepressants as a last resort, to be used if psychotherapy does not work. Each side has a point. Pharmacotherapy is quick and easy and, at least compared to prolonged psychotherapy, relatively inexpensive. On the other hand, psychotherapy can resolve the problem causing the depression. This can give the patient the opportunity to make real, productive personal and professional changes, which can also help prevent a subsequent attack. One modern approach, not useful for all patients, is to combine psychotherapy and pharmacotherapy to deal simultaneously with the underlying reasons for the depression and help the patient feel better fast.

The decision to give pharmacotherapy should not be made simply because of the belief that all depression is the result of a chemical imbalance which is correctable by pharmacotherapy. It may be, but to the best of my knowledge no pathognomonic chemical imbalance has to date been identified with any degree of certainty. Furthermore, what is causing the depression makes less difference than we think when it comes to choosing between pharmacotherapy and psychotherapy. Psychotherapy can affect one's chemical balance (via one's emotions), and pharmacotherapy can be effective even in the absence of a chemical imbalance—working independent of cause just as a drink before boarding a plane relieves flight anxiety although the anxiety is due to a strictly emotional fear of flying. This is why a depression that is clearly a response to real life factors, such as lack of money or not having had a compliment from the boss all year, may respond to appropriate pharmacotherapy simply because, as Dr. Richard Wagman (personal communication, 1994) says, it moves the patient "from here to there."

Antidepressants alone, without covering medication and supportive psychotherapy, should be avoided for workers who are potentially or actually schizophrenic.

A patient was not depressed, he was schizophrenic. His voices, however, told him to tell his doctor he was depressed so that he could get fluoxetine and be "one of the boys." That is, he lived in Greenwich Village in New York and everyone in the neighborhood was taking fluoxetine and he wanted to belong. One week later, possibly because he became excited and paranoid from the drug, he hung himself.

A schizophrenic veteran was able to avoid being openly paranoid by isolating himself from the world. He felt, "Since the war is over I have no gun. I could only face the world when I had a gun. Now that they took my gun away from me I can no longer go out of doors at all." But he could at least write, and he was working on a book about his years as prisoner of war—telling a fascinating story of his forced march through the ice and snow, his days of isolation when he did not know what time or month it was, and how he subsisted on a gruel of a few potatoes boiled in water and the plants and bugs he could glean from the landscape. He described his inner personal triumph over isolation and torture, and how he got through the days until his release at the end of the war.

But his psychiatrist, concerned that he was neglecting his interpersonal relationships, "got on my case" and pushed him to develop his relationships with others. She told him first that he was depressed, and second that he was depressed because he was not getting out more and relating better. And she gave him "more fluoxetine than I usually give because you are *very* depressed."

The medicine agitated him physically and mentally because he believed his therapist was trying to push him too quickly, and unsupported, into dangerous waters. To be a good patient, he complied and waded in. Then, panicky and paranoid because of the medication effect and because he felt he had no life raft and was drowning, he tried suicide, but failed, and then decompensated into a full-blown paranoid psychosis requiring hospitalization.

It is always wise to remember that there is a dark side to getting over depression. Depression is not entirely a bad thing when it serves a creative purpose. This may be the case with tithing, whereby individuals allow themselves to continue to be effective professionally as long as they arrange to suffer personally. Or depression can broaden perspective and vision, for depressive hypersensitivity is close to creative perceptiveness, and depressive alarmism, the kind that blows up minor things out of proportion, is very close to creativity itself (at least that kind that succeeds by conjuring up tempests out of teapots).

## AN OVERVIEW

In this overview I summarize points I have already made and add some new ones. The importance of depression warrants this summary, even at the risk of repeating some material.

In this chapter I have explored the insidious factor of depression and how, even though it explains many cases of occupational disorder, it is often unrecognized and improperly treated. I note that real and imagined occupational disappointments and losses exist to make all workers depressed, and some of them deeply so. I note that in diagnosing depression we must distinguish between having a few depressive symptoms and having the full-blown depressive disorder. I describe some of the signs of depression and some of the symptoms depressed workers report. Depressives tend to be blue. They may also have angry and paranoid feelings, but as I point out, any one "out there" these days does have real enemies. They have not only a depressive self-attitude with low self-esteem but a narcissistic character structure with elevated self-esteem, which in turn exposes them more than others to disappointment and leads to more low self-esteem. This combination of feeling blue, paranoid, and both more and less worthy than others is diagnostic.

Depression is manifest as an inability to do one's work well (or at all) when depressives conclude that they do not deserve to accomplish much or that what they do accomplish is not any good and so should not be shown or promoted or should be destroyed after being finished.

Depression is also manifest as pseudophysical symptoms such as chronic fatigue, which may mimic Epstein-Barr; back pain; and even certain forms of carpal tunnel syndrome or repetitive strain injury. In the depression context, these are called depressive equivalents—that is, they are physical manifestations of depressive conflicts, such as the one between getting anger out and keeping it in, the latter for practical reasons (to keep one's colleagues) or for emotional reasons (to satisfy guilt). Or they are simply manifestations of a general depressive stagnation, burnout, or withdrawal, which are in turn a manifestation of depressive despair, on the one hand, and a depressive need for self-punishment, on the other.

A differential diagnostic point is that hysterics with physical symptoms are often accused of malingering their physical symptoms when no physical basis is found for their symptoms. In contrast, depressives under the same circumstances are accused instead of being crybabies—that is, of taking a little discomfort (one that is within normal limits) and making much too much out of it.

Dynamically, we have to seek the source of depression both from within, in the individual, and from without, in the individual's environment. Some observers make much of the distinction between exogenous (reactive, external) and endogenous (internal) depression. They are right to do so because, while in any one depression endogenous are often combined with exogenous factors, therapists still have to distinguish what is nature and what is nurture (or lack of it) to make sense of a depression and to develop a case-specific treatment approach.

As just mentioned, most workers do have reasons to be depressed exogenously. Individuals insensitive and hostile enough to depress anyone abound on any job. There is often a selfish and critical boss to contend with. Workers are abused, or downsized, because they are in the way of a boss who wants to get ahead; the boss thinks they are making too much money and so are less desirable than a younger person with a lower salary; the boss wants to hire a family member or friend of the family; or the boss feels that the workers are too competent and threaten his or her job or self-esteem. In the latter case, the way to defend oneself best is not to improve one's skill sets but to soft-pedal the skills that one already has. In such circumstances a degree of discouragement and depression will likely appear in everyone, and the argument that depression does not take hold unless the worker is vulnerable to abuse because of something from his or her early life is a specious one. However, while not being promoted or actually being forced out against one's will is tragic enough, thinking that it was a personal thing due to incompetence makes the tragedy even more poignant and more difficult to bear.

In many cases the depression is endogenous and the corporation, or individuals within the corporation, are blamed a lot when they have only done little. Workers contribute to their own depression by being vulnerable to criticism. They fail to consider the source, such as that their boss does not know how to handle people or is a complete jerk who was—following Laurence J. Peter and Raymond Hull's Peter Principle[1] (Peter & Hull, 1969)—promoted to his or her level of incompetence. Instead they parentalize the boss and become like children who think their parents are infallible and who conclude that they themselves must be the ones with the problem; this causes their self-esteem to fall even lower than it already is. Depression appears when workers want to be loved and forget both where they are and that, at least outside of the worker-of-the-month award, there is little time or inclination to go be-

---

1. "In a hierarchy, every employee tends to rise to his level of incompetence" (p. 172).

yond a worker's mistakes to mention the positive nature of a job well done. It appears when hypersensitive workers conclude that any constructive criticism is destructive, that professional is personal criticism, that criticism is not criticism but rejection, and when they forget (especially true for writers) that rejection does come with the territory.

Workers need help through these periods of depression, and throughout this chapter and this book I offer some treatment approaches therapists can use to help their patients overcome the acute and chronic phases of the disorder. Depression can be successfully treated, but only with dynamically sound approaches that at least give some consideration to the deep psychology of depression and deal with losses where indicated—not only the obvious ones, like the loss of a loved one, but the less obvious ones, like the loss of self-esteem because of an imagined or real loss of esteem in the eyes of others.

An important therapeutic goal is for workers to gain perspective so that they will not be so personally affected by their relationships with others in authority (although sometimes those relationship will still sting). Instead of thinking that rejection is deserved, workers should develop a more realistic assessment of their own talents.

Therapists who treat depression must separate myths from facts. It is a myth that self-help approaches which urge workers to "look at the bright side" and "adopt a positive attitude" are sufficient by themselves to snap a patient out of depression. It is a myth that depression is caused by a catastrophic event and therefore treatment involves ferreting out and understanding life's major tragedies; for in reality, depression may be (and often is) triggered by a seemingly unimportant incident. It is a myth that when it comes to one's work, it is abnormal to be sensitive and take things too personally. This is a myth perpetuated by those who abuse workers for their own purposes, like the boss who does not want to pay them too much, or the media critic who wants free reign to attack them. But all good workers identify with their work and so take rejection of their work personally. Calling them foolish for having done so only adds another layer of criticism to what they are already suffering. It is a myth that understanding the internal causes of depression is the same thing as blaming a depressive for being depressed. It is beside the point that depressives cannot help themselves and are victims, not criminals. They must take responsibility for their own depression. But at the same time they should realize that mental disorders are not evil deeds, and if the patient contributes to them, that is part of the problem that must be faced and handled. It is a myth that insight therapy alone is enough to cure depression. While it is helpful in the chronic stages of depression, especially in the acute stage treatment should include support because most workers with depressive occupational disorder need a friend and ally. A good friend and ally to have is an individual therapist who can provide a warm and supportive holding environment, without overstepping the boundaries of professional etiquette.

In conclusion, depression is a universal occupational hazard in the workplace. Central to all occupational disorders, and the chief reason for some, it is a theme in disorders ranging from repetitive strain injury to burnout, yet it is too rarely recognized and too often improperly treated.

In a sense, attributing occupational disorders to depression is an optimistic view, for depression is not only a universal property and cause of occupational disorders, it is also their Achilles' heel. Because depression can be treated, so can the occupational disorders that it creates.

# 4

# Anxiety
# Occupational Disorder

## MANIFESTATIONS

Anxiety is familiar to most of us, for most of us have experienced some anxiety both while awake and while asleep. While awake some of us have experienced stage fright—the fear that we will not be able to perform in front of an audience because we will get dizzy or faint. While asleep we have had a nightmare—for example, that we are at the edge of a precipice and about to fall off or in a cave without an exit, or that we are taking, but not passing, an examination and thus will not graduate from school or get the job we always wanted.

For most individuals, anxiety is painful but not excessively disruptive. For example, pianists tremble before getting up on the stage and during the first five minutes of a performance. But they go on anyway, and while their shaky hands may mar the first notes played, the anxiety disappears at least in time for the second movement, and all goes smoothly from then on. But sometimes anxiety becomes so severe that it becomes disorganizing. The transition from nondisruptive to disorganizing anxiety is familiar to anyone who has tried to find a wallet or a purse misplaced somewhere in the house. At first, when we cannot locate it we become anxious about the possibility that we have lost it, but nevertheless we methodically look for it, calmly trying to remember where we put it. But when we cannot find it, our anxiety increases and becomes panic. Now we rush about, getting progressively more excited. The more we get excited, the more our anxiety increases and the harder it is both to remember where we put the wallet or purse and to search for it methodically.

Often, anxious patients actually feel anxious. They feel dizzy or have palpitations and similar symptoms. But sometimes anxious patients are unaware that they are anxious because they use one or more defenses to handle their anxiety. In turn, anxiety is sometimes mainly or only recognizable by the defenses that are used to handle it. The different defenses (and the specific anxieties that they are brought into play to handle) in fact characterize and distinguish the different occupational disorders. For example, the defense of doing and undoing as a way to handle anxiety about accomplishing good things characterizes the obsessive-compulsive occupational disorders and distinguishes them from depression, which is characterized by the defense of introjection as a way to handle anxiety about one's anger.

When repression is used to handle anxiety about competing with and besting others, motivation and creative ability are buried and patients develop performance inhibitions, like writer's block, or somatic conversion symptoms, like writer's cramp.

When denial is used to handle anxiety about successfully accomplishing one's goals, the mind goes blank and work in progress stalls as good ideas are withdrawn, one's work is refuted, or work that has been completed is lost or destroyed.

When projection is used to handle anxiety about being "defective" (as the patient sees it), patients see themselves as being in an unfriendly, hypercritical environment and then blame that unfriendly environment for all their troubles. Stress and trauma rule in such a world, and people who live there develop occupational disorders that are believed to be an appropriate response to difficult circumstances, although the difficult circumstances are of their own making and they are overreacting. Patients cannot work because their room is too hot or noisy, or the world is not a good place into which to bring their children, their creations. Success does not make them anxious; others want them to fail. Their hands freeze to avoid typing something because they feel they will be subsequently criticized for saying what they have to say. They do not do stupid things; they do brilliant things for people who are too stupid to recognize and appreciate them. If fired, they are not fired because they have been chosen to go because of their bad past performance; rather they are let go because the boss is picking on them and does not love them. Rarely, if ever, do they ask if it is true that they are being picked on and unloved and, if it is true, if they did anything to provoke it. They rarely ask if there is something that they can do to improve their behavior and their performance. For such people life becomes a constant battle against, instead of a cooperative venture with, the establishment. They fight not with their occupational inhibitions but with those who are believed to be inhibiting them, although often these "malignant" people do not even know that they exist, or they are actually their allies. Such people like to fight this way. For if it is "not me" with the problem then "I don't have to change to get along with the world. All I have to do is sit back and make demands on the world to change, to get along with me."

When displacement (and projection) are used to handle anxiety about forbidden sexual or hostile feelings, workers become phobic and develop a symptom like stage fright or a fear of the computer. Their fear simultaneously expresses and handles their anxiety, and it does so in a symbolic way. For example, workers who cannot use the computer because of the fear that it will blow up on them if they hit the wrong key are simultaneously expressing their anger at the computer and the company that makes them use it and the fear that the computer will take revenge on them for their negative feelings about it. They are also expressing other symbolic fears, such as fear of castration and the existential fear of humankind's powerlessness in a forbidding world.

When substitution is used to handle anxiety about positive feelings, hostility takes the place of forbidden love, and the patient develops a personality disorder characterized by becoming cranky and difficult to get along with to avoid getting too close.

> A local bookstore fails to make up for in charm what it lacks in literary significance. It has a musty smell. The paint is peeling. The books are tattered and never dusted because no one imagines they will be sold. And the individual who runs the bookstore is personally driving business away. Whenever a customer enters she merely sits behind the desk and continues *her* reading, never looking up either to smile or to ask what the customers want—that is, to show concern for *their* reading. She would like to be friendlier, she tells her therapist, but something checks her, so that each time the impulse to be warm and open occurs to her, in spite of herself, she avoids it by putting her eyes down and on the page, hoping the new customer will get the message and go away.

When avoidance is used to handle anxiety about accomplishing things, patients become passive as a way to keep from being active. Such patients tend not to do what they want to do, but only what others want them to do. They work when they are asked to, but otherwise they do not do a thing.

The defense of rationalization supports the other defenses—that is, it justifies the defensiveness. For example, individuals may rationalize stage fright, a phobic defense, as a desire to change careers or retire. Pianists who have to abort their careers because of stage fright say that they want to become conductors, and CEOs who have to abort theirs for the same reason say that they want to leave the business world and go into research, or retire to devote more time to their family or to improving their golf game. Older individuals retire not because they are afraid of being criticized for being old, but to enjoy leisure time while they are still young enough to be able to do so.

All these defenses, and the rationalizations that support them, work up to a point but then become maladaptive. They are maladaptive because they relieve some anxiety but solve few problems and create many new ones. They help deal with feeling overwhelmed, but in exchange they waste time and energy without enhancing, and often while diminishing, production. They sacrifice too much to the comfort of limits and the pleasure of smug self-satisfaction. For example, avoidant workers, operating within comfortable limits, if they produce at all, restrict their production to what feels safe and become safe but sorry people artificially limited in what they do and working beneath their capacity. Paranoids, defending themselves against their critics, say, "There is something wrong with you, not me," and they get a great deal of smug satisfaction in blaming others, but no working projects emerge. Even these comforts and satisfactions are illusory, for failure is the price of relief of anxiety, and with failure comes an even deeper pain than that due to the original anxiety. People like paranoids create the very problems that they feel caused their anxiety. While their critics, bosses, or other authority figures may indeed be a hostile lot at the start, paranoids seal their own fate by making them more so in response to the paranoid's odd behavior.

## CAUSES

### External Causes

There are few, if any, cases of anxiety that are purely externally caused. Usually both external and internal causes are contributory, so that both stress and the individual's emotional makeup are significant factors in creating a given episode of anxiety. Agoraphobics who stay indoors because they feel the streets are dangerous are usually both partly right and afraid of the sexual and hostile fantasies that might get out of control should they leave the protection of home. Opera singers who develop stage fright because of a dread of being booed by hostile audiences at the first sign that the voice is letting them down are often both right to be afraid and too sensitive about what other's think. Even a soldier in combat who develops DaCosta's syndrome (cardiac palpitations) does so only partly as a response to the conditions during battle; as one of my patients (who was a veteran) put it, "In my case at least the anxiety was also partly a manifestation of my personal cowardice."

The realities associated with having to work for a living are a source of anxiety for most workers. Work is usually hard, the pay is often inadequate, and these days no one can be certain of having a job tomorrow. But even the most difficult or impossible jobs create anxiety only for those who are anxiety prone.

A psychiatric clinic where I once worked was a source of real stress for some of its workers. This was a satellite clinic, about 50 miles south of the mother clinic, where most of the administrative bureaucracy resided. The bureaucracy in the mother clinic would arbitrarily decide that workers at the satellite clinic would have to spend one or more days a week at the mother clinic, and without warning they would change the workers' assignments and disrupt their schedule and their personal lives accordingly. No one knew when they would be "summoned" and have to do a 50-mile (or more) commute each way, every day, adding 4 hours a day to their work schedule.

A few people handled the uncertainty and the commute fairly well and survived, although with minor deficit—for example, they had an increased startle reaction, or they had examination dreams, some because they feared losing and others because they wanted to lose their jobs but were too dependent on them to tolerate the loss, or too guilty about themselves to tolerate their secret wishes. But others could not handle it well at all. These were the individuals who had spouses who hated to be left alone all day; who themselves were so dependent on their spouses that they did not like to leave them for too long a time; who disliked not being in control of all aspects of their lives; and who had driving phobias that made it difficult for them to travel back and forth such long distances. Some handled the problem by transferring to the mother clinic and moving close by. Others handled it by working out their intolerance of uncertainty or their driving phobias, or by helping their spouses to work out their dependency. Still others handled it by finding another job. But some were stuck, on all fronts, and they were the ones that suffered the most. They simply panicked. One day they would be here, another day they would be there. One day they could sleep until 7 A.M., and be home at 5 P.M.; another day they would have to get up at 5 A.M., and not be home until 7 P.M. They constantly felt anxious, and sometimes shook and cried at work and complained to anyone who would listen, until no one would listen any longer. Many developed headaches. One, a physician, developed severe back pain and was out of work for months on disability. Morale at the satellite clinic deteriorated, and every one's work suffered. The patients sensed what was happening and became anxious and depressed themselves, and then began demanding more care just to reassure themselves that their world was still intact and that someone would always be there to help them.

## Internal Causes

Anxious patients are often alarmists who make much out of little. They turn inherently neutral into stressful situations and then become uncomfortable. On the positive side, alarmists are often creative people with a fantasy life that is active and so allows them to visualize problems in advance and then solve them expeditiously. But on the negative side, alarmists have difficulty functioning because they become paralyzed in situations in which nothing much, or at all, is likely to happen, thinking that every step that they take is a dangerous one and that every move that they make will be their last. For example, they do not speak in public, but hold back because they think that their careers will end because they will forget their lines or make a Freudian slip at a crucial moment and hurt someone's feelings.

Alarmists have made a neutral job into a source of anxiety because they have made it into the object of personal conflict. For example, some writers make their pen their sword and thus working becomes a hostile act; then they cannot work because of anxiety due to their conflicts about hostility. Or a clerk makes work into a test of love rather than one of competency; then she cannot work because working becomes a dependent act, as anxiety about being rejected takes over. In effect, such workers have made their jobs antigenic and have become allergic to them. Like actual antigens, antigenic work finds, attracts, or produces "antibodies," and then antigen and antibody interact to make an inert substance that sinks to the bottom, taking the creative work down with it. For example, the antigen "fear of murdering a rival" combines with the antibody "guilt over hostility" to produce the inert paralyzed hand, and all word processing, or piano playing, stops.

The contaminating antigens are the familiar sexual ones, like excessive dependency, and the familiar hostile ones, like jealousy of a rival and an excessive need to compete with or control others. Guilt is the antibody most often responsible for occupational inhibition, and there are different guilts for workers to contend with. Guilt may be zero-sum guilt, in which the individual believes that there is a finite amount of something in the world and "what I get you lose"; survivor guilt, in which the individual who actually gains something at another person's expense cannot enjoy the gain because of an excessive and exclusive preoccupation with the other's loss; instinctual guilt, in which the conscience condemns sexual or angry feelings as excessive or improper; and guilt about success, in which any achievement is forbidden.

The following case illustrates what I mean by guilt about success.

A patient, a journalist, feared success because she associated it with expressing her emotions, which she saw as shameful. Each time an "I" appeared on the page, each time she told the reader of one of her experiences, she felt a pang of anxiety. Each time she submitted a work for publication she could not sleep, and each time a rejection slip came back for something she wrote she saw it as further proof that she should not have bothered, really she should not have dared, to speak her mind.

So she set out to write in a way that would assure that her writing would not expose her personally. To do this she did not say what she felt she had to say, but instead held back, using such excuses as "Everybody knows that already," or "I would be humiliated if I ever had to actually face one of my readers."

As she planned all along, her books failed because, as she herself complained, they were "prune-like" texts that reflected "how I am afraid of being a plum—rich and juicy enough to be in danger of being eaten up."

The aforementioned patient maintained her comfort level by writing in a fashion that was accurate but dull in the extreme. Others with similar problems might accomplish essentially the same thing by being personally indecisive, first as a way to avoid the anxiety about doing something and second, when they do something, as a way to avoid the anxiety about taking responsibility for what they have done.

A journalist's personal life was a "fearful symphony" of undoing because of his panic about accomplishing and all that it signified. For example, he answered the question "Where is your wife?" by saying not "I don't know," but, "I cannot be certain of her present whereabouts," as a way to avoid taking a stand for which he would also have to take responsibility, and as a way to at least partially withdraw before satisfactorily doing even something as simple as answering a question. Along similar lines, each time he scheduled a vacation he canceled it at the last minute, driving his wife to distraction. He was an aficionado of rainy places, like Scotland, not because he fundamentally liked rainy places but because he was too spartan to enjoy places that were sunny. For example, he called Spain "too open and friendly." As he put it, "all those damn fandangos." Not surprisingly, his sexual relationships with his wife were similarly affected. They were both infrequent and unsuccessful because he could not get or hold an erection or come to orgasm, because both meant commitment.

His fearful reticence similarly affected his professional life. Once when he appeared on live television he was so tense that his wife commented that he looked like he had "a pole up his rear end." His job required him to write a story quickly, but he could do little better than revise it endlessly until the deadline had passed, or, when there was no deadline, beyond the time that the story had relevance. The writing itself showed his inhibitions. It was full of creaky segues that gave away how much effort it had cost. It virtually breathed revision, and strain, and the inability to relax. As his editor said, "No participles dangle. In fact nothing dangles at all. Instead, the whole thing sinks right to the bottom."

He brooded endlessly about giving up his newspaper job and going free-lance versus giving up his free-lance work to keep his newspaper job.

He dreaded working the daily job because of an editor who constantly criticized him. But he equally dreaded being out there on his own, as he put it, "up there, exposed, with no one to keep me from doing wrong, no one to criticize me and show me my mistakes, and no one to blame for the mistakes I make, after I make them."

He was so uncertain about what to do that he was collecting opinions from four psychiatrists simultaneously. He had four psychiatrists because he had second thoughts about the wisdom of any one doctor's plan, so he went to another psychiatrist for a second (and a third and a fourth) opinion. Finally, he made his "own plan." First he gave up his newspaper job. Then he tried to get it back a few months later. Then he gave up writing for months on end and instead preoccupied himself with banning the red dye in the ham his father's company packaged, believing it to be the cause of deaths all over the world. He was full of his own problems and appalled by his own defects. Yet he seemed to be fixing what was broken in other people's lives. This was, of course, just another way to avoid accomplishing—in this case the accomplishment of fixing what was wrong in his own life.

Patients who fear loss of self-esteem can fear failure rather than success and make their work a test of self-worth. Then they go beyond the normal concerns about having done their job well and see the possibility of being humiliated and made into a big nobody in every professional act. Thus they cannot do much, if any, work because of a fear of rejection. Writers whose inspiration flags temporarily, company CEOs overconcerned about an important meeting, and clerks trying to find a lost file they fear is gone for ever are among those who have become anxious about failing. The fear of completion that is part of every thesis block is often really anxiety about being embarrassed, found defective, and rejected should one's work become coherent and complete enough to be handed in for evaluation.

One student writer could not complete her thesis because she was afraid her teacher would humiliate her. She took notes but could not organize them into a coherent work because she was afraid to present her ideas in a comprehensible, final form. As she put it, "They can't drop the blade on you unless and until you actually put your head into the guillotine." In effect, she thought that it was "better not to have loved at all than to have loved and lost."

A source of anxiety other than guilty sexual or hostile wishes arises from a fear of being flooded from within. A creative rush often makes people feel as if they are in a choppy ocean, being hit by a wave, about to lose control, go under, and drown. They completely forget that they are not in the ocean but rather that the ocean is in them.

## CURE

### Dealing with Maladaptive Defenses

Patients should stop the excessive use of defenses as a way to avoid experiencing the slightest degree of anxiety, because doing so sacrifices overall effectiveness for overall comfort. Deniers should stop destroying what they have done just so that they can deny that they did it. Instead they should save everything they do. They might instead hide it in a bottom drawer, label it "for posterity," plan to recycle it later, and then return to it when they feel calmer and are better able to accept their own accomplishments.

Projectors should stop projecting and collecting injustices. They have to stop blaming the world for their own difficulty in writing a project, completing a task, or painting or composing. Workers who erase work by mistake on the computer should stop blaming computers for being difficult to operate. Instead they should take the blame for not knowing how to compute and learn how to do it. Projecting improves their self-esteem, but the improvement of self-esteem is at the expense of improving their performance. Such individuals have to do some honest self-assessment, take responsibility for their feelings and actions, and ultimately learn that maybe the world is going to change for them eventually, or maybe not, but certainly in the meantime changing for the world is a good thing to do.

Avoidants have to stop ducking all stress and allow themselves to experience some, as long as it is within tolerable limits. So many workers leave sick when they get stuck in what they are doing or call in sick when they fear an upcoming assignment. By doing this they relieve their own anxiety, but the relief is only temporary. They create anxiety in others as well as a great deal of resentment, especially when they leave before they finish or do not show up at all and force others to do their work for them (work which sometimes can take others hours to do, when they could have done it in a matter of minutes).

Depressives should stop introjecting as a way to deal with their difficult reality. Depressives stuck in a bad job who cannot change jobs can at least stop blaming themselves for their job-related problems and make plans accordingly.

### Other Therapeutic Approaches

All workers have to deal with the tendency to make their work a source of conflict. No one can eliminate all anxiety and stress from their professional lives, and a small amount of stress does not mean that all is lost. It is not necessarily a bad thing. But workers should avoid creating imaginary stress where little or none exists. To do this they have to work just to work, not to impress others, "kill off" the opposition, or get love. Anything else is either a waste of time or ultimately threatening to the individual. For example, often writers who write not to write but to impress others soon find that this is either a waste of time, because no one is looking, or it has the reverse effect, because others are smirking and calling the writers eggheads or bookworms.

All workers should correct the cognitive errors that create unnecessary anxiety. (Cognitive errors are discussed at length in Chapter 14.) For example, a some = all approach to self-evaluation is particularly self-destructive. Most workers attach base gratuitous motives to their work. But that is no reason to condemn themselves entirely because of the belief that if they are not all good then they are all bad. They should recognize that even if they are working to kill off the opposition, the killing is figurative, not literal. Patients should not globalize, believing that if they are not effective right now, they will never be effective again. That just creates two problems from one: the work disorder itself, and the depressive feeling that having the work disorder now means having it forever.

Workers should deal with problems with low self-esteem in the ways discussed more fully in Chapter 17. They should avoid simultaneously appealing for love and evaluating themselves strictly on the basis of whether or not others love them; taking rejections too seriously and too much to heart; and installing others who disappoint and dislike them as poisonous introjects, bad little voices (like the ones that writers hear telling them, "No good, it has been done before").

> An advertising executive was in danger of ruining her career by making her work a test of love. She was presenting her ideas when they were still in an early stage to see if others could divine what the completed results would be. She was doing this to see if they could appreciate the "real me" behind the surface, the real genius that lay behind the apparent chaos. If they could, it meant that they loved her for who she was, not for what she did. Instead most rejected the ideas as incomplete, and she felt rejected and blocked. She had to start submitting acceptable work, not submitting unacceptable work hoping it would be accepted as proof that she herself was acceptable.

### Formal Psychotherapy

Generally speaking, therapists should use a gentle approach to anxious patients. Self-exploration is particularly difficult and painful for anxious workers, and if it is to be done at all it has to be done in a way that avoids making such patients more anxious than they already are. Going slow is especially the order of the day for patients who fear success. They will resist treatment if therapists try to take their symptoms away too quickly. They consciously and unconsciously object, in part because they do not want to succeed, and in part because they hold their therapists to the same neurotic standards as the ones to which they hold themselves (so they don't want them to succeed either).

# 5

## Phobic
## Occupational Disorder

Most patients with a phobic occupational disorder can go to work, but their phobias interfere with their ability to do their work properly and with their ability to pursue their careers successfully. Once at work they have to avoid an aspect of their work that causes them anxiety, which makes it difficult or virtually impossible for them to do the things that would gain them attention and respect in the business world. While they can function, they can only do so in a limited way, and within self-imposed parameters within which they feel comfortable. They can type, but they fear using the computer. Or they can speak to single individuals or to small groups, but not to large audiences. They remain anxiety free until forced to go outside their limits, whereupon they become panicky. Sometimes they continue to work through the panic. At other times they make an excuse or get sick to avoid doing what they feel they cannot handle. Sometimes they even quit their jobs to find another (but not necessarily better) one in which they can retreat and feel protected from having to face what they fear.

Phobics have at least six sources of job stress. The first is the job stress that all workers have. The second is the stress associated with the object or situation that they fear. The third is the constant stress they are under from having to avoid making contact with that object or becoming involved with that situation—for example, having to say no to the boss who asks them to give a presentation that day. The fourth is the stress that results from the consequences of their avoidance—their work usually suffers, and they do not come highly recommended when they try to get another job. The fifth is the stress they experience when they are no longer able to avoid what they fear. The sixth is the real danger that results when their overconcern with irrational fears is (as is usually the case) associated with an underconcern for rational ones.

A psychologist constantly worried about his records being destroyed by a fire but never about the homicidal patients he was seeing unprotected in his office, behind closed doors and without guards or a working alarm system. He also constantly worried about losing his job because of downsizing, but never for the real reason that he might lose it—that he would be not downsized but fired because he was constantly calling in sick, without giving enough notice for coverage to be arranged, and because he was spotted shopping when he was supposed to be at home recuperating.

Phobics become anxious when faced with objects and situations that most people can handle. Most people can handle them because in reality there is very little danger associated with them. But phobics cannot handle them because of what they stand for symbolically. For example, some phobics cannot take a job in a big city because they cannot ride in elevators. While elevators do occasionally fall, mostly they are safe, and usually people ride in them without incident. But phobics avoid elevators, speaking in public, working at the computer, or working in closed spaces because they have invested these neutral objects, or situations, with personal meaning. They have attributed something they fear within themselves to the outside world. They have done so so that they can deal with the fear, by going around it or avoiding it entirely.

A phobic feared being stifled and smothered in a closed space—that is, he became claustrophobic. He functioned well as long as he did not have to be in a small room with the door closed. Eventually his claustrophobia interfered with his work because he got to the point that he could not interview job candidates unless he left the office door open and sat near the exit, placing the interviewee in the middle of the room—just the reverse of the position interviewees are supposed to be in. Consciously he was only aware that he sat where he sat so that he could "escape easily." Unconsciously his phobia originated in his childhood relationship with his father. He hated his father and wanted to kill him because the father confined him to the house for long periods as punishment (really as a way to keep him dependent and in tow). Today's phobia expressed elements first of his original confinement, and second of his longing to be free from it. However, being free from it meant strangling his father, a guilty wish he projected to become a fear that he himself would be smothered or strangled.

A pharmacist who lived on Staten Island in New York, an island served by both bridges and a ferry, developed a bridge but not a ferry phobia. She could get to work, but only after a round-about, exhausting commute by boat. She arrived at work, but she arrived there tired and frazzled. Once there she could function, but only in the role of underling. She did this so well that she was often offered a promotion to the next higher level. But each time she was offered a promotion she panicked and then avoided accepting the promotion by quitting and getting a new job. She avoided being promoted because she knew that she could only work well when she was in the shadows, and her work could only deteriorate if she went to a higher level. In effect, she felt safer at home than out in the sun, where she believed herself in danger because she felt exposed, out there where every one could see her and her flaws—really, her secret unacceptable desires.

This patient's therapist traced the roots of her phobia to her relationship with her mother. Her mother hoped the patient would be a housewife who would get married, stay at home, and have the many grandchildren the mother always wanted her to have. The patient rebelled, however, and wanted not marriage but a career. The next message from her mother was loud and clear: "You are defying and killing me." For the patient the bridge symbolized "getting from here to there rapidly and easily," and she welcomed the bridge phobia because it kept her from "going out on her own" and "getting out from under." She did allow herself to use the ferry, however, because she was too healthy to become entirely paralyzed, and the ferry was an acceptable compromise because it represented a kind of tithing—that is, taking the ferry was a way to get to work but it was slow and ponderous and entailed a degree of suffering. The suffering involved allowed her to go work and arrive there guilt free, because she could reassure herself as she went that she did not go too quickly, too comfortably, or too successfully—that is, that she was not flying, but crawling.

## SPECIFIC PHOBIAS

The following are some of the things phobics fear: (1) those things specific to the individual; (2) those specific to the human race; (3) real fears that phobics share with normals.

### Fears Specific to the Individual

#### Fear of Bodily Harm

All phobics, but especially successophobics, try to avoid achieving and accomplishing too much because they fear bodily harm.

A journalist wanted to quit his day job and go free-lance. But when he considered making the attempt, he looked before he leapt. First he looked back to his childhood, to a time when his father told him (speaking of the dangerous world out there) not to fly in planes, he'd get injured or killed; not to go out of the house, he'd get polio; not to put his head on the back of a movie seat, he'd get a fungus; and to be a doctor so that he could treat these things in the likely event that he should get any or all of them.

Second he looked forward, out at society, and it told him what was in effect the same thing: "Becoming a free-lancer is putting yourself at risk. You will starve, and die."

Together his father and society convinced him that the world of the free-lancer was a dangerous one. They convinced him that bad things happen to active, ambitious people who strike out on their own in spite of all the warnings. So ultimately he took the safe route and listened to another piece of advice from both his father and his society: "Don't give up your day job."

## Fear of Rejection

Some phobics respond to a minor slight or rejection like some people respond to a black cat crossing their path: They feel it is not just a passing thing but something that puts them in real and serious danger.

A phobic writer had good ideas but she never developed them because she was afraid to say what was on her mind. She was afraid to do this because she was afraid that she would be criticized and rejected. She either stifled her creative explosions or refined them to make them safer and more palatable. On those rare occasions when she submitted her works for evaluation for publication, she became fearful of getting the mail because it might contain a rejection slip. And when she received a rejection slip she got depressed and had one of her recurrent nightmares. She dreamt she worked in a blitz of ticker tape of papers saying "No!" flying about her head and covering and stifling her art in piles of waste. Or she dreamt her family was all dead and her friends hated her, and everyone she called had changed his or her phone number. She was all alone, with no place to live and no money, and she had just celebrated a birthday with a zero at the end of the number, signifying that she herself was getting older and was well on her way to becoming disabled and dying.

Rejection slips or bad evaluations at work are never pleasant. But they are even less so when workers develop a phobia about them and overreact to them not as if they are mere snakes, but poisonous snakes. In reality, just as most snakes are not poisonous, a single rejection slip, like a single bad evaluation at work, rarely seals the fate of the individual receiving it. It rarely spells the difference between success and failure, and certainly not between life and death. It only feels that way, and it feels that way because the individual views the rejection slip or bad evaluation not as a minor incident but as a major catastrophe and thus feels humiliated, castrated, or extruded.

Workers can get depressed when rejected, but they cannot stay depressed all day. That is not what they are being paid to do. They cannot (to quote artists who speak of all the bad reviews they get) prevent an episode of rejection from ruining their breakfast, but they can refuse to let it also ruin their lunch. They will not let it ruin their lunch if they can recognize two things: (1) Work has its ups and downs, and there are good and bad days on any job; and (2) it is possible and necessary to sort the reality of the rejection slip from the fantasy of what it means about oneself, keeping in mind that rejection slips and bad evaluations hit those who take them personally the hardest. Individuals with successophobia take them personally and to heart because the rejections revive the original fears that contribute to their fear of success, and what resounds is, "I told you so." These original fears are of being grown-up, which means having to leave a protective, sheltering womb; being a survivor (survivor guilt), which means leaving people with less behind and in the lurch; and being in reality, for most of us have learned by experience that few people can tolerate or appreciate another's achievements, and that many actually become hostile to others who are smart and effective people and then keep up with the Joneses by cutting the Joneses down to size.

In addition, individuals with low self-esteem take rejections personally because they feel that last year's acclaim is no longer relevant and see this year's criticism as applicable to their entire career, so that one bad review or significant failure means they have accomplished nothing and will never accomplish anything. Such individuals, when rejected, naturally assume that their attackers both have a reason to reject them and the expertise to do so. They assume that their critics are entitled to be critics because they are critics, and they are critics because of their personal virtues and knowledge. In attributing wisdom to authority, they forget that sometimes authority's wisdom is imperfect, that authority can be self-conferred, and that self-importance rivals authority's importance. They do not disagree with their critics but assume that they got what they deserved. In particular, phobic writers submitting works for publication are especially vulnerable because they award their publishers a higher status than they merit and then see them as omnipotent—smart, experienced, perfect experts who always know what they are saying and doing. When rejected, they feel truly impotent and completely defenseless because they forget that even publishers are only human and can, and have, made some very human mistakes.

Furthermore, individuals who are excessively guilty take rejections personally. Workers who think that they deserve to be rejected because they think that they are being punished often suffer the most. For them rejections are not part of the work but are a personal retaliation for something bad they think they did while working.

Finally, individuals who are superstitious and believe in magic take rejections personally. They demonize them like others demonize black cats crossing their path, ladders, heights, or the stage. They see them as mysterious things with a powerful hold. Yet they never ask, "What is the source of their power?" and "What can they really do to me?"

## Fears Specific to the Human Race

The evolutionary child within, which may be especially active and strong in the phobic, beckons the phobic, who will as a consequence regress too easily to an ancestral time when humans lived like wolves in packs. Humans needed to be in the pack then, because it was a matter of life and death. They needed to avoid rejection by the leader of the pack because their fate depended on it. But phobics see packs, and leaders of the pack, everywhere and feel that the leaders hold their lives in their hands. They make authority the pack leader and then think that authority can (with not even a word but merely with a sign—a mere look or a nod of the head) demolish them, and end their lives by ejecting them and putting them out in the cold, where they will be hungry, alone, and die. In effect, phobics become like children, dependent on parents, and then see every one as their parents. Thus they give almost everyone power over them and the ability to destroy them.

Such people reason that if parents do not support them, it is because there is something wrong with them—because they are defective and, as defectives, they deserve to be ejected from the pack. Then, to hide their defects and avoid being rejected, they become silent. They arrange to be neither seen nor heard so that they do not call attention to themselves. As adult workers, they behave accordingly. They remain in the shadows. Work phobias keep them down, but warm and protected. They want, in other words, their occupational disorder. It keeps them from calling attention to themselves and from risking total annihilation—the annihilation of exile.

Thus we can begin to see why a phobia such as stage fright (that elusive, incomprehensible, and even faintly ridiculous anxiety that keeps so many people from public speaking even though their work depends on it) can occur in the most sensible people, and why it has (though it is in fact anxiety about nothing), as Agatha Christie put it, such a "physical" hold (Christie, 1977, p. 152).

It is so powerful because it *is* about something. It is about a terrible thing happening—the end of our career or of our lives. We are standing before the leader of the pack, being judged either to be acceptable and accepted or to be lacking and thus worthy of ejection.

Another reason it is powerful is that it represents something that is desirable. We are fighting something we want, which is harder than fighting something we do not want. Such a phobia represents desirable silence. We want to fall unconscious, for it eases the pain. We want to black out because it is a way to avoid offending, antagonizing, or killing off others on whom we depend. Furthermore, such a phobia is restitutive. If we are carried off on a stretcher, we are, at least for now, part of a group. We are loved, not hated, no matter what the personal cost, and we belong to the pack once again. It is a way, if not actually to be elected, then at least to get the sympathy vote. Our wolf leader hears our cry, feels our pain, comes to the rescue, holds us up as we are about to fall—and by doing this tells us that we are loved.

Of course, in reality getting sick can have the reverse effect. Phobic workers think they are safe because they are being cooperative and hiding in the shadows where no one can see them. They think they are safe because they do not make trouble. But they overlook that ultimately they are going to fail *because* no one can see them. They forget that they are in even more danger because they are acting so weak, needy, and vulnerable. Sickness is a poor defense. It provides sadists with a new opportunity for rejecting. All sadists are at bottom cowards, and all cowards only feel comfortable and safe attacking those who cannot defend themselves. Getting sick encourages wolves to eject the person in order to keep the pack healthy and functioning.

## Fears Based in Reality

It is not always fantastic to personalize rejections. Often rejections *are* personal, and those who personalize them are right to do so and be afraid. But even in this case, phobics forget something—that the personal element is not a real but a transferential one, and they are being rejected by others not for the reasons given but because others use them like a blank screen on which they, the critics, project their deepest fantasies. People who get rejected often get rejected not because of who they are or what they have done, but because they remind their critics (their bosses, for example) of a parent or of a sibling. (Considering the source as a way to master fear is a topic discussed throughout this text.) Of course, it can be difficult to identify what is a real and what is an imagined problem. For example, old age is a real burden for some, but phobics also make too much out of old age, just as they make too much out of a black cat. They become convinced that in old age their fate is progressive incapacity wherein they will grow tired and unresponsive because they have heard and seen it all, or because their adolescent brashness will tarnish and become not a patina of wisdom but a dullness that covers their shine. They prove their own point when they view all the real problems everyone has at work as proof that life as they knew it is over. Then they act accordingly and cower in a corner or flee the scene of their presumed humiliation.

## TREATMENT

Phobias are difficult to treat. But they are even more difficult to treat when they are not treated properly.

An insight-oriented approach is rarely effective by itself. Phobic patients often require a parameter—that is, one or more supportive or behavioral techniques that help reduce anxiety or increase mastery. Some therapists have found the following techniques helpful and effective.

### Associating with New People

When phobic illness originates in identification with passive, fearful, discouraging people in the patient's life, the patient should avoid such people and instead associate with others who are active, unafraid, and encouraging.

One easily cowed artist lived in a shore resort where there was no art. She said, in effect, "I thought anyplace by the sea would be full of artists. I guess that while all artists paint by the sea, all seas don't have artists painting by them. I knew I was in the wrong place when I saw all the bumper stickers that said, 'The worst day fishing is better than the best day working.'" She was constantly depressed—and with reason. Not only did the townspeople avoid saying hello when they passed her on the street because they seemed to know she was different (there was no positive feedback from people who liked her, even if they were only casual acquaintances), but people actually stared at her and muttered things under their breath as she passed by. She began to work effectively again when she moved back to the city, where she belonged, and became once again a kindred soul—no longer, as she put it, misquoting John Keats, "Ruth, put out to pasture among the alien corn."

A patient had became withdrawn at work. He could not speak up when indicated, and he was unable to finish projects—a problem that mostly started when he became lover to another man who figuratively "couldn't drive through green lights" (that is, who was too easily discouraged because he was excessively fearful of everything and everybody). The day of the "wedding," the patient started to have nightmares. For example, he dreamt he was in San Francisco (he was rejected for three jobs there) and in a hotel during an earthquake. The top of the hotel, in which he resided, broke off and fell. He remembered in his dream (in effect, consciously for the first time in years) how his father pursued, caught, and beat him for stealing money from his grandmother to buy stamps for his stamp collection. Then, still in the dream, he saw his stamp collection getting wet and being ruined: "All the glue melted off in the rain." He began to work more effectively again when he developed friendships with others who were more assertive.

## Developing Healthy Counterphobic Mechanisms

Counterphobics have learned how to turn passive terror into active mastery by denying fear and becoming less passive and more assertive.

The man who was lover to the man who could not drive through green lights (the preceeding case) forced himself to speak up to others who were taking advantage of him and criticizing him unduly. He showed them who was in charge and who, besides them, had something valuable to say and would be "doing some of the talking." This both increased his activity level in a general way and helped him complete some of the projects he had dropped by getting him past his "phobic hump."

Phobics who face their fears get over their "phobic hump" and emerge fearless, until the next time. The model consists of people forcing themselves to attend an affair that frightens them and then finding that they go from "You'll never drag me to that dinner party, you know I am afraid of people" to "I am certainly glad I went, I didn't want to go, but I had a good time and I am glad I didn't say no and stay home." The patient who forces himself or herself to speak up, drive over a bridge, or complete a project will panic to a point, and then afterward "go over the hump" and feel calm, and even euphoric, with a sense of accomplishment replacing the feeling of despair.)

The process must not be carried too far, however, or the individual may become hypomanic, aggressive, or avoidant.

A patient who was excessively fearful about getting older handled his fear by demeaning talented younger people, whom he saw as the competition. This made him a negative person, difficult to get along with. Finally he lost his job because of his mistreatment of underlings. Another dealt with his fear of getting older by acting like a perpetual juvenile, wearing toupees to hide both his age and his low self-esteem, though they hid neither. Then he sexually harassed women as if to say, "Maybe I can't remember figures, or come up with new ideas, but I still have all my hormones." His hyper-sexuality was a way to deny feeling impotent and to deal actively with his feeling helpless in the face of what he perceived to be his progressive physical deterioration. In the end he retired early, just to avoid being fired for being too old.

## Changing One's Profession

Psychotherapy had little effect on the CEO mentioned previously, who was unable to interview applicants because after a few minutes he felt trapped in the room with them, feared he would faint, and was only able to master this by sitting next to the door so that he could get out in case of an "emergency" (at the expense of making his interviewees uncomfortable sitting in the middle of the room while he sat on the periphery). Pharmacotherapy worked, but it made him intellectually dull. His discomfort subsided and his general emotional state improved only after he gave up working with people entirely and took a job working for a pharmaceutical company, evaluating their research projects.

## Increasing Self-Esteem

A particularly effective form of therapy focuses on the phobic's low self-esteem and other similarly negative self-attitudes.

Phobias do not exist independently of the phobic, but are the product of the individual's personality. So a person's phobias tell us something about the person. For example, people who cower when dogs come over and wag their tails tend to be not forceful, insensitive people but passive, suggestible, hypersensitive people with negative self-attitudes and low self-esteem. Insensitive, narcissistic, self-important people trend away from phobias and instead develop more grandiose symptoms, like megalomanic delusions. Therapists treating phobics have to ask not only, "What kind of phobia do you have" but also, "What kind of you does your phobia have?" and treat accordingly. Failure to do so is one reason why phobics have such a notoriously poor response to therapy. It is not enough to note that the phobic fears a boat, as John Nemiah wrote (1985, p. 897) because it symbolizes both a penis and a vagina. Phobics also have to learn why they are such fearful souls in the first place, and the answer is as much low self-confidence as it is castration anxiety. To get better, phobics must not only stop seeing every boat as a hermaphroditic symbol, but also start believing in themselves, and get in the boat and row. Besides insight into their castration anxiety and penis envy, they also need a protective grandiosity, the kind that can keep them from constantly questioning and second guessing themselves as people and professionals, or (for those more psychoanalytically inclined) the kind that can keep them from constantly believing that their personal parts are out there exposed and vulnerable to any vandal who comes along.

For example, a patient with stage fright tried everything to get over the anxiety that plagued him for the first minutes of his speeches. He tried in-deral, behavioral therapy (giving at first short and then longer and longer speeches), cognitive therapy (exploring his distortions, such as the fear that if he made a little mistake all would be lost), and going back in time analytically to trace his stage fright to his lying in bed masturbating as he overheard his parents having sexual intercourse, deathly afraid they would discover what he was doing and "expose him" to horrible, abject shame. None of this worked. What did work, however, was his learning that he had something to offer his audience. Now instead of cowering in a corner afraid of his shadow, he could stride proudly forth and display his wares for all to see. In part his cure was a transference cure, whereby his self-con-fidence increased because the therapist was showing confidence in him. (While it is true that transference cure is not on a par with basic change, some therapists at least feel that it is better than no cure at all.)

When phobias are a manifestation of personal low self-esteem, a cor-nerstone of their treatment involves elevating self-esteem through a cor-rective new relationship with a benign, nonthreatening, nonrejecting, encouraging "wolf" in the person of the therapist. The therapist can give the patient permission and encouragement to feel less vulnerable and more special. Therapists can say something like, "You don't have to feel in danger all the time; nothing much is going to happen to you today or tomorrow; and not only won't I reject you, but I don't think you deserve to be rejected. I think you are good; I think you are an adult; I think you are capable of succeeding; I think you deserve to function." It does not matter as much as we sometimes think if the therapist uses analytic methods ("You are not incompetent, you are fixated and regressed"); cognitive methods ("Just because one critic doesn't love you doesn't mean all critics don't love you"); or the paradoxical methods of Jay Haley ("I tell you to think of yourself as a fool because I really want you to see how ridiculous that is") (Haley, personal communication) as long as the message is conveyed somehow, verbally or nonverbally.

Therapists (who, it is hoped, are themselves less vulnerable and not afraid of their own shadow) can both serve as positive identification fig-ures and encourage their patients to develop relationships outside of therapy with others who encourage them to function while not making them pay back for every success.

In conclusion, continuing our wolf-pack analogy, one method of treating phobias—an approach that will help some, but not all, pa-tients—involves changing patients' fundamental negative self-attitudes until they feel beyond ejection, helping them master their feelings of vulnerability until they believe themselves too worthy to be considered for exile. This happens when phobics find a wolf that accepts them and makes them feel loved and important on their own. They are less cowed by authority than authority would like and, feeling less frightened by the world, they become less frightened by things like stages or elevators that symbolize the world. Now they can stand proudly before the leader of their wolf pack, and think, "This person will want to accept me because of who and what I am. These wolves are lucky to have me in the pack."

A supplemental therapeutic approach accomplishes essentially the same thing, not by elevating the patient's stature but by diminishing the stature of others (like authority) in the patient's eyes.

> A patient, a writer, got a rejection slip one day. It said, "Maybe your writing is no good; but maybe it's because we have such a small list that we can't accommodate your book." She was upset until her therapist pointed out that there was another possibility they did not mention. As the therapist put it, "Maybe it's because 'we' are a bunch of amateurs."

Stories of how the critics were mistaken when they criticized the greats help here. Essentially little more than stories of how the abusive parents, not the victimized children, were the ones with the problem, such stories serve to invalidate the negative effects of the parent on the patient and increase the patient's self-esteem by diminishing the stature of the source of the low self-esteem in the patient's eyes, so that the patient no longer cares if this particular pack wolf ejects him or her.

Both techniques help patients become less impressed with and frightened of others. They become more confident and can be found when it is time to speak at a corporate meeting. They will not forget their lines, feel faint on the stage, or have to cower near the door when they interview candidates. They get up, look up, and speak out. They do not have stage fright—they have stage presence. They do not care about the wolf at the head of the table. They *are* the wolf at the head of the table.

## Treating Stage Fright

A certain amount of stage fright is normal because there is always anxiety about accomplishing great things. Wanting to be important and successful is, in effect, deciding to choose the life of a deep-sea diver— beautiful but dangerous. Anxiety is part of such a life, just as stuffed ears are part of flying on a plane or sore muscles are part of exercising at the gym. Performing is never painless. Being a stage presence is always dangerous. Expecting otherwise is usually frustrating.

However, extensive stage fright is abnormal. It spreads beyond the stage to affect one's professional life in areas other than public speaking and one's personal life and relationships as well. Dynamically, it is an issue in many neuroses and all phobias, for all phobias are about being on top, being in authority, and being exposed.

Clinically, stage fright is characterized by performance anxiety. Individuals feel faint, fear they will wet their pants, and are convinced that they will misspeak or forget their lines and that all will be lost. Dynamically, the workers who are the most afflicted are those who are intelligent, ambitious, and successful by nature because they are people who also, by nature, blow things up out of proportion. This is partly what makes them successful. But at the same time, it is also what makes them anxious. They feel anxious when giving a speech because they attach too much importance to the speech, which is usually less significant in the infinite scheme of things than they think it is. Then they feel that they are performing in a bathysphere, hot house, or pressure cooker. They blow things up out of proportion because of a need to be perfect. But being perfect is not really possible or necessary. When it comes to perfection, there is always a certain amount of leeway, and almost perfect is usually good enough. Forgetting a line by itself will not affect the performance unless the performer thinks it will, believes that one mistake means all is lost, and handles the situation accordingly and badly.

Therapeutically, I have found that insight-oriented approaches alone do not usually work for stage fright. Individuals who work on their anxiety until they are ready to perform usually find that stage fright is the last symptom to go. In her book *Writer's Block and How to Use It*, Victoria Nelson (1986) says, "First allow yourself to do nothing at all until you feel a deep and genuine urge to write something" (p. 32). Her advice applies more to writers who are blocked because they are obsessional than to workers who are blocked because they are phobic. Phobics must face anxiety if they want to get better. They must force themselves to perform and to experience performance anxiety. They may tolerate it. But if they do not, they can at least bring it back into therapy and work it out, so that the next time the prospects of performance can become less frightening and the performance itself can become easier.

As previously mentioned, therapists have to handle the lack of narcissism that afflicts some individuals with stage fright. Phobics who are fearful are fearful because of their low self-esteem. Some speakers, for example, anoint their audiences as "the experts" they need to please while simultaneously despairing of ever pleasing them. Next, instead of doing their job and expecting that all will be well, they become certain they will fail, and they panic. Therapists also have to handle the excessive narcissism of stage fright that usually accompanies low self-esteem (the two are not incompatible). Some narcissism is natural and to be expected in performers because, for the moment, they are the center of things (a quintessential narcissistic position). But excessive narcissism is self-referential. For example, some people fear plane crashes because they think that their presence on a plane will somehow influence the outcome of their flight. In like manner, the message in worrying about fainting or losing one's place while performing is, "This occasion is important enough to worry about because this is *my* occasion." Patients who become less convinced that they are uniquely important in the infinite scheme of things will become less anxious about what they say and do.

There are some tricks therapists can recommend for those with performance anxiety. It helps some speakers to admit their fear right from the start. Admitting to nerves and not making patently false excuses, such as blaming laryngitis for an inability to speak, allows all concerned (performer and audience alike) to relax. It also converts the audience from adversary to friend merely by eliciting its sympathy.

Sometimes speakers find it helpful to ask themselves, "What is the worst that can happen?" as a way to self-reassure. They can also self-reassure that if a speech or performance goes badly, they can do better the next time. Another refuge is the feeling that this time, if they actually faint (which can happen in stage fright, although it is rare), then at least they will the get sympathy vote and be remembered (a sense of humor can help see them through).

For some, visualizing a supportive person in the audience—say, speaking to an imagined friend—is reassuring. For others, ridiculing the audience helps more. Seeing members of the audience naked, for example, can make them less threatening by bringing them down a peg or two.

Knowing about audiences (considering the source) helps, too. Often, performers remember that audiences are ambivalent about them, but they forget that ambivalence has a positive as well as a negative side. While it is true that audiences want the performer to fail because audiences are competitive and are looking for an object with which they can express a disdain already in place, they also want the performer to succeed because they paid for their ticket and they want to avoid feeling guilty about being hostile (guilty, hostile audiences fear for the performer and want the performance to go well, if only to avoid having to blame themselves for anything that goes wrong).

For example, a group that hired a speaker who kept clawing at his collar because he was nervous throughout blamed not him and his nerves but themselves for not providing him with an air-conditioned auditorium. Throughout the performance they were on the edge of their seats, hoping that he would not pass out, less because they cared about him and more because they did not want to go home guilt-ridden about what they did to him.

Medication helps with stage fright like alcohol helps the person afraid of flying get on the plane and get through the flight. But flying is a passive experience, while performing is an active one. Performing in an altered (intoxicated) state often shows and usually has disastrous consequences. In this sense, sobriety with deficit is preferable to using the addictive solution (intoxication with deficit).

The practical and realistic therapist knows that sooner or later most public speakers have to accept that stage fright never disappears completely. Performers have a choice. They can do the following:

1. Give up working entirely.
2. Force themselves to perform and tolerate the unpleasant anxiety associated with performing (mostly during the beginning of the performance).
3. Decide to fit their work to their phobia, rather than the other way around. Just as other phobics (for example, those who cannot drive over a bridge) learn that there is always a tunnel or another journey without a bridge, workers with stage fright can learn to alter their professional lives so that they do not have to speak in public (or its equivalent). Performers can become recording artists, or stage managers; teachers can become administrators. This only presents a problem when the switch cannot be made, or cannot be made guilt free, and when compulsive attempts at mastery replace the exercise of good judgment and practical common sense.

### SUMMARY

Phobic occupational disorder is one way to handle fear and anxiety. In it the worker exchanges the problems associated with impaired work performance for the comfort associated with lessened anxiety. Phobias are difficult to treat because they relieve anxiety and because there has been too much reliance in the past on insight and cognitive approaches, which may not help workers believe in themselves and in their work so that they can tolerate necessary anxiety for their ultimate benefit or avoid becoming anxious at all. I have suggested some alternative approaches, but they may not work in every case.

# 6

## Obsessive-Compulsive Occupational Disorder

### MANIFESTATIONS

For didactic purposes, in this chapter I divide patients with an obsessive-compulsive occupational disorder into three broad categories: indecisive/perfectionistic, stubborn/resistant, and controlling/tyrannical.

### Indecisive/Perfectionistic

Indecisive/perfectionistic individuals cannot start or finish a task because they are convinced that anything they do will be imperfect and thus are doubtful that anything they do will be worthwhile.

A writer could not decide to keep his day job as a waiter or leave it to be an artist full time. So he tried a little of both, and did neither right. First he waited on tables while waiting to be discovered. Then he gave up his day job waiting because although he was making enough money, he was not making enough art. Then he gave up his art to take a day job waiting, because although he was creating beautiful things, he was not making enough money. After each move he felt he had made a complete mistake and then spent an inordinate amount of time and energy regretting his error and correcting it, all the while brooding about the meaning of his life and preoccupied with such imponderables as, "Art doesn't pay, and what pays isn't art." He alternately resented himself for being unable to compromise, because he was sick, and resented society for making him have to compromise, because it was sick.

A perfectionistic writer could not start her work until there were no distractions, but she could never get started because there were always some distractions, either inside or outside the house. After starting her work, she could not say what she wanted to say because of having to say it in a certain way, and she wrote little because if she wrote an essay she thought that she should be doing something commercial, like a work of fiction, but if she wrote a commercial work of fiction she thought she should be doing something meaningful, like writing an essay. Or she became bogged down in correcting her work, endlessly fixing what was perfectly satisfactory. For example, she developed checking obsessions to reassure herself that she did not say something on one page and something else on another, really to be certain that she was both doing all things right and doing all the right things. She also wanted to have it all (i.e., to get something without having to give something else up). For example, she tried to write a complex plot with deep characterizations, refusing to admit that with complex plot some of her deep characterizations had to go if the work were to be kept within manageable limits. She worked too hard to achieve complete originality, forgetting that there really was no such thing as a completely original story and that most readers do not care if a plot is derivative. She did this until she suddenly remembered that something too original can be too outré for the audience, at which time she tried to make what she wrote seem as much as possible like the last best-seller, only to become concerned that she was plagiarizing. Sometimes the conflicting options went beyond causing her to get bogged down. Instead they caused her to throw perfectly valid endeavors away merely as a way to achieve closure. When on those rare occasions she finally managed to complete something and was correcting proofs, as she put it, she "forgot that it was possible to win a Pulitzer for a work with a typo in it." She tried to correct all flaws, though some were merely relative, or, when they were absolute, made less difference than she thought. She dallied so long that she returned the corrected copy too late to meet the publisher's deadline, driving her editor to distraction and making herself known as "a difficult person," which it made it that much harder for her to get her next work accepted for publication.

A writer's perfectionism shaded into grandiosity. He rewrote and revised constantly to win a writer's prize, be rich and famous, be invited to cocktail parties and "knock them dead," go down in history, and be immortal—or, failing that, at least to get his picture in the obituary section of the *New York Times* and to pen the perfect epitaph for his tombstone, one that, as he humorously put it, "would be the envy of all the new kids on the plot." Beneath his grandiosity lay a serious problem with low self-esteem, the result of his realization that in writing there were cons for every pro. This led him to conclude that whatever he, and other writers, did, he, and they, could have done it better, and so should not have done it at all. Each time he wrote something he feared:

"It's been done before (and so is trite);
It's never been done before (and so is risky);
It's too sour (will turn people off);

It's too sweet (will be vomit provoking);
It's too deep (no one can understand it);
It's too superficial (junk!);
It's too long (no one will be able to get through it);
It's too short (who wants to pay all that money for 150 pages of all big print?);
It's too popular (pandering);
It's too academic (for rocket scientists only);
It's too much feeling (too autobiographical, self-indulgent, and self-centered);
It's too little feeling (not enough of myself in it);
It's too romantic (like molasses);
It's not romantic enough (like dry crumbs);
It's too clear (and obvious);
It's too obscure (and unreadable);
It's too dirty (will offend);
It's too clean (won't be offensive enough to be interesting and sell);
It's too much plot/action (no character development);
It's too static (too much character development, no plot/action)."

He overlooked that there were successful works that had been done before (*Jaws* was *Moby Dick*) and had never been done before (*Finnegans Wake*) or since (*Finnegans Wake*); too sour (Arnold Schoenberg's *Erwartung* was once a best-seller); too sweet (*Snow White* has always been a best-seller); too deep (again, *Finnegans Wake*); and too superficial (many popular novels). He overlooked that, although there were few completely new ideas anywhere, an old idea, with proper timing and clever marketing, could be at least made to seem fresh, if not 100% creative.

Perfectionistic workers can benefit by learning not to take themselves so seriously. Humor sometimes serves this goal well. For example, one writer who regularly could not meet a deadline developed a helpful mantra to reduce her anxiety and allow her to concentrate: She thought not "All is lost," but "Instead of doing 29 projects, I will do 28 and leave the last one unfinished, keeping posterity guessing what it would have been like if I had completed it instead of leaving it unfinished at my death."

Perfectionists must learn to compromise their all-or-nothing approach to their work so that they do not give up at the first sign of a problem. Those who compromise can continue, simply by accepting that they are working beneath their capacity, just like every one else.

### Stubborn/Resistant

Stubborn individuals, such as stubborn underlings, resent cooperating in a joint endeavor with their bosses and their organization. They will not do it either for altruistic reasons (that is, for the good of the company) or for selfish reasons (that is, for their own good). They will not do it in part because they make every interaction into a confrontation, and this happens because they equate cooperation with submission and being asked to do something with being told to do it (being ordered about).

The following patient developed a number of compulsions engineered to avoid doing the work she was supposed to be doing:

> A compulsive, parsimonious clerk could only use paper clips if she found them on the floor, not if they were already on her desk. But there were few clips on the floor; so when she needed a clip she had, as inconspicuously as possible, to push one off the desk so that she could then pick it up off the floor and use it. Her "reasoning" was that the office paid for clips on the desk, but clips on the floor were found objects and so were free. She was proud of saving the firm money. Secretly, of course, she was costing them even more. For they were paying her to do her clerical work, not to push paper clips around.

When individuals become just as stubborn with themselves as they are with others, they cannot do what they want to do just because they want to do it. This often happens so unconsciously and automatically that it seems completely outside of their awareness and not subject to their control. In a typical scenario, when the work day is over and other things demand their attention, creative ideas come flooding in, but the individuals are not at their computer and so they cannot put their ideas to disk. The next day, when they return to their desk and their computer, the block is back. Although the opportunity is there to put their ideas down, the ideas are gone.

> One writer with "a stubborn mind" sat all day in the library, forcing herself to write but unable to write, green with envy about how all the other people were writing away while she was silent. Just before the library closed, thoughts flooded her mind—only now it was too late to do anything about them because she had to put the reference books she needed away. Of course, she could always write her thoughts down the next morning. But by next morning, back in the library, her mind was again a blank—that is, until closing, when again her "stubborn mind" did just the opposite of what she wanted it to do.

Stubborn writers who become paralyzed with anxiety when they struggle to do something they want to do (as when they want to finish but they cannot even start) should, rather than struggling with themselves, nonchalantly move on to another project until the first one presses in again on its own. Pushing themselves too hard to work can be counterproductive, for two reasons. First, it involves writers mistreating themselves, like some people mistreat stubborn children, only to find that they yield the least when they are expected to yield the most (as Betty Kaplan's 1995 article in the *New York Times* illustrates). The second reason involves what I call paradoxical inertia, a term which I use to describe the stubborn mind that refuses to think when requested to do so and only gives what is wanted when the individual acts like he or she no longer wants it. In a familiar form of this inertia, people find that when they forget a name, a good way to bring it back is to act nonchalantly about wanting to think of it, at which time it promptly reappears, seemingly as if on its own. Panicking and pushing are two of the ultimate ways to act like we want something, and so two of the least effective ways to bring something back—what Sandra Blakeslee's (1995) article calls "traffic jams in brain networks" (pp. C1, C9). As in trying to bring back a name, telling blocked minds "Who cares?" is often the best way to get the mind to oblige. Writers who relax by thinking, "If you can't finish this one, go on to another one, then come back to the first" can surmount an impasse. In contrast, writers who insist that they must have their mathematical proof, and they must have it by Tuesday, only inspire their mind to shut down, stay shut, and refuse to open again.

Mark A. Kishlansky (1996) when he finds he cannot write for some hours, plays solitaire or invader games on his computer or goes out for coffee (p. 34). According to Gregory Jaynes (1995), the author Michael Crichton was blocked for some years; but instead of forcing it he did other things for a while, and his creativity returned (p. 66). Most workers cannot wait so long, but the general principle is a good one.


## Controlling/Tyrannical

Some tyrants are little more than scrupulous, arbitrary, critical, argumentative, bossy, controlling obsessives in a position of authority.

A boss who at home was known to clean the bathroom floor with a toothbrush at work rewrote all the referral notes that her colleagues took from callers to the clinic, and she redid all the questionnaires that her colleagues filled out when taking histories from the patients in the clinic. When asked why she did this, she said, in essence, that she was afraid others would make a mistake and hurt the patients. What she did not say was that she believed that she was the chosen one the company needed to control the defective incompetents who were running and ruining it.

Another patient, a hardware store owner, made encounters with his customers into semantic arguments, which he often won. But he was turning sales opportunities into debating sessions, and so effectively ruining the business. Once a customer asked for "those picture hooks that supposedly don't leave holes in the wall. You know what I mean." The salesperson knew what she meant. But instead of saying "Yes, I have them," or, "No I don't," he debated: "Of course they do. All hooks have nails, and all nails leave a hole in the wall."

## CAUSE

All people with obsessive-compulsive occupational disorders do too much intrapsychic and too little real work. They devote too much time to pathological personal concerns and too little to the healthy concerns of the company. Their personal preoccupations range from mundane ones (as when a patient spent half the day keeping her desk space free from clutter and aligning all the remaining objects on the desk so that they faced in the same direction) to global existential ones, such as concerns about the meaning of life (as when a life insurance clerk could not do her work because with each policy she processed she brooded about the transient nature of life, and with each claim she settled she brooded about the inevitability of death). Some are completely imagining the things they worry about; others are blowing real and appropriate concerns way out of proportion, making everything they do too significant and so excessively fraught with danger. This is the problem when a worker cannot greet new workers because she cannot shake their hands for fear of germs, or a doctor cannot examine a female patient properly, even with his nurse present, because he fears being charged with rape.

Dynamically, obsessives are like phobics in that they worry about the same humiliation, defeat, and rejection and have the same conflicts about sexual desires and hostile wishes, which they resolve by displacement onto something external and symbolic. But the phobic patient displaces the anxiety onto concrete objects, like a dog, or concrete situations, like being trapped in an elevator, while the obsessive-compulsive patient instead displaces the anxiety onto abstractions, like the value of cleanliness or parsimoniousness. For example, Freud's Little Hans (1957) dealt with his hostility to his father by displacing and projecting his hostility onto horses, and he developed a fear that horses would bite him. His counterpart, an obsessive patient also hostile to his father, instead worried too much not about being attacked by a horse but about "man's cruelty to man." Then he backed that up by becoming excessively antimanagement because he was too preoccupied for anyone's good with the rights and safety of what he believed to be the downtrodden workers in his company.

Another difference between phobics and obsessives is that phobics handle their fear of failure by avoiding a test of self. A phobic senses the possibility of failure, and he or she leaves. In contrast, the obsessive-compulsive handles the same problem not by avoiding it but by taking the test—only he or she studies and studies for it and then repeats it until he or she gets all the answers right. The phobic file clerk who is afraid the files will not be in alphabetical order might develop a symptom that keeps him or her from filing, such as a phobic hand paralysis. The obsessive file clerk with the same problem might instead do the filing and then constantly check to see if the files were all placed correctly. Both would do little useful work or none at all, for similar reasons, but they would do the little or no useful work in different ways.

Cognitively, obsessive-compulsives become anxious because they look at things too close up and worry them to death. For example, they measure what they accomplish in life by what they accomplish today, and what they accomplish today by what they want to accomplish in life. For this and similar reasons, they become like a centipede that thinks about each step it takes, confusing itself until it cannot walk; or like a traveler who takes excess baggage on a trip in preparedness for all contingencies, making what could have been an enjoyable venture into an unpleasant and painful journey.

## TREATMENT

### Transference Problems

Obsessives make daunting patients because in the transference they do to their therapists the same thing that they do to their bosses, their co-workers, their underlings, themselves, and their work. Not surprisingly, it becomes difficult to help them with their problems, because of their problems.

As workers, they try very hard because they want to do well, and sometimes they succeed. On the other hand, they are always ruining what they do because they want to defeat themselves and others. As a result, when they are at their best, their achievements can be impressive. But when they are at their worst, they are usually too tied up in knots and self-destructive to work up to their full potential. Essentially the same thing happens when they are in therapy. As patients, they want to work hard in treatment and to get better both to please their therapist and to help themselves. But unconsciously they also want to defeat their therapists and themselves. The result is that therapy proceeds in stops and starts and often never goes very far.

One patient put her therapist between the devil of her depressive fear that she was a failure, which made her want to improve her self-esteem, herself, and her lot, and the deep blue sea of her guilty fear of success, which made her unwilling and unable to self-improve at all. As indecisive about being in treatment as she was about everything else, she at first could not decide whether to stay in therapy or to go. Her compromise was to stay in treatment but to remain uncommitted to it throughout, prolonging it while making sure it did not do too much good. She complained about and made fun of her interminable psychoanalysis, but she wanted to take 5 years out of her life just waiting for something to happen. The therapeutic problem with this patient was how to get her unstuck without pushing her too hard and running into the stone wall of her guilt—in short, how to be active enough with her so that she did not retreat and waste 5 years of her life in useless therapy while being passive enough with her to avoid running afoul of her guilty conscience.

Another patient was too perfectionistic to develop realistic treatment goals because she discovered that, in this imperfect world, to get something she had to give up something else, so that there seemed to be no way to gain without losing as well. And she was so stubborn that she preferred the illusory freedom of staying sick as an alternative to what she saw as being criticized and controlled by her therapist and giving in to him. As a defense, she played the part of the controlling one and got into power struggles with the therapist, whom she soon came to view not as the expert she came to consult, but as "the hired help" to be ordered about and pushed around until he gave her what she wanted. Her reaction to her therapist went "nicely" with her tendency to stubbornly self-defeat by denying herself what she wanted because she wanted it, so that she did not meet the goals she set for herself just because that meant "giving in" to herself.

One way to bypass these and similar traps is to focus away from the obsessive behavior itself and onto the reason it occurs. Some therapists have found that a good place to start is the obsessive's conflict between the humiliation of being a "big nobody" and the simultaneous fear of being somebody, a conflict that can only result in the typical obsessive swinging between doing (accomplishing) and undoing (apologizing).

This conflict should first be identified and then analyzed developmentally because it originates in early relationships; analyzed cognitively, as the outcome of logical distortions (like the belief that minor are major transgressions); and treated behaviorally, so that patients can be helped to act guilt free even while feeling inappropriately guilty, or encouraged to finish what they start (a behavioral approach)—but not because the therapist says so, and not because it is good for them to do so, but so that they can discuss their anxiety about completion in therapy (a psychodynamic approach).

The patient's conflicts will predictably take the form of transference resistances, creating therapy block (which is the rough equivalent of writer's block) and leading the patient either to prolong therapy without discernible results or to quit treatment entirely. A writer who delays submitting work although it is substantially perfect and complete and misses a deadline because of a fear of success becomes in therapy the patient who has diversionary power struggles with the therapist, ranging from coming to a session and arguing with the therapist about a minor point throughout to missing the session completely and then returning and wasting the next session by talking about why he or she missed the last one. Such behavior should be analyzed as a transferential manifestation of occupational disorder, just another compromise between action and inaction, but this time with the therapist.

An ambivalent, hostile newspaper reporter started treatment because he could not decide whether to stay at his bread-and-butter job as a reporter (where he was not much of a success) or go into free-lance work (which he was having trouble doing, in part because he was only able to do it in what free time he could spare from his work as a reporter). He complained that staying at his full-time job interfered with his concentration, but he feared leaving it because it was leaving a job that paid well, in exchange for probable artistic failure and an uncertain financial future. With a job, he could pay his rent but not do his writing. Without one, the opposite was true and was equally devastating. He had, in other words, what we might call "Alexander Borodin Block," in which (as happened to the composer) composing detracts from doing chemistry, and doing chemistry detracts from composing, and the individual postpones choosing indefinitely but remains constantly uncertain which fork in the road to take—shifting, weaving, and retracing steps instead of, and as a way to avoid, moving forward.

Always wanting advice to help him make up his mind about what to do, yet stubborn and unyielding when he got the advice he wanted, the reporter was in effect defeating his therapist in the same way that he was defeating himself, and so he was not seeking cure but was instead displaying his occupational disorder in yet another context.

In particular, he defeated his therapist by having a bad word to say about every good idea that his therapist put forth. For example, he complained that when he forced himself to write an article, the effort showed, and every word he wrote looked like it was (and it was) put through a cotton gin—stretched, shrunk, turned this way and that, until what he had was a patchwork that revealed how it was stitched together from component parts. In reply, his therapist suggested that instead of forcing himself to work, he should wait for inspiration. But the patient demeaned this suggestion with, "But suppose nothing happens for a long time?" When his therapist, doing an about face, instead suggested he force himself to work and on schedule, he replied that that was both painful and a waste of time because artificial controls imposed from without provoked him to self-defeat from within.

When his therapist suggested that he might try to get his feelings out in his writing, he replied that when he did he felt flooded by old painful memories. Then when the therapist agreed he might be better off writing about neutral things that did not promote anxiety, he disagreed, saying "That makes for bland writing, as empty of idea as it is of feeling."

When his therapist was active, he accused him of trying to control him. When the therapist was passive, remained neutral, and suggested he make his own decisions, which he would then help him implement, he accused him of abandoning him at times of crisis and reminded him that he needed to have his hand held and be told what to do in order to avoid feeling rejected and unloved.

When he got the constructive criticism he asked his therapist to give him, he replied that criticism made him tense, and being too tense held him back. So the therapist became more supportive instead, only to have him reply that he needed and could use the criticism because hostile critics inspired him, if only to prove them wrong.

In effect, this patient was playing Eric Berne's (1965) masochistic game of "Why don't you—yes but." In this game the therapist makes many suggestions, but all of them are discounted until the patient wins by showing the therapist that there is nothing that can be said or done that will be helpful.

There were only two ways out of this game for the therapist. The first involved not playing but interpreting the game. The therapist told the patient that in his opinion, while he wanted to be cured of his occupational disorder because it limited him, he relinquished it reluctantly because it provided him with what Ronald Hayman (1993, p. 69) says Tennessee Williams called the "comfort of limits." The second involved playing another game instead—with the rules set by the therapist, not by the patient. This "game" is called "the game of psychotherapy," and the main rule is to pay strict attention to the reason why the patient cannot work on the problems that need the attention. The goal was to keep the therapist out of a quagmire distilled from the dark sides of all good things, and to give the patient a simple, accurate, incontestable overview that might actually help him. This patient could not solve his problems because he needed to remain sick because of his guilt about achievement, a need which he in turn satisfied by making sure that nothing helped. The solution was not to focus on the details of his defensive debating, and try to deal with these directly, but to step back and look not at the content of the debate, but at how the debate satisfied his pathological guilt about achievement. It was this that the therapist focused on. The patient, neither able to deny his self-destructiveness nor make it the subject of an interpersonal battle, gave up his resistant struggle with the therapist. Relieved of guilt about even the slightest degree of success, he was able to make a satisfactory compromise in his life, without destroying all concerned along the way. Without further ado, he left his newspaper job to became a minor success doing short free-lance articles on such interesting but hardly earth-shattering topics as Australia's train system.

For patients who are handling a difficult job situation badly, the best approach can be to focus away from the obsessive behavior itself to deal strictly with the real problems that exist for the patient in the workplace. The therapist pinpoints what starts or worsens obsessions and deals with that. Often it is what makes the patient angry. In one case it was a co-worker snapping gum, and dealing with the gum snapper—not the patient's reactions to the gum snapping—removed the reason to obsess.

A writer who worked at home could not concentrate because his dog barked at every noise. First he felt like muzzling her, then he felt guilty about his hostility to helpless beasts. First he yelled "shut up" at her, then he thought of punishments for himself for thinking and saying bad things to a poor, dumb creature, who could do no better.

In short, he was spending the day unproductively brooding about right and wrong and whether he was a good or bad person, broadly preoccupied with his overview of himself when he should have been more narrowly focused on the work he was supposed to be doing.

His therapist told him, "Ignore the barking, don't pay so much attention to it," but he heard this as a criticism of him for being hypersensitive to noise. Then his therapist told him, "Be nice to your dog and don't say mean things to her, especially in a hostile voice, because she is just a dumb, innocent animal," but he heard this as a criticism that he was mistreating a creature who cannot defend itself.

Then his therapist said, trying to support him, "I understand how terrible this must be for you," to which he replied, "I didn't know it was so terrible until you mentioned it. Maybe I am underreacting. Maybe I'm not sensitive enough. And what kind of artist is not sensitive?" And he added, for good measure, "You are giving me the same advice you would give to someone normal. The problem is that I'm not normal."

He responded better when the therapist shifted from the emotional uncertainty to the actual difficulty—the dog's barking—and advised him to set up a room in the house and strip the doors, just like the therapist stripped his own door, the one that opened into and led from his office, to keep the sound from coming in or getting out. Moreover, if he could work with music playing, he was advised to turn on music to drown out the extraneous noise while letting the dog bark all she wanted. "Now both of you are merrily doing what comes naturally. Now both of you are functioning without inhibition."

Some patients respond to a firm hand that stays them from obsessing. They are not allowed to obsess unless the obsessing accomplishes something—that is, unless it is a way to think through and solve a real problem. A patient is allowed to brood about whether to try to keep his senile mother at home or place her in a nursing home. A patient is allowed to brood about whether only melody, or also rhythm and pitch, should be respected in the development of his musical twelve-tone rows. But a patient is discouraged from brooding about why a desk chair at work has four legs, not three, or if his advancing on the job is the same thing as murdering his father, and whether symbolic murder is prohibited because it is close to actual murder or is permitted because it is only symbolic. Problem solving is encouraged. Abstract musing is permitted. Concrete self-torture is forbidden. Patients are asked to do their real, instead of their intrapsychic, work.

> A free-lance author could only write with a contract because she needed a defined goal. Without a contract, as she put it, she felt as if she were "self-unemployed." So she saturated the field with her manuscripts before it was time to submit them. But she was submitting work in progress, sending it out for acceptance before it was ready to be put to the test. While some editors could see her potential, others read her manuscript not as a work necessarily imperfect because it was still in progress, but as an imperfect finished product, and they rejected it for the very imperfections she planned all along to fix. So she went back to finishing things before sending them in, only to discover she could not finish them unless she had a contract in the drawer.
>
> The problem was resolved not by analyzing why she was unable to work unless she felt accepted, but by getting her to change her method of working. First she renamed the rejection slips she already got and was going to get in the future "suggestion slips" to emphasize their impersonal nature. Now she could use the valuable ideas they contained to improve her work. Second, she was only allowed to send up one "trial balloon" manuscript at a time. In this way her balloon was punctured, and she fell to earth, only about once a month. This left her time to recover and do some work before the next balloon went up and was punctured again.

Some therapists advise their patients to deal with their obsessing by making a list of alternatives and then using the list to make priorities. Those who cannot decide whether to quit and go into business for themselves or stick with a safe bread-and-butter job, one they can depend on, can list the pluses and minuses of staying and of quitting.

Therapists should advise their patients that they have another job to do after making their lists: They have to use the list they have made properly. Most people know how to make the lists. Few actually know what to do with them afterward.

> One patient, unable to decide whether to keep a full-time job and do free-lance work part time or to go free-lance full time and quit his job com-

pletely, made a list that read as follows: "Some pluses of having the bread-and-butter job are having a 'family' at work, having money, and if you quit your job to stay at home you could get lonely, and depressed, so that you cannot do the very thing that you quit your job to do. And some minuses are being constantly tired from lack of sleep, or from hangovers from the pills you have to take to sleep, so that you are unable to do either your work at work or at home."

But his lists served him no good purpose. First, he was making lists instead of working. And second, he did not know what to do with the lists once he made them. Follow the longer side? But what about all the concerns on the shorter side? Tear up or burn the short side of the list? How will that help? He asked, "Isn't that like voodoo?" and remarked humorously in passing that "if it is like voodoo, maybe instead of tearing the lists up I should stick pins in them."

Individuals with occupational disorders cannot get over their disorder by only doing what the overwhelming evidence suggests they have to do while dismissing the shorter side of the list. Sometimes the considerations on the shorter side take care of themselves once a decision is made. But at other times, unless the shorter side is addressed directly, it will interfere with implementing the longer side.

In the preceding case the worker's list had most of the entries on the side that suggested quitting, but he could not leave until he dealt with the side that suggested staying. He had to rethink the "family at work" idea. He had to recognize that the "work family" is a myth. Deep affections do form between co-workers, but they are as brittle as they are intense. They do not often survive outside of the workplace. When he learned not to make his work family a reason to keep a job he could not stand, especially one that was also keeping him back, he was able to quit and to do so guilt free.

Practical solutions and procedural adjustments are not always possible. But when they are, they should be tried. Doing so avoids endless self-analysis of one's neurosis, including rooting around in, and reviving, an often unpleasant and mostly frightening past—a process that can cause more occupational problems than it solves.

# 7

## Sexual Disorders
## Occupational Disorders

### MANIFESTATIONS

Work can be inhibited in ways that are reminiscent of how sex can be inhibited. There are six stages of work, just as there are six stages of sex, and there is a stage-specific work inhibition to match each stage-specific sexual inhibition. The six stages of work are (1) deciding on a project; (2) getting started working on the project; (3) saying/doing something significant; (4) finishing what has been started; (5) issuing, exposing, and promoting one's work; and (6) doing the first five not just once but over and over again. The six stages of sex, which roughly match the six stages of work, are (1) desire, (2) excitement, (3) performance, (4) orgasm, (5) resolution, and (6) repetition. The matching stage-specific inhibitions of work and sex are as follows:

- Workers with Stage I inhibition hesitate to do something with their careers. They do not feel like having a career, just as some people do not feel like having a sexual encounter. They do not feel stimulated.
- Workers with Stage II inhibition want to work, but they cannot get started working. They sharpen pencils and make notes, but that is as far as they go. They are like lovers who are stimulated but get bogged down in courting or in foreplay.
- Workers with Stage III inhibition get started working but are unable to perform satisfactorily. They have nothing to say, and their minds feel blank. They feel like women who perform sexually but are "anesthetic," or men who perform sexually but detumesce before orgasm.
- Workers with Stage IV inhibition cannot finish their work, just as some individuals cannot climax sexually.

- Workers with Stage V inhibition do finish, but then (flush with embarrassment) they feel sheepish and cannot face the world, or if they can, they fret and worry constantly about having unduly exposed themselves. Ashamed, they put their work in a drawer to hide it from themselves, or they lose it to cover their tracks from and avoid showing it to others. They worry about their work like some people worry about the consequences of being discovered having, or having had, sex. "Did I do a bad thing?" "What will they say about me?" "Will I be punished physically or morally?"
- Workers with Stage VI inhibition successfully complete one task, project, or opus, but then ask, "Should I become creatively abstinent?" as some people ask, "Should I become sexually celibate?" They decide, "One great work is enough. I will retire, I never want to do this again," just as some people try sex once, recoil, and say they will never try it again.

## CAUSE

Some clinicians think the match between work and work inhibitions and sex and sexual inhibitions is without significance and occurs because there are six stages of any behavior—work, sex, or playing tennis. Others think the match is significant for the following reasons:

1. The work inhibition appears because work is unconsciously sexualized and then inhibited because of sexual guilt. Evidence for this is that some workers themselves describe work inhibitions in terms equally suitable for describing sexual inhibitions. Men compare their inability to work with sexual impotence and women their lack of inspiration when working with sexual anesthesia.
2. The work inhibition is merely one symptom of a primary sexual disorder, such as impotence, premature ejaculation, or sexual anesthesia. For example, there is evidence that sexual paraphilias can be manifest occupationally. Sexual fetishism can surface at work, too, as an irrational emphasis on a particular aspect of one's work. A mental health worker I once knew who had what seemed to be a "foreplay fetish" made it impossible for me to start my meetings because she would not let me get past a discussion of whether or not the meeting should have an agenda. A group of psychiatric residents I once taught made it impossible for me to proceed with the body of a discussion I wanted to have because they could not decide on the correct pronunciation of the word, *primer*, as in the title of a book we were reading, *A Primer of Psychotherapy*. Exhibitionism can spill over from the sexual arena to

become an overconcern with what people think and how they react, both to the detriment of doing the job at hand.

3. Both the work and the sexual inhibition arise from a larger underlying exogenous problem, so that being criticized interferes both
with work and with sex.

4. Both the work and the sexual inhibition arise from a larger endogenous psychological problem, which is in turn manifest in a number
of ways (both at work and when having sex). It is a well-known fact
that personality traits like dominance, passivity, or anal retentive-
ness and the intrapsychic conflicts from which they arise, such as
fear of passivity, fear of activity, or fear of spontaneity, can affect
both one's job and one's sexual performance because so often individuals remain true to form wherever they go and whatever they do.

The patient presented in Chapter 6, the obsessive-compulsive journalist,
agonized for months on end about what to do with his life while in effect
remaining stuck in place, able only to doubt himself and change his
mind, because he resented someone else making demands on him and
refused to meet their demands just because they were being made. In
parallel fashion, he noted how he could never come to orgasm when having intercourse with his wife but was able to ejaculate when masturbating. As he saw it, that was because he was by himself, without someone
else's welfare to consider, and without someone else making demands on
him to perform.

## TREATMENT

The resemblance of occupational to sexual disorder suggests at least
a theoretical approach to the treatment of occupational disorders. The
therapist and patient first think of what decreases the patient's sexual
urge and see if something similar does not stymie creative inspiration.
Then they think of what increases sexual urge and see if something similar does not encourage creative inspiration, or bring it back if it is gone.
Being praised, for example, helps considerably to increase sexual ap-
petite, desire, and performance and their equivalent at work. I think not
being praised enough, or not being praised properly, is the single greatest mistake that most corporations make with their workers and is the
most overlooked cause of work inhibition. I also think that being praised
honestly and sufficiently at work is the most overlooked, the simplest,
and the cheapest approach known for both preventing and curing occupational disorders.

# 8

## Personality Disorders
## Occupational Disorders

Many workers are hypersensitive, suspicious, or suffer from low self-esteem because of the belief that others do not like them. This by itself is not enough to constitute a personality disorder occupational disorder, which only exists when patients think about themselves and react to others in a fixed, repetitive, and maladaptive way that interferes with their ability to work up to par or at all.

There are several ways to classify these disorders. One is according to the main presenting personality trait—for example, passive-aggressiveness or masochism. Another is according to whether the disorder affects the patient, others in the patient's environment, or both. One such classification (more an underground than an official one) uses three familiar foods—onions, garlic, and red pepper—as paradigms. Onions, which can upset the stomach and give bad breath, are the model for patients whose illness causes them and others around them to suffer. Hysterical personality disorder is often an onion disorder, affecting as it does the patient, the patient's family, and the society in which the patient lives. Garlic, which rarely upsets the stomach but often "pollutes" the environment, is the model for patients whose illness mainly causes others to suffer while sparing the individual. Successful psychopathy is a garlic disorder. (In this chapter I will discuss unsuccessful psychopathy citing as an example the boss who was fired for using a psychiatric clinic as his personal source of patient referrals for himself and his wife, in effect ruining the clinic for everyone else working there.) Red pepper, which upsets the stomach but has no effect on the environment, is the model for patients whose illness mainly causes problems for themselves but not for others. Schizotypal disorder, in which the patient becomes a harmless eccentric unable to do useful work, is an example of this kind of disorder. In this chapter I will emphasize how a individual's personality disorder can cause that individual personal anguish. In Chapter 11 I will emphasize how one individual's personality disorder can "bust" another individual's career.

## SCHIZOPHRENIA AND
## THE SCHIZOPHRENIC SPECTRUM[1]

Some patients with schizophrenia are not able to work. Therapists should suspect schizophrenia when severe occupational functional impairment is present, even in the absence of determinable hard signs of schizophrenia, such as delusions or hallucinations. In other words, schizophrenia is part of the differential diagnosis of all patients who are chronically unemployed.

Some schizophrenics are able to work, but on the job they have difficulty getting along with people or in doing their assigned tasks. Difficulties in working may occur because they are

- Dereistic (divorced from reality)
- Autistic (self-preoccupied)
- Anhedonic (suffering from an innate inability to experience pleasure, either in-born or due to guilt about thinking pleasurable thoughts or doing pleasurable things, and so unmotivated to get involved with their work and the people there)
- Delusional and hallucinating
- Suffering from schizophrenic low self-esteem, which is notably different from depressive low self-esteem in that it represents a kind of delusional self-persecution
- Unable to filter selectively (ignore) both external and internal perceptions, which leads to flooding—becoming overwhelmed by too much going on at the same time. (Flooding is often accompanied by a thought disorder, such as overinclusiveness or disorganization of thinking. Removing the patient to a quiet room and assigning him or her simple tasks simplifies the environment, diminishes arousal, minimizes confusion, and allows healing repression, and with it personal reorganization. Putting the patient in a busy office and pushing him or her too hard to get involved and function has the opposite effect. This is why at least some schizophrenic workers do their best when they work in isolation, as when they stay at

---

1. Though schizophrenia is not a personality disorder I include it here as the "parent disorder" of paranoid, schizoid, and schizotypal personality disorder occupational disorders.

home writing, work in a pet shop with animals, not people, or are assigned to the back room of a post office and sort mail at night.)

- Infantile, and think like children (for example, concretely); relate like children (for example, to only a part of an object, such as its warmth-giving qualities); and regress, using regressive, childlike defenses to deal with their anxiety (such as helplessness) instead of more mature defenses (such as reaction formation)

- Grandiose, and cannot work because they think they are too good to have to work or too lovable to have to do their share

- Paranoid, and cannot work because they feel their enemies at work are holding them back or otherwise humiliating or defeating them

- Impulsive, and cannot work because they lack the ability to control themselves. (Most of these patients can control themselves until someone unwisely provokes them by refusing an appropriate request, or abuses them sadistically, and then they become agitated or even violent.)

## Paranoid Personality Disorder[2]

Workers with a paranoid personality disorder are not team players because they feel their world is full of enemies. They misconstrue constructive criticism as blame and necessary blame as persecution. If they accept criticism or blame at all, they do so with sweeping self-extenuation so that they may acknowledge that their failure to take some action resulted in disaster but will likely point to inadequate information (poor briefing or training), childhood trauma, and so on as the culprits. They also confront, blame, and criticize co-workers. They are suspicious of others and prove their suspicions illogically, by relying heavily on overgeneralizing from the part to the whole while omitting contrary facts that prove them wrong and rejecting elements that do not suit their interpretations. They might become miniature psychoanalysts who overinterpret everything said and (disregarding conscious motivation) see only unconscious intent. Or they might choose to emphasize one aspect of mixed conscious motivation, so that they see another's profit motive as entirely destructive because it contains the element of self-interest, or see another's desire for success not as a wish for self-actualization but purely as a wish to destroy a rival. Their suspicions are also the result of projection. They attribute their guilty wishes to others and both criticize them instead of themselves and feel others are criticizing them in turn, and for the same thing.

---

2. This discussion is adapted from my book *Diagnosis and Treatment of the Personality Disorders* (1992).

Because on one level they suspect that their paranoid beliefs are ridiculous, they form office cabals or cliques whose chief purpose is to secure the agreement of others and thus enlist outside support for their false ideas. The validators they choose are often third parties, but sometimes they even demand a degree of acceptance from their victims. The persons called on are in a difficult position, for to agree is impossible while to challenge not only makes the subject more anxious but is likely to be interpreted as siding with the enemy. When the object of their cabal gets wind of what is happening and does challenge them, they often apologize in a superficial way to deflect criticism, but they have no intention of changing their beliefs or behavior.

Finally, there is the matter of the self-fulfilling prophecy, in which the paranoid premise is seemingly validated by circumstances, but in fact it remains untrue because (1) pessimistic predictions, when made in sufficient quantity, will be borne out in impressive numbers by chance alone, and (2) the patient has created his or her own circumstances by antagonizing others, changing not only his or her perception of reality but reality itself, as a way to validate the pessimistic and angry assumptions. If patients believe that an individual or group has it in for them, they do not have difficulty antagonizing that person or group.

Such people are dangerous because of their often considerable influence. They can win us over to their unreal view of the world by throwing us off balance with the sheer force of their convictions and their well-rehearsed arguments, which challenge our elementary principles and put us in a kind of logical shock in which we fail to respond rationally and constructively.

### Schizoid Personality Disorder/ Avoidant Personality Disorder

Schizoid patients are shy and withdrawn because of a dilute (attenuated) "schizophrenic" anhedonia, which interferes with their ability to relate by compromising their capacity for anticipating or experiencing joy in human relationships. Clinically, they seem unpressured and laconic and may seem to lack intelligence. Avoidants are more reserved, withdrawn, and shy; however, their withdrawal and shyness are fringed with an aura of anxiety, paranoia, and depression. Both do well when they fit in with their jobs. (For example, many schizoids fail as waiters but succeed as clerks.)

### Schizotypal Personality Disorder

In schizotypal patients, the interpersonal reserve and semi-isolation of the schizoid patient also appear but are further marked by strange and eccentric private and public beliefs and habit patterns. In other words, these patients have a schizoid trunk festooned with odd, quirky branches. They have odd illogical theories that are not adversarial, as they are in the paranoid patient, but closely linked to a wishful, capricious, magical, mysterious, fictive world. As a result, their solutions to problems are not formed from a detached spirit of inquiry but are fanciful and wish-fulfilling dreamy eccentricities. Such people can either be very creative or too eccentric to do their job properly. Again, many have been saved by being carefully matched to their jobs. Schizotypals who cannot be waiters can often function very well behind the counter in a trendy boutique or health food store.

## OTHER PERSONALITY DISORDERS

### Psychopathic/Antisocial Personality Disorder

Psychopaths use physical illness as an excuse and emotional illness as an evasion. For them, RSI is not a conversion but a cover; and paranoia is not a way to deal with forbidden homosexual impulses but a way to project blame onto others for their own careless or criminal activity.

One worker was fired because she did things wrong and then, when brought up short, lied to save face and blamed others for her misdeeds. She left parts of office equipment that was needed for out-reach work in her car and drove home with them overnight and on the weekend, so that they became unavailable to the person on duty. When this was called to her attention, instead of admitting she was wrong and offering to improve next time, she claimed that "hypoglycemia made me forgetful." Once she ran a computerized test, and the tracing came out flat because the leads were not properly placed. Instead of admitting her error and redoing the test, she said, "It was working when I started it," so "It must be the people who came after me who messed up the machine."

The head of a clinic where I worked was fired because he criticized many of his staff personally and to the patients in the clinic, not because they represented rival siblings from his childhood but because he saw competent staff as rivals who were in the way of his satisfying his desire to fill up his and his wife's private practice. His method of crushing the competition was by never saying a good word, and always putting in a bad word, about them while indefinitely postponing any need to offer an overall assessment that included both their good and bad features. This worked because no one jumped to the victim's defense (because everyone wanted to curry the boss's favor); because they were afraid of defying him and becoming his next victim; because his victims were their rivals, too; and because at heart they were simply sadists who liked to see others suffer.

## Borderline Personality Disorder

Some borderlines present mainly with problems in their interpersonal relationships, which are characterized by an unpredictable alternating and shifting between a dependency so complete that their individual identity is lost and an independence so complete that they become remote, removed from the influence of others, and even disdainful of them or full of hate for them. They are reliable workers when they are identified with the company; and they are irresponsible, uncooperative, and self-destructive when they are not. When merged with an individual they admire, they overvalue that individual and form a fierce loyalty to that person and to his or her ideals, while devaluing all that individual's rivals. Depending on who is their mentor, they can become the champion of a pro-company cause or, when they are merged with a destructive mentor, become half of a masochistic dyad that undermines or destroys itself (and the organization).

> An angry borderline nurse merged with an anti-American nurse administrator, and the two were downsized for being troublemakers who tried to rid their hospital of as many American-born physicians as possible, driving some of the most competent doctors out of the hospital. Their manifest reason was, "They are too expensive; we can get foreigners for a lot less." But their real reason was a combination of (1) antisemitism directed to Jewish Americans; (2) oedipal fixation, so that positive attachments were only possible with those who were as unlike their fathers as possible (neurotic exogamy)—and foreigners had personal characteristics that fit their bill; and (3) their ability to control foreigners, who were too unsure of themselves (because of their immigration status) to give them a hard time.

## Hysterical (Histrionic) Personality Disorder

Hysterics are primarily self-constructive, but then something interferes—and they allow it to—or they cause something to interfere—because they need it to. They do this because they are afraid of self-fulfillment, and they are afraid of self-fulfillment because they are afraid of success. Because they fear success, they need and want to be failures, and they act accordingly. Because their fear of success has oedipal roots—that is, because it originates in competitive triangular relationships—they need to see themselves as defective in relationship to someone else, and compulsively compare themselves to others, in a way that assures that they will look like the relative failures they want to be. Often they compare themselves to the best features of others, taken individually and out of context.

Orenstein (1991) says that Maurice Ravel, who may have been a hysteric and who stopped writing for the last 6 years of his life, compared his own to Mozart's effortless superhuman prodigious output (p. 123). The author Herman Melville (1981; originally published 1851) complained that he was not Nathaniel Hawthorne because he was not as popular as the other man (p. 534). A psychiatrist complains that he does not make the money a cardiologist makes, while a cardiologist complains that he cannot deal with difficult patients as conveniently as a psychiatrist can. He has to cater to them (i.e., coddle them) while the psychiatrist, as he sees it, can put them down, and in their place, by identifying them as "the crazy person in this relationship." A subordinate wants to climb the corporate ladder to the top and be powerful like the boss. A former boss, a psychiatrist, who used to administer big organizations and was on top and in charge of many subordinates, later in his career wants to join the rank and file and see patients (leaving the administration, and with it the political clout, and decision making, to others) because he now believes that clinical work is more fulfilling than administrative work and envies the lot of the clinician, left alone with only one person's needs and demands to consider at a time.

## Narcissistic Personality Disorder

Both of the following statements are true: To succeed at what you do, you must not be so selfish and narcissistic that you become offensive to others. To succeed at what you do, you have to be self-centered and narcissistic enough that you can be good to, and have confidence in, yourself.

Both are true because there are ineffective (or bad) and effective (or good) narcissists. Ineffective narcissists too easily feel unloved, hurt, and abandoned. Before giving other people a chance to speak and to redeem anything they might have said that could be interpreted or misinterpreted as an attack or a rejection of them, they sulk in a corner, refuse to come out of their office, or stay home sick to avoid being attacked and/ or to get revenge on their co-workers by making them do the absent person's work.

But narcissism is not necessarily a bad thing. Friends and associates tell workers that they are too narcissistic because they envy them and are trying to defeat them, and bosses tell them that they are too narcissistic to avoid paying them. But all successful people are effectively narcissistic to a degree. Effective narcissism is the kind associated with high self-esteem—the kind that helps workers do their work without constantly looking over their shoulders to see who is criticizing them. Part of the necessary grandiosity of success, it makes workers pleased with themselves, even when they have less reason to feel this way than they think. It allows them to demand that others treat them well even when they should be treated badly. It allows them to do so without feeling the slightest pangs of conscience or regret.

## Passive-Dependent Personality Disorder

Severely passive-dependent people are what I call "placental characters"—their transcendent goal in life is to remain in a kind of womb, hooked up to the mother by an umbilical cord, and not having to do much more than move about and occasionally kick hard in protest.

A patient, not overtly delusional or hallucinating, was unemployed for more than 10 years, although at least on the surface he was intelligent, personable, and physically capable of working. But instead of working he spent all day at home fantasizing about getting lucky and hitting it big as a radio announcer. He convinced himself that he was working because he was trying to find work, something he had been trying to do for years (but without success) and because he sat at the computer planning his daily schedule, updating his address book, and surfing the Internet, all of which, he complained, tired him out and put him under considerable stress. Whenever his wife suggested that a young man who stays home all day re-arranging his schedule and surfing the Internet has a problem, he told her that she did not understand him, had it in for him, and was the kind of small-minded person who would have defeated any one of a number of great artists just starting out.

Early in his career he did take a few low-level jobs with radio stations, but there was a problem with every one of them. He and the boss had a personality clash; the job was beneath someone with his abilities; it took him away from studying radio announcing and from auditioning; and so on. The real problem, however, was his laziness. Even at home he did not help with the chores when his wife went to work to support the family. For example, they had one child, and while he was waiting for his career to take flight he could have taken care of the baby while his wife was at work. But instead he handed the child over to his father-in-law, sighing, "That kid is a job and a half, and unless you take care of him I won't be able to get any work done at all." Consciously, he really believed he needed the peace and quiet to do his work at home. But unconsciously he felt that the baby competed with him for the treasured position of "the only child in the family."

The less severe passives are immature adults who, even when they have enough expertise to be out there on their own, still act like little children who want and need to have their hands held. They make better apprentices than full-fledged peers. They forever sit at their mentors' knees, submissive to authority. They have trouble growing up and taking charge. They avoid being in a position in which they tell others "what I think, and what I think you should know." Instead they assume that everyone knows more than they do, and they even take others' claims of superior power and knowledge at face value and to heart and allow themselves to be pushed around without challenging or fighting back, even where possible and when indicated. Overly eager to please, or afraid to displease, they become fearful of speaking their minds, which to them means challenging their parents. They have difficulty being active in a self-promoting way, and even when they attempt to stand their ground, they quickly retreat at the first sign of opposition. They will not put up a fight against working conditions they do not like, or people at work who are making their lives miserable. At the most they grouse, blaming their job and their company in an almost paranoid way, but they conclude that it is not safe to discuss the problem because that will only make a bad situation even worse. Ultimately, they get a reputation for ineffectualness, and others say of them that they seem to want a mother more than a career.

Even the greats can seem to be affected by the persistent infantilism that characterizes passivity. For example, Johannes Brahms, who may or may not have been passive, did not write a symphony until age 40, out of a fear of being found unequal to the task and to Ludwig van Beethoven. This may have been because he saw himself not as Brahms, but as one of Beethoven's disciples or children.

To get better, passives have to learn to speak up and say what they think—without becoming counterproductively aggressive, as can happen when they fail to distinguish between productive assertion and counterproductive aggression (e.g., they write not memos but diatribes, or have not air-clearing discussions but air-fouling tantrums). Assertiveness is counterproductive with friends who are misperceived as enemies, and it is dangerous with enemies who are misperceived as safe (although they are in a powerful position and have the inclination to do the individual harm, given the slightest excuse and opportunity). Workers cannot overlook the reality of how the other person will and will not respond. Some people feel threatened by those who speak up and stand their ground. Others admire them for it, although these people are probably rare. Workers must distinguish between those who are in a position of real power and those who merely have a psychic hold over them.

Passives can be difficult to treat when they think that the therapist should do all the therapeutic work for them and that all they have to do is sit back and take the cure, without having to participate in it. The therapist says, "You have to start becoming more of a presence at work." The patient retorts, "I came to you with the problem of not being able to be a high-profile worker, and you expect me just to do it?" The therapist replies, "You are telling me that because of your problems you can't get help with your problems?" The patient says, "You are telling me that to get help with my problems I have to have no problems?" An impasse—a miniature version of the original occupational disorder—quickly develops in the transference.

## Passive-Aggressive Personality Disorder

Passive-aggressives are self-destructive people, as well as people who express their anger indirectly—for example, by not doing something that is expected of them or by messing up something they did do. Passive-aggressives are identifiable by the effect they have on others. They victimize others and then make others feel not victimized but guilty, and they are often so good at and subtle about it that their victims' reaction, when there is one, is delayed, until long after it is too late to defend themselves properly or counterattack effectively. For these reasons, one might say that passive-aggressives' bite is truly worse than their bark.

A clerk in a stationery store was angry with her boss. To get back at him, she deliberately cut off the margins on documents when using the copying machine, and then she replied to a customer's legitimate complaints that "You cut off the margin on this document" with, "Why did you need that part of it anyway?" The customer thought her funny at first but complained about it later, saying to her boss, "The nerve of her. . . " (one month later she developed a carpal tunnel syndrome that kept her from doing any copying).

A salesperson was told by a customer, "I can get those for one-third the price [at a different store]." Instead of suggesting a compromise discount, or explaining why getting them at this store was advantageous for both of them regardless of price, she first replied with stony silence and then said, "Perhaps you would be happier going elsewhere." When asked by a customer "What's the price on this item?" she did not simply tell her the price, although she knew it well from having sold many of the same items that day. Instead she told her to turn the item over and look at the price tag underneath (more work for the customer, less work for her). When customers saw something they liked that was not in their size and asked her if their size were in stock, she invariably replied not with "I'll look in the back of the store and see" but with, "If you don't see it on the rack, then we don't have it in the store." This left the customer feeling angry and disappointed, thinking, "She doesn't care," and feeling stupid, thinking, "Perhaps I should have known that already, or at least I should have known that that is how she would answer my question, so that I could have avoided asking in the first place."

The bus driver mentioned in Chapter 3 (who, when asked "When does the next bus leave?" replied not with "In two minutes" but first by silently pointing to a bus schedule hanging on a rack in front of the bus and then by advising the customer to read it "instead of asking me") did not make his job easier for himself. For his response took just as much, or even more, time and effort as answering the question. But it did allow him to express a little hostility toward those he believed were "interrupting my siesta and forcing me to coddle them"—something that he considered to be beneath him and "not my job." "My job," he admitted privately, "is driving the bus, not catering to a bunch of idiots." His intent was to make his customers guilty for bothering him, although it was he who was ultimately criticized for not wanting to be bothered.

A customer entered a restaurant, where a man behind a counter was taking orders and was asking those giving the orders, "Here or to go?". The customer assumed (not without reason) that there was no table service, and so she ordered her food and took it to a table herself. Afterward the waitress appeared and ruined her meal by sarcastically chiding her for bypassing her. The customer saw the waitress's point at the time, but despite her intellectual insight she never returned to the establishment.

## Sadomasochistic Personality Disorder

Not all companies are brought down by bad business decisions, social shifts in tastes, or the ups and down of the economics of consumer spending. Many are brought down by the sadistic individuals who work there. (Sadists are discussed in Chapter 11.) As we shall see in Chapter 11, companies can be as sadistic as the people who work for them. The company that plans a downsizing and announces it in advance (but only in a vaguely defined future, keeping everyone guessing and on edge) is as sadistic as the key worker who keeps the company on edge, or pushes it off the edge, by threatening to quit but then staying on and doing damage.

Masochism is both a specific dynamic factor in certain occupational inhibitions (ranging from typist's cramp to emotionally induced RSI) and a general cause for suffering among workers. Masochists are self-destructive individuals who look for any way they can find to hurt themselves. Of course, their occupation provides them with an excellent, ready-made medium and opportunity for such self-destructiveness.

Some masochists work up to par but arrange to suffer from their work by seeking unpleasantness. They make a masochistic career move by selecting a job that hurts and sticking with it instead of taking another that would be less painful. Or they find a decent job and then handle it in an unhealthy, self-destructive way. Others work below par. They stop short of success, or they fail outright as a way to hurt themselves deliberately or unconsciously. Some damage their anatomy in ways that range from the more to the less obvious. For the more obvious, they can have accidents. If they are the composer Robert Schumann, they can maim their fourth finger in the guise of strengthening it. If they are the composer Carl Maria Von Weber, they can accidentally drink a glass of nitric acid to ruin their singing voice. If they are the composer Ernest Chausson, they can ride their bicycle into a wall and kill themselves. If they are one of my patients, they can, in preparing for a craft show pick up a saw and unthinkingly cut off a piece of their thumb. Or they hurt themselves in less obvious ways. They can damage the part of their anatomy they need most not by bashing their head or cutting off a thumb but by tensing instead of relaxing at the computer keyboard—a character armoring, as Reich might put it, that is both why they develop a hand syndrome and why rolfing (a method of deep muscle massage intended to serve as physical and emotional therapy) sometimes works therapeutically (as, according to rumor, it did for the pianist Leon Fleischer).

A doctor with a self-defeating personality disorder went stale because as a way to self-defeat he made a pact with himself to not keep up with the advances in his field. Also, when trying to write papers, he slowed down at the keyboard not because of the emotionally caused repetitive strain injury his therapist diagnosed but as a way to see to it that he would be disappointed and exasperated with himself. In like manner, although he was talented and knowledgeable, he rarely spoke in public because of a progressively worsening stage fright put into place to assure that he would not get his message across. When attending conferences, he made jokes when he should have been acting serious, and he made fun of the speakers to associates sitting next to him so that they would think him a regular guy with a great sense of humor. It seems as if the only thing he really took seriously was his need to hurt himself by being defiant of authority. Of course, his lack of seriousness and his defiance got back to the head of the department and created bad feelings, earning him a place not at the head of the table, but at the top of the next downsizing list.

An unsuccessful writer who felt he was doing the best job he could under the impossible circumstances that prevailed in the literary world blamed his lack of success on his problems with publishers and critics and thought that realizing his dreams was hopeless. What he failed to realize was that his failure was self-created. He acted out sexually and then justified his nightly philandering by saying he was living for the moment and improving his self-image through sexual conquest—as if being a professional "conquistador" was not a good way to improve his self-image. And he arranged to have to take a demeaning, draining day job, and get overly involved with it instead of just doing it, by refusing to accept financial help from his wealthy family (due to excessive pride) and by buying things that he did not need, just to maintain his life-style at the expense of pursuing his professional goals.

A wife known for her narcissism was selfish right up to the moment of truth, when she decided to quit her day job to go into business for herself. As soon as she was about to sign the final papers, she became altruistic. She decided to keep her day job, telling herself, "I want to stay here so that I can buy my husband the things he always wanted to have, but that I was too self-centered in the past to get for him."

Many masochists rationalize their masochism away. Those with little insight think they fail because they have no talent or ability, and to back up their contention they call themselves bad names like philistine, lazy, incompetent, shiftless, and stupid. Many convince themselves that unpleasantness is a good thing for them. They say to themselves, "It's the unpleasant jobs that do, after all, have a measure of security and come with an excellent retirement plan, and it's good to be future oriented, sacrificing pleasure now by saving it for pleasure later." When they say, "Instead of enjoying myself now I will postpone enjoyment until later," they mean, "Instead of enjoying myself when I can, I will postpone enjoyment until I can't." It is the bright future they are always waiting for, and in the meantime (as an exchange) they suffer in a drab job or career. But they know the bright future will never come. That is why they agree to the exchange.

## Treatment of Sadomasochism

Sadists first need insight into how sadistic they are, and then they need to develop control over their sadistic behavior by setting limits on it.

Because masochism is often too deeply ingrained to be overcome easily, a first step is for patients to avoid doing irreparable harm to themselves while under its spell and before it is resolved. For example, in the long run few workers regret having resisted the impulse to lose or tear up partially or wholly finished projects. Friends and therapists can help by gently encouraging masochists to be good to themselves, much in the same way that friends and therapists of obsessionals can help by gently encouraging them to be less guilty and more self-accepting. Often this stems the self-destructive tide long enough that insight or cognitive therapy can have a chance to work.

Masochists need to learn less destructive ways of dealing with sadists. They cannot encourage sadists to attack by looking or acting vulnerable.

They have to stand up to sadists, such as career-busting bosses who demean them because they do not want to lose them (e.g., the boss who, when a worker got too good and caught the eye of a rival company, wrote bad letters of recommendation so that the worker could not move on). They have to fight back rivals who try to crush them, such as book reviewers who give their books bad reviews because they are writing a rival book, or co-workers who undermine them so that they can get ahead in their stead. They should deal with their sadistic critics not by trying to please them to get love but either by ignoring them completely or facing them down (perhaps verbally) or, better, by succeeding regardless of what they think and, when possible, even regardless of what they do.

Insight-oriented treatment improperly done can make masochism worse. Masochistic patients who learn about their oedipal conflicts may feel not better but worse, if finding out that as a child they were part of an infantile murderous plot against a rival sibling or a parent of the opposite sex only causes them to become more guilty. If oedipus is to be analyzed at all, it is helpful to identify and trace its vicissitudes, not merely to show how early oedipal strivings persist into the present but also to show that the oedipal strivings were not abnormal; that the patient was not a bad child for having them; and that what gave the most difficulty was not the oedipal strivings themselves but the parents' critical reactions to the strivings. As one therapist put it, "All children want to have incestuous relationships and murder their parents. So what? This only becomes a problem when parents take these wishes seriously and to heart, react to them excessively, and retaliate."

Some therapists find it helpful to analyze masochism developmentally. Present masochism is seen as a way to suffer to please others now, as it was a way to suffer to please one's parents in the past. The problem often comes up when children have competitive envious parents who put them down (or "castrate" them) for being younger and stronger than the parents are.

> A composer was asked to speak before a group on his latest work. That night he had a dream that he was asked to conduct before the group, but he did not know how to conduct. The group coalesced into his father, who was booing him and complaining that he should not have been asked to conduct before him, first because he did not know how to conduct, and second because his shoes were the wrong color (brown, not black); were the wrong style; had a stain on them; and were covering a malformed foot, one "with a toe cut off."

# 9

## Job Dissatisfaction

Job dissatisfaction, although unfortunate, is not inevitable. Yet too many workers think that it is. They see work as a predictable complication of life, and job dissatisfaction as a predictable complication of work. Therapists, on the other hand, are of two minds about job dissatisfaction. Some agree with their patients that all jobs are difficult and draining, and they tell the patient to shrug this off: "Of course, otherwise, why would they pay you?" But others dismiss all patients who complain about their jobs as misfits, cranks, and malcontents whose only problem is the excessive expectations they bring to and demands they make on their work. Both workers and therapists overlook that job dissatisfaction is a symptom of an occupational disorder that stands beside other occupational symptoms, like phobia and depression, and can be dealt with as an abnormal condition that needs treatment.

### MANIFESTATIONS

Job dissatisfaction, although it is a chronic, mild, and diffuse occupational symptom or disorder, is nevertheless cumulatively devastating. Although it simmers rather than boils, it can nevertheless disrupt life. Although it may not cut deeply like a knife, it can spread laterally like a rash and gradually and insidiously affect one's career and the pleasure taken in pursuing it.

Job dissatisfaction keeps workers back in different ways. Some workers work effectively but are unhappy professionally. They do their work, and sometimes they do it well, but they do it half-heartedly and without enjoyment. They find their job dull and boring, not really for them, and they do not want to (but have to) force themselves to do their work. Clerks have to drag themselves out of bed in the morning, and writers have to drag themselves to their desks. At 5:00 P.M. on Friday, office workers heave a sigh of relief that the work week is over, only to break out in a cold sweat at 6:00 P.M. in anticipation of Monday morning. This TGIF syndrome is generally passed off as familiar to all but of no particular significance. Although we hear an amusing litany of seemingly trivial complaints whose purpose seems to be to blow off steam, underneath there is an alarm sounding, warning of serious personal and professional consequences, imminent or in place already.

Many even quit their jobs and rationalize quitting as a reasonable thing to do: They give up their career to have a baby; or to retire early because they are getting "too old"; or, if working for themselves, to work for others and thus make a steady income; or, if working for others, to work for themselves for the satisfaction and freedom from 9 to 5 constraints. Real or distorted images of society can play a role in these rationalizations too, as in, "I won't continue in politics unless I can do so honestly. But you can't get ahead in politics if you are honest. Therefore, I won't run for office again."

Some workers work ineffectively—that is, beneath their potential—with everything they do flawed in some way, either absolutely or compared to what might have been. For example, some writers do finally get to their desks and begin, only to write routinely and joylessly; thus they wonder if they should be doing something else for a living. An actress supporting herself as a waitress can get out of bed in the morning to go to work, but once there she hates to cater to people who just want to "stuff their face." She excuses herself for how she feels by reminding herself that "all creative people hate to wait on tables." She hardly works at all and makes too many mistakes while doing the little work she does. A CEO devotes half his time and energy to thinking about and doing his work, but the other half to thinking about and managing his pension plan, so that he can retire early and not have to do any work at all. Such people may keep their jobs but not get ahead. Or they may be downsized or fired outright for being lazy or incompetent.

An advertising man held himself back because he feared being successful. His fear of success did not take the form of a cramped hand or an "accident on purpose" on the job. Instead he felt dissatisfied with his career, burned out, chronically fatigued, and he worked below capacity because he was constantly obsessing about what to do with his life. He wrote advertising copy and made a reasonable impression on others and a living for himself, but he constantly talked about how tiresome his job had become and how he wanted to write a novel. He complained, "I am a blocked novelist," and he got treated for writer's block, when in fact he was a blocked advertising man who was using the possible novel to explain and justify his advertising block. He used the usual array of rationalizations or excuses to justify his being in a rut: "It's impossible to be honest in the advertising profession nowadays," or "There's never any satisfaction to be had from jobs that pay as much as mine," or "my last project fell short of expectations so the next one will probably do the same thing, so why bother trying to do something worthwhile? I'll just show up, put in my time, go home, and at least try to enjoy my life after hours."

Some workers have fallow periods intermeshed with periods of normal (or even higher than normal) productivity: They do some work, but they do it intermittently. Their work is spotty because they work on a high level but do so only occasionally, writing two proposals instead of twenty—that is, doing great things, but doing them only once in a while. Others work constantly but fail to achieve much of anything because they do too many things, so that everything they do is compromised or flawed because they do not give it their full attention.

Some cannot work much or at all because they develop chronic headaches or chronic fatigue, somatic symptoms that are a way to say, "This job gives me a headache" or "This job is so dull that it puts me to sleep." Or they develop a burnout syndrome that, in addition to dissatisfaction, contains a significant component of depression. They blame themselves for their fate; blame their co-workers and superiors for making their job hell; or blame their wives, lovers, and children for not being supportive enough or for keeping them back.

As with the other occupational symptoms and disorders, sometimes the symptom of job dissatisfaction looks like a reactive or exogenous one although it is mainly an endogenous one. There are true exogenous disorders where the dissatisfaction is a response to difficult, stressful working conditions, and workers are dissatisfied for a good reason.

In one case dissatisfaction resulted from company policy that gratuitously ruined what could have been a perfectly good job for almost all the doctors who worked in a clinic. The patients were allowed, and even encouraged, to dictate the terms of their medical care because that served the administration's selfish needs. Patients who got what they wanted personally, such as financial compensation and drugs to maintain their drug addiction, gave the administration good reports, forgetting that they did not get what they needed medically—namely, psychotherapy for their compensation disorder and drug withdrawal for their drug addiction.

But in many cases job dissatisfaction is endogenous. The job is adequate, but the person is inadequate to the job. Endogenous job dissatisfaction is a symptom not much different from symptoms like scrupulosity or excessive brooding. It is found in such workers as those who overreact to a normal amount of on-the-job stress; and those who, out of a sense of guilt, masochistically take and stay on a bad job when a better one is available, or who masochistically take a good job and make it into a bad one (an action tantamount to committing professional suicide).

> To suffer, a man deliberately selected a dull boring job, convincing himself that it was for the money, that he did not have talent for a better one in the first place, and that the life of the individual in the field he wanted, and was good in, was impossible, out of reach, unrealistic, and undesirable because that sort of work was ultimately an unproductive thing to do. A potentially fine artist, he nevertheless decided, "The world doesn't want another painter," and he stuck to a nursing job, as he put it, "helping a bunch of kids get over colds." He justified his remaining at what he believed to be this unsatisfactory job by saying that he felt hopeless about his outside prospects. He then concluded that he should be thankful for the job he had and not make things worse for himself by complaining about it or trying to better his lot.

In addition, endogenous job dissatisfaction is found in workers who are basically too narcissistic for their own good, and would complain about any job and compulsively search for a new and better one, no matter what job they already had.

Like other endogenous symptoms, endogenous job dissatisfaction has an origin, developmental history, cause, and differential diagnosis. It serves a dynamic function, follows a specific (usually downhill) course when it goes untreated, and tends to respond to one or more specific methods of treatment. As for its developmental origin, it often begins in adolescence, when adolescents make the wrong career choice because of conflicts with their parents and then have to live with the consequences of their early mistakes for the rest of their lives. As for the differential diagnosis, there are different endogenous job dissatisfactions, and the character of each depends on the larger underlying emotional disorder of which it is a part. Depressives, or narcissists, are as dissatisfied with their jobs as they are with their lives—in the same way and for the same reasons. For example, depressives think that they are too insignificant for their jobs, while narcissists think that they are too important for their jobs. As for the dynamic function served, job dissatisfaction, like any other symptom, resolves conflict via compromise formation (for example, cases in which individuals in conflict between being successful and being guilty about success work, but they make sure their work is not up to standard).

Sometimes job dissatisfaction is a composite of external and internal influences—that is, it is both reactive and self-induced. Each part of the picture must be recognized and addressed. In a typical scenario, a worker finds a partly stressful job to be completely stressful because of personal anxiety, which makes even the most minor stress into major stress. Having endogenous problems predisposes to having exogenous ones, while being under stress tends to release endogenous problems that would otherwise have remained latent.

## PSYCHOTHERAPY

In treatment, these patients tend to repeat their dissatisfaction about their jobs in the transference to their therapists. On the positive side, transference material is useful for understanding the disorder in question and provides grist for the mill of interpretation of the patient's dynamics. On the negative side, it is an impediment to treatment because the patients, instead of working out their problems in therapy, relive them once again and become surly, difficult to please, and too resistant to get what they want and need out of treatment.

# 10

## Non–*DSM-IV* Occupational Disorders

### WORKAHOLISM

Workaholism is not a pathological condition and should not be the focus of treatment when the patient wants to work hard; likes working hard; feels, "What else is there to life?" and "Where else but in my work can I get this much satisfaction?"; and is not hurting anyone in the process.

> A journalist used exhaustion, not the clock, to tell her it was quitting time and refused to schedule even a two-week vacation every year because that would take her away from her work for too long. Her therapist diagnosed her as a workaholic and insisted that to get better she would have to go away on vacation for at least one week twice a year and not take her work with her. She refused to go along with her therapist, countering that she would only pace the floors, counting the hours and minutes until she could get back to her desk and start working again.

Workaholism is a pathological condition that should be the focus of treatment when the patient feels that work is excessive and complains about it; cannot stop working even though he or she wants to stop; and/or is hurting loved ones in the process but continues to work excessively although they complain (for example, about his or her continuing to work on holidays and special occasions).

### OVERLOAD

Overload is an often pathological state in which patients pile on detail after detail and activity after activity to keep their lives as cluttered as possible. The problem is illustrated by the CEO traveling around the country who tries to do his in-office work as well as the itinerant work, and hence everything suffers; and by the day worker who parties and dances all night in a disco, oblivious to the upcoming work day and unable to function efficiently at work after the night out. For both, simplifying life is the logical solution, but this is easier said than done. Most overloaders continue to suffer because they simply will not face the choices they must make in the interest of job effectiveness.

> One pianist went on concert tours and fooled himself into thinking, "I can compose in between performances—after all, you can only compose for a few hours a day anyway."
> But his concert schedule affected his composing adversely. Even his piano playing became an on-and-off thing because of his composing. Eventually he gave up composing entirely for performing in public. What is wrong with that? Although it may be somewhat arbitrary to say so, I think that the following judgmental hierarchy is valid: Producing is above reproducing, especially in those cases where performing the works (or collecting the products of) others is a compulsive avoidance of creating something of one's own.

> A woman starting her own business bought a professional office at the height of the commercial office market, and she paid a good price for it. Then she decided to write law books instead of developing her law practice. She rented the office out for income, which she needed to support herself while she pursued her career. Unfortunately, she got an unreliable tenant who paid the rent irregularly. Instead of summarily evicting him, she became personally involved in his troubles (saying, "After all, he has a wife and children") and even made excuses for him (saying, "After all, he does eventually pay, though sometimes over a month late"). Instead of cutting the asking price, selling the office, and eliminating him from her life, she hung on, hoping the real estate market would turn. She expected herself to have infinite patience and capacity for stress and tension, as well as few needs of her own. But she found that she was no more or less human than anyone else. Only after many months in therapy did she come to recognize that she should sell the office at a loss and view the loss as the cost of doing business and as the price to pay for her sanity.

> An overloaded creator was a pioneer who thought he had to do everything for himself. A writer, he could not get help from consultants because he thought that that would be cheating. He had to do all his own research, and he had to do it the hard way. For example, he had to look up everything on his own instead of having a computerized literature search done for him. So he paced the library stacks, as people did in the days before databases. He did it this way to do it the hard way, because he felt that the

hard way built character and backbone. When confronted with his behavior, he excused it by saying, "I hate the computer," but he really meant, "I hate being nice to myself." He thought, "There is a reward in heaven for unnecessarily complicating my life." But in effect his only reward was the pleasure of masochistic self-defeat and the smug satisfaction the inveterate moralist gets by righteously insisting that one should judge a book not by its cover but by its spine.

Dynamically, overloaders take on more than they can handle for reasons that range from pathological perfectionism to an excessive, even masochistic, desire to be a nice person who wants to please each person who asks for something.

Successful therapy of overloaders involves getting them to simplify their lives. If they are trying to do too much, they should try to do less. That means giving up something to get something. Yet most overloaders want it all.

One overloader wanted to finish an impossible book all by herself, without asking for help and without leaving out what she could not do, while maintaining her standards throughout and denying that "something had to give." Another wanted to set up his own company but could not give up his full-time job for a part-time position so that he could have the time and the energy to start his own business. He knew he had to temporarily "give up money for the sake of art," but he, like most overloaders, could not do so easily. All he could do was brood about the advantages and disadvantages of each point in his plan. Nothing ever changed, and eventually he gave up his plan as hopeless.

Because overloaders who are asked to do less will resist, therapists should at first suggest that their patients do less with a limited goal in mind: examining the anxiety that will appear when they attempt to do less. Doing less is at first primarily a way to learn what is causing the anxiety about not doing more.

## DEPLETION

Occupational disorder due to true depletion is popularly called burnout, but there is a significant difference between the two. True depletion is an occupational hazard, but not a pathological condition. Burnout (my next topic) is both of these things.

In true depletion, a talented person runs out of good ideas and is not suppressing or inhibiting them for one reason or another. The one-idea CEO or the one-novel author may just be the victim of depletion. This problem is not pathological, because it can exist for all creative people.

They often cannot help it, and sometimes they cannot be effectively treated. There seems to be a creative pool from which material emerges until it is gone, and the pool cannot be refilled. Their creativity is, metaphorically speaking, a kind of fossil fuel formed only in infancy and childhood—a substance that is laid down only in the early years; once the well is drained, it will never yield more. Perhaps as adults they have different experiences from and are not as impressionable as children, so later experiences do not have the impact of early ones and cannot form new inspirational pools. Depletion occurs when the pools of fossil fuel run dry and cannot be refilled by reading, interviewing, listening, looking, or drinking in impressions because none of these things put back what was there before—and even if they do add something, its inspirational value does not live up to the "old times."

However, only a few workers are really depleted in a literal sense. In most cases depletion is really false depletion due to inhibition. It is the result not of dried pools but of discounting fertile fields of ideas still inside. Curing this kind of depletion involves not refilling with something but removing something else (i.e., it requires relieving inhibitions). Such individuals do not have to stop and refill. They have to stop discounting what is already there.

Although this view may not reflect every case of apparent depletion, it is the most helpful (if not the only) therapeutic way to think about the problems of patients who claim to be depleted. It is possible (even easy) to remove inhibitions, but it is virtually impossible and extremely difficult to infuse absent motivation, ability, and ideas. Thus, seeing depletion as inhibition is not buying into a patient's occupational disorder.

## BURNOUT

Unlike true depletion, burnout is a pathological condition. Burnout is often why individuals with talent and a desire to work reach a certain level of achievement and then stall or backslide—often suddenly, completely, and finally, and for seemingly no good reason. They cannot continue at, and possibly interrupt, their career.

In one writer, the bud (so to speak) opened but fell off rapidly after fully flowering. He had talent and the desire to work and had achieved a level of success in his chosen field. He did great things once, but he did not seem to be able to do them again. He sunk to a lower level, feeling that something interfered with his inspiration, and his ability was compromised. What followed was a string of mediocre ideas. He continued to work, but no one any longer viewed him as a genius. Eventually he retired, saying, "I'm too exhausted to continue to work. I'll play golf instead and fix up my house. I could be perfectly happy just doing that."

It is too easy to dismiss all burned-out patients as depressed. Some are, but others are simply responding appropriately to demoralizing, numbing rejection with what is the occupational equivalent of an adjustment disorder or a posttraumatic stress disorder.

## FLOODING

Flooding is in some ways the opposite of depletion. In flooding, an excess of strong feelings is aroused, and the patient cannot properly integrate or satisfactorily discharge them, so the feelings become overwhelming. Integrating and discharging feelings is always difficult in the workplace. Feelings cannot be integrated in the workplace because people have to continue to do their work until quitting time, and they cannot afford to take the time or spare the energy that integration requires. Feelings cannot be discharged in the workplace because workers cannot speak up because they fear offending the powers that be.

People who work at home (artists and writers among them) have a special problem with flooding, but for somewhat different reasons. They cannot integrate or discharge their feelings, not because they are too busy or afraid to speak their minds or it is dangerous to do so but because they have no one to hear what they have to say. They are without even those few safe opportunities that the average worker has for dissipating tension and blowing off steam. For the former group—flooded company workers—less input is the cure. For the latter group—flooded workers at home—more output is the answer.

PART TWO

---

# Exogenous (Reactive)
# Occupational Disorders

# 11

## Exogenous (Reactive) Occupational Disorders

The exogenous occupational disorders, unlike the endogenous occupational disorders, are not primarily due to a mental disorder, such as anxiety disorder or depression, although these can play a facilitating role or be the result of an exogenous disorder once formed. They are primarily due to real on-the-job work problems, which may be either impersonal or interpersonal and can range from diffuse, ongoing, job-related stress that demoralizes workers (such as the stress of sexism) to discrete, one-time, job-related trauma that jolts workers into retreat (such as the experience of being downsized).

As I emphasize throughout this book, it is difficult to distinguish whether exogenous or endogenous factors mainly contribute to a given disorder. Although this is a cliché, what often counts is the interaction between an individual and his or her work environment. Of course, when stress or trauma are severe, the worker's contribution may be negligible. But more often a precipitating "stressful" or "traumatic" event is a minor one. It is not necessarily a downsizing in which workers lose their job. It may instead be something subtle, like an indirect putdown, which only becomes a stressor when the individual cannot handle it in a healthy way.

In one case a boss asked a broker into his office and posed a question that appeared innocent on the surface: "Why do some of our clients prefer your colleagues to you?" One worker would shrug this off as a mild knuckle-rapping and pass it off with "You can have a bad day now and then on every job" and "Every boss can have a nasty disposition at times." But this broker reacted more negatively than that. He was too insightful to take what was said at face value without also reading between the lines; too sensitive to not mind an attack even though it was merely a covert one, implied rather than stated; and too paranoid to not see hidden meanings even though they were meant to be kept hidden. He did not emerge from the encounter unscathed. Instead he became anxious and angry, and this episode became the grain of sand around which he, like an oyster making a pearl, elaborated a full-blown "exogenous" depressive occupational disorder.

## THE LITERATURE

The *DSM-IV* (American Psychiatric Association, 1994) includes the exogenous occupational disorders with the situational (adjustment and posttraumatic stress) disorders and with the V-codes, or occupational problems of everyday life—that is, the job difficulties normal people have as a result of the occupational hazards present all the time on every job.

The lay literature tends to overemphasize the role of job-related stress in occupational disorders and downplay the role of the personality and/or pathology of the victim of that stress. In any given case of occupational disorder the stress is blamed too much for the problem and the victim of that stress is exonerated too readily for allowing the problem to take hold and develop.

The lay literature also overemphasizes how an employee's occupational disorder results from the tension between management and workers while overlooking another source of tension: the tension that arises between co-workers. Some workers' problems are due to a career-busting boss, but many are due to career-jamming colleagues or career-undermining underlings. In addition, the lay literature studies employee stress at the hands of management more than management's stress at the hands of employees. Bosses can be affected by bottom-to-top interpersonal difficulties, and they can suffer as much at the hands of difficult underlings.

In contrast, the technical literature (particularly the psychoanalytic literature) tends to minimize the role of external stress and emphasize the role of the individual in creating, provoking, and/or overreacting to stress. The psychoanalytic literature can even blame the victim. It implies that victims have provoked their job-related stress when in fact they are not responsible because they have no control over their unhappy circumstances. If it does not blame them entirely for provoking their stress, then it at least blames them for being unable to handle and adapt to unprovoked stress, even in situations that would be difficult for almost anyone to manage.

## SPECIFIC SOURCES OF STRESS AND TRAUMA

### Positive Stressors

The Peter Principle (Peter & Hull, 1969) suggests that workers do not do well after a promotion because they have been promoted to their "level of incompetence"—that is, they have been promoted to a new, higher level position based on how they did in their old, lower level one, even though that is a poor predictor of future performance (pp. 19–27). But there are other reasons why individuals may not do well after a promotion, and a fear of success is the most usual one. (Fear of success is discussed in Chapters 5 and 8.)

## Negative Stressors

### Home Life

Sometimes troublemakers in the patient's life are not co-workers or bosses but spouses and children. Just as people can wreck their home life by bringing their work home with them, workers can wreck their jobs by bringing their home life back into their work. Marital problems, for example, often weaken workers both directly and indirectly (the latter by leaving them vulnerable to on-the-job stress).

> A physicist was complaining to me that he thought he must be creatively blocked because at times he could not come up with the proofs he needed when he needed them and had to turn to a colleague for help. His wife, sitting next to him in the session, put him down, saying, "He's interested in block in creative artists—not in uncreative physicists." In a flash, I understood one reason for the physicist's work inhibition and something about what needed to be done about it.

In such cases patients can think that having an affair is an effective solution. They see lack of support from their partners as the problem and look to the affair for the support they feel they are missing and think they need. But this is no solution. First, they are trying to solve a problem with one person by having a relationship with another. Second, the compliant in the affair is as likely to be solving his or her own problems as helping the other out. Third, real complications abound (as when affairs interfere with concentrating on work and getting enough sleep). Fourth, the immorality and resultant guilt are likely to spill over from the affair to the job, so that the worker feels generally uncomfortable. Fifth, affairs are blocked relationships, and practicing one block is hardly likely to improve another.

### On-the-Job Relationships

Work disorders are often the result of interpersonal problems with authority, peers, and underlings on the job, whom I collectively call non-sexual harassers. In Chapter 8 I distinguished three classes of personality disorders according to how the disorder affects the patient and the others in the patient's environment, and I distinguished between the onion disorders (which affect both the patient and the environment), the garlic disorders (which mainly affect others in the patient's environment), and the red pepper disorders (which mainly affect the patient). In Chapter 8 I focused on the red pepper aspects of personality disorders that caused workers to self-defeat. In this chapter I mainly focus on the garlic aspects of personality disorders, which cause workers to hurt others (especially those who get in their way).

Promotion becomes a negative stressor not only when the worker has a fear of success but also when former co-workers snub individuals who have been promoted because they are envious of their success; avoid them because they are angry with them for selling out and being a traitor to the old gang; defeat them because they refuse to work gladly for someone who used to be a colleague; and criticize and humiliate them (calling them "nerds," "teacher's pet," or "mama's boy") because they see them as having joined the conspirational "establishment," which seems to embody all of the negative feelings about authority carried over from past encounters with adults.

## Others' Personality Disorder

*Paranoid personality disorder.*   Knocking the competition is hysterical (as described in greater detail in this section) when it is mainly competitive. But it is paranoid when it is mainly a way to deny one's flaws by attributing them to others, and when the motive is to deny a sense of personal defectiveness by demeaning the effectiveness of others.

*Psychopathic/antisocial personality disorder.*   Psychopathic bosses are immoral people who abuse others as part of their plan for gain (such as power or money) and then, also as part of their plan, cover their true motives by blaming their victims to demoralize them further and reduce their sense of self-worth so that they complain less about how they are being mistreated.

The head of a psychiatric clinic who put other psychiatrists down so that he could get all the referrals for his and his wife's practice attacked others for the same purpose using two clever tricks of logic. The first consisted of turning their positive into negative attributes. Women who worked hard in his clinic were too aggressive and too pushy; and men who worked hard in his clinic were too passive and too cooperative. In like manner, workers who made a mistake, reconsidered, and changed their minds were called not flexible but unreliable, and they were condemned not for seeing the light but for having been in the dark in the first place. Once, when he wanted to fire one psychiatrist but could not, he first picked on him. That psychiatrist, after he moved to the country, first tried to sell his New York cooperative apartment and then changed his mind and decided to keep it as a pied à terre. This boss decided to put him down for his changeability. "Why did you move out of your apartment if you like it here; or why, if you don't like it here, did you come back?" The boss overlooked that most of us are ambivalent about everything and have a right to change our minds without being condemned for it; and that the ability to change is the hallmark of the big, broad mind, while consistency is the hallmark of the little, narrow one. Next the boss gave him menial jobs, in effect demoting him. Then he marked him down for being unable to do the low-level work at a high level, although in most circumstances being unable to work effectively beneath one's capacity would be considered an attribute, not a liability.

The second trick was to condemn others for single flaws without regard for their performance as a whole, focusing on the negatives, which are usually mixed in with positives, in a way that would violate federal regulations. He condemned older workers because they used the medical insurance policies too much, while overlooking that they were more stable, mature, and experienced than younger workers and thus worth any extra money they might cost. He condemned younger workers as inexperienced, immature, and untrustworthy based solely on their age but without regard for the kind of ability that can be conferred on younger people by virtue of their wide-eyed innocence, freshness, and unfettered excitement. He viewed females as defective compared to males because they got pregnant, and males as defective compared to females because they do not have much in the way of maternal instincts.

A critic who wanted to defeat a pianist who was his wife's rival used the first trick of making an individual's strong into a weak suit. Instead of saying that the rival played rubato (stretching out a phrase like a sigh) because he was a romantic, he said that the rival did this because he had no respect for the printed page.

*Hysterical (histrionic) personality disorder.*    Creative genius, as Victor Hugo (1982, originally published 1862) said, elicits hostility (p. 995), especially from people who cannot stand the competition. Chief among these are hysterics, who make every interaction with co-workers into a competitive one in which there is only one prize and there are at least two contenders for it. Upon hearing of others' success, hysterics think not, "Isn't that wonderful?" but "How can I get back at you for getting what is rightfully mine?" We often hear how successful people abandon their best friends upon becoming famous and successful. But we rarely hear about how their best friends abandon them *because* they have become famous and successful.

Hysterics who feel themselves defeated feel less defeated if everyone around them is defeated, too. The reasoning is, "If I can't have it, then no one else can have it," "If I'm going to suffer, I want everyone else to suffer, too," or, "If I am going to go down at sea, then I want the rest of the world to be in the same boat." At work they reason, "If I have to work late, then I want everyone else here with me at the office," or "If I am going to be fired, then I hope the whole place shuts down."

Hysterics cloak their competitive, jealous hostility rationally by finding defects in their rivals. Where there is both good and bad in others, they find a minor glitch or omission in what they did or a presumed flaw in who or what they are or stand for. They are right, but only to a degree. Their science is what I call hysterical aesthetics, a science of flaw finding: However much they may justify it, it is not a search for immutable truth but merely a way to rationalize their competitiveness and jealousy; a game played to win, in which the only rule is to knock the competition as sour grapes while presenting the sour grapes as critical plums.

The experience of one of my patients when she was trying to sell her apartment illustrates this principle.

> People were so critical of the apartment that she could not stand to be home for potential buyers. They were quick to see its flaws, but slow to admit its virtues. After recovering her aplomb, she analyzed the situation and thought, "What is the reason for this?" She recognized jealousy as the common thread. They tore the apartment down to avoid admitting to themselves, and to her, that they liked it and would buy it if they could afford it. The problem, as they tried to convince her and themselves, was in her apartment, not in their bank account.

> As an undergraduate, a critic (who was later to become a household name in the annals of rock criticism) ran a college music station. Another man was an aspiring announcer who started his own rock music program, playing his favorite, then modern, rock records. The critic-to-be tuned in one night and, pleased with what he heard but fearing that the other man was an upstart who would take his audience away, literally came running to see what was happening and to put a stop to it. He did this by undercutting the originality of the programming and the effectiveness of the program, first to the young announcer's face and then behind his back—over the air in gratuitous asides during the critic's own program. The encounter was so disruptive to the younger man that he gave up his radio program and all aspirations to be an announcer and was started well on his way to developing what would later prove to be a crippling stage fright.

The budding announcer was not surprised to hear (many years later) the same man, who had become a well-known radio and newspaper critic, making nasty remarks about famous, accomplished people. For example, he demolished one famous, accomplished rock composer by saying that his greatest product was not his music, but his students.

Was that a description of the rock composer in a nutshell? Or was the critic revealing more about himself than about his victim? Was his envy and jealousy surfacing along with his recognition that he, the critic, was capable only of criticizing, not of doing?

We should not count on the rock composer, if he were still alive, recognizing the emotional (neurotic) origin of this powerful critic's supposedly intellectual, aesthetic assessment of his work. We should instead count on his taking the criticism as valid, getting depressed and having trouble doing his work at all.

Jealousy will reveal itself in any number of ways. One is through the jealous individual's associations on being told of another's success. Such individuals are self-referential. They respond to a report of another's promotion with an assessment of their own prospects. They remark wistfully, "I wish that would happen to me." Or they ominously note, "You, like every one else, are doing better than I am." After that they may go on to demean the other's accomplishments—demeaning aesthetic triumphs as low paying and financial triumphs as devoid of aesthetic value.

Most workers are innocents. They think that being successful is all that is required of them, and that there is nothing that breeds success like success. But it does not work that way with hysterics.

A gay Jewish writer thought, "If I become famous, I will be impressive enough to be invited to cocktail parties." He did become famous, only to discover that either he was not invited to cocktail parties (so that he did not show up the host) or that he was, but only to be used, ridiculed, or otherwise victimized (as a way to make a host who felt insignificant feel less so). To this day he resents that at a Christmas party he attended, the host called to him from another room to "come listen to the Hanukkah song they are playing on the radio just for you." He claims that he overheard the host refer to him as a "quill queen."

Most workers forget that their success breeds the envy and jealousy of hysterical co-workers. They forget that hysterical superiors are hostile to those below them who are doing well. They forget that people who get to the top are people who want to be on the top, and people who want to be on the top do not usually take kindly to talent lurking below, because they see it as competition for their lofty position. They also forget that their own underlings are breathing fire at them. They forget that underlings are people who stay in a routine job for a reason. Often they do so to avoid figurative "father and mother murder." Such people are morally outraged by those who want to succeed and have succeeded. To them that only means they do not care if they might kill, or have killed, their parents (in an oedipal sense).

It is so easy for workers, especially those in the middle, to forget that the best way (but one that is not recommended) to avoid trouble is to be an unoriginal plodder who does no more than his or her assignment and, when pressed to do more, spouts the protective litany of the bureaucrat: "That's not my job." This is to avoid being humiliated by superiors; stabbed by co-workers; or abused by underlings.

*Narcissistic personality disorder.*   Narcissistic bad bosses are self-serving people who undercut and otherwise work at cross-purposes to their employees because they put personal satisfaction over professional responsibility. Their workers are only there to serve them and enhance their glory.

If such bosses want to see their workers succeed, it is for all the wrong reasons. It is because their success is the beacon that sheds the light by which they glow. If such bosses criticize workers, it is because their failure reflects badly on them or because they hope to get admiration from *their* bosses—for their perceptiveness, insight, sensitivity, and their ability to remain independently negative when every one else has jumped on the bandwagon of praise.

*Passive-dependent personality disorder.*   Passive-dependent bosses, in a role reversal from what would be expected, see their workers as their mothers. They do not want to give to but want to take from them. They evaluate them like a child evaluates a mother's breast and breast milk: in terms of availability of the breast and quality and quantity of the milk produced, dispensing with the breast when it runs dry, and biting it, angered because it has nothing more to give. Concern about their workers' well-being matches a baby's concern for the well-being of the mother's breast. Figuratively speaking, these bosses stay warm and grow fat, while their workers grow cold and their breasts shrink and dry up.

One such boss had a personal life that reflected his professional dependency. On the job he worked his people unmercifully and for little pay, while stealing computer software for his use at home. In like manner, he refused to donate to the educational television shows he avidly watched because he felt entitled to see them for free. He also frequently called up radio stations, complaining that they were playing something not to his liking and virtually demanding that they play what he wanted to hear and when he wanted to hear it.

*Passive-aggressive personality disorder.*  The term *passive-aggressive* refers to angry people who do not keep their anger in or express it directly but get their anger out by expressing it indirectly.

Passive-aggressive undermining of talent and success goes on all the time in the inside (corporate) as it does in the outside (personal) world. Many workers must contend not only with parents and relatives outside of work who undermine them (for example, believing their particular job is too feminine or too masculine) but also with a career-busting boss, envious co-workers, and disrespectful underlings, who put the worker down every chance they get. Some are well-meaning people who have no idea that they have invalidated sincere endeavors and trivialized important pursuits. But others simply do not like a talented administrator or successful underling or peer. They attack deliberately and consciously, almost as if they are saying, "Your success means my failure." None are direct about their attacks ("I hate you for making more money than I do"). Most are subtle and sly about it, or even two-faced.

There is an Armenian word meaning, "the covered word," or indirect insult, that refers to those who express hostility passive-aggressively.

One co-worker told another that a friend they had in common "said you were no good, but I defended you." Her motivation was to discourage her victim so that she could leap over her head and go to the next highest rung of the corporate ladder, elevating herself without actually having to do anything uplifting. Then, to cover her real motives and protect herself from possible retaliation, she added, "Don't kill me, I am just the messenger."

The victim replied, perceptively, "Yes, but 'don't kill me I am only the messenger' only applies to those who were asked to deliver a message. You volunteered. And people who volunteer to deliver such messages are responsible for the messages they deliver and for their consequences."

The following dialogue took place between a neighbor and her friend just after the neighbor finished her first children's book:

*Writer:* I just finished my first children's book. I could do this forever. I loved writing it and I have many more books inside.
*Friend (soon to become former friend):* I would like to see you do something really challenging with your life, like become a legal secretary.

An author told her mother that she planned to spend the rest of the afternoon working on her book. Her mother called her back that evening to discuss the day. The mother asked, "How did it go?" "How did what go?" the daughter asked her mother. "It," repeated the mother. The mother, who did not want her daughter to write, refused to actually say the words *writing* or *book,* hoping that if she did not mention them, the daughter would forget all about writing and do something else.

When a psychologist left government service, he had the following experience many times, which illustrates the low esteem in which the world holds people who work for themselves and who write, and how self-employment in general (and self-employment in the artistic fields in particular) is considered to be "self-unemployment"—that is, not a serious or important undertaking, at least not as serious/important as practicing law with a law firm or doing accounting for a large corporation.

    *Doctor:* I am leaving my work here.
    *Colleague:* What will you be doing?
    *Doctor:* I will be writing full time.
    *Colleague:* The best of luck on your retirement.

A critic, when openly aggressive, made sardonic jokes about the complete work, not works, of certain composers. With relish he quoted the pianist Glenn Gould, who rumor has it said, "Mozart didn't die too young; he lived to be too old." He condemned all live artists and American conductors by stating his position that the only good artist is a dead artist and that the only good conductors are from Europe.

    When passive-aggressive, he replied to the mother who wanted her daughter, when she grew up, to be a conductor of a symphony orchestra by saying, "I hope it won't be hard to find an orchestra" (really his own version of, "That's nice, but when are you going to get yourself a real job, one that is reliable and comes with benefits and a paycheck?"). He subtly belittled his musician friends by implying that when it comes to music, "Anyone can do it." Not himself musically talented, he nevertheless dreamt of writing a popular song and making a million, proving that the composer Robert Schumann was on target when he supposedly said, "What the musician does is easy to do. All you have to do is to think of a nice tune no one thought of before." He focused on creative peoples' vulnerabilities while overlooking their accomplishments, part of his plan to put their real accomplishments down whenever he could. Having heard that a friend had just written a nice little book proving a musical theory (a book likely, however, only to sell 500 copies), he told him, "I would like to see you write something big, something with a plot, something that can be made into a movie."

    He liked to remind any co-worker who appeared on the verge of succeeding or who had actually succeeded of his or her humble origins: "I can't believe that you, little Bunky, my classmate, made it." He jokingly reminded one up-and-coming critic he worked with, "I still remember the time many years ago, when we were classmates and you were just starting out, you got drunk at the hockey game and threw a fish on the ice."

    In effect, he did the same thing to himself. Each time he tried to advance himself, there was a little voice in him that got revenge on himself by asking an innocent-appearing but ultimately devastatingly hostile question, like, "Are you sure you are doing the right thing? Are you sure you are up to it? Wouldn't you be safer, if not financially better off, staying put and right where you are?"

A therapist admitted that she could not stand patients who were doing better than she was doing because she saw them as her rivals. She envied patients who did not have to work a regular job because she thought them independently wealthy. *She* had to go to her office on a daily basis, so why should *they* not have to do the same thing? So she demeaned those who worked at home as idle or retired. Sometimes she unconsciously (but nevertheless deliberately) gave them bad advice, secretly hoping they would take it and fail, steering them wrong and undermining them with sincere, helpful-sounding suggestions/criticisms that were really intended to cripple them. For example, she encouraged her patients to give up their bread-and-butter job although they needed the money. She said, "devote yourself full time to your art," hoping that they would starve and be too physically weak to go on and so not threaten her by showing her up. In one case she identified workaholism as a problem and treated it in a worker who was a workaholic but had no problems with it. She told her, "You do not want to spend your whole life working 16 hours a day." But that was exactly what the worker wanted to do.

Passive-aggressive bosses express hostility indirectly and covertly instead of openly. They develop an ongoing, generally hypercritical attitude that substitutes for the focused assault. They often attack by picking, or stubbornly refuse to be pleased no matter what. They might learn their victims' sensitive points and speak to these. They might attack in the form of the hostile "it was just a question" question. They might use wry irony, starting their sentences with, "Can you believe that. . . " (for example, the musicologist who said, "Can you believe that Beethoven had to revise some of his tunes 200 times before getting them right?"). They might hide a criticism by first making it and then taking it back, as when a boss told a gay worker that he used to hate queers but now he was much more tolerant, because he came to realize that some gays are good workers and nice people. Or they might express anger in the form of its opposite, as when they express sadism in the form of pity—in effect, fusing their hatred toward others and the guilt about it into one pronouncement that says, "I feel sorry for defectives."

A predictable and diagnostic reaction to indirectly expressed hostility of this sort is not knowing what hit. Workers think, "I wonder what was meant by that?" and suspect that they have been put down. Yet they never really know if it is justified for them to feel annoyed and appropriate for them to get angry, or if they are being too sensitive or expecting too much. They never know if they should swallow their anger and simmer in silence or speak up.

Encounters with passive-aggressives are more depressing than at first seems justified. Of course, the depression is an appropriate response, if not to what is said then to what is meant and intended. It can only get worse if the worker expects the passive-aggressive to change. Passive-aggressives do not change anything. Instead they become more defensive—and they know how to defend themselves. When confronted, they deny all and/or attack their victims as they feel attacked, sometimes so cleverly that it is difficult not to buy into their self-defense that you, not they, are the one with the problem.

*Sadomasochistic personality disorder.*    Some of the milder sadists, instead of supporting or helping workers when they are down, pick on them. They issue orders for them to get up, knowing they are too weak to stand. Bosses tell workers who are depressed to cheer up, not because they want them cheerful but to attack them for being gloomy, which they do because they find their gloom annoying.

Other milder sadists make no attempt to create suffering in others. They are content with *schadenfreude,* or pleasure from the suffering of others (in the cause of which they had no detectable hand). They rejoice when they see power overthrown, beauty fade, and talent dry up. They gloat when a new rock group fails, saying aloud and with relish, "That's what happens to you when you get big." They celebrate when the boss makes a bad business decision and wrecks himself or herself, sometimes even when the boss takes the company down, too.

> In his personal life a boss liked being a spectator. He enjoyed watching TV pictures of roof-top jumpers, and he spoke many times of the pleasure he could have gotten if the law allowed him to witness executions. He equally enjoyed seeing others fail on a lesser, more symbolic, level, so that when he went to the opera he hoped to hear bad notes, and when he went to concerts he hoped to hear musicianly slips. With glee he spoke of how one popular artist's second record, her sophomore "trial," was not as popular as her first, and how he loved it when a promising political candidate made a fatal Freudian slip. His devotion to *schadenfreude* was a way to make himself feel better about himself because he saw himself as a failure in life. As he saw it, others' pratfalls put him in a comparatively flattering light, as well as proved an existential point he wanted to make, also to put himself in a favorable light—a point about the failed pretensions of humankind and the comeuppance for the pride that he believed regularly went before a fall.

The more serious sadists do not wait for fate to act but instead take fate into their own hands. They gleefully make others suffer, putting them down, kicking them when they are down, hitting them again when they try to get up, and being abusive once more when they complain. They dismiss them with, "If you can't stand the heat, then get out of the kitchen." Then they call them paranoid and suggest that their reaction to the abuse is inappropriate while denying that the abuse itself is excessive.

A boss hated those he saw as competing with him, and then he deprived them of what they needed, using his considerable political influence within the hospital (his family was on the board of trustees). Those who were "it" knew they had been targeted when, after a conference, they found his doodles: scraps of paper on the floor or on his desk with their name carved (really dug) into the scraps, as if they themselves were being mutilated.

A father hired his son to work for him and then acted out a sadomasochistic, oedipally tinged father-son rivalry because he wanted to be top dog, regardless of how this affected the business. He deliberately weakened the son by assigning him to do the things the son hated to do. Once he even put him in "Siberia," an out-of-the-way warehouse where he sent him to supervise all the intractable workers, who were there because they had done something to get banished. Basically, this was the father's way to get revenge on the son for being younger and stronger. The patient's brother went along as a way to gain advantage over and to get revenge on the patient for being the rival sibling. Soon enough, all three stopped seeing each other socially and then stopped speaking to each other professionally at work. No business got done, and soon afterward the business failed completely.

A woman, a sadistic antifeminist, liked being independent herself but held women who worked for her to a different standard, one destructive of their independence. It was the standard that when she was a child she held her own mother to. It was the housewife standard—the one that says that "Real women stay at home and cook and clean." She was a liberationist, but her interest in women's liberation was not a true one. Rather it was a reaction formation—a way to deal with her guilt about wanting women subservient. Ultimately, she developed an occupational inhibition, a typist's cramp, which represented her own "declaration of dependence"—that is, it was a way for her to put down the pen and take up the broom.

A racist doctor in a medical clinic made a black nurse feel defective for being black by disagreeing with everything she said, to the point that she went home angry and depressed every night. When the nurse pointed out that an interviewee was beginning to cry, he corrected it to, "No she wasn't beginning to cry, she was tearing." (Another colleague later wryly commented that this man seemed to be one of those few people gifted enough to be able to distinguish objective from goal, guarantee from warranty, and opera from operetta.)

The doctor once asked the nurse, whose training and experience were considerable, for her diagnosis of a patient. When she gave it to him he retorted, "What, you must be crazy"—to which the nurse naturally replied, "If you think I am crazy, why did you ask me for my diagnosis?" He replied, "Because I didn't know until then how bad you were at diagnosing and how paranoid you got when people who are just trying to start a discussion with you even hint that they disagree with what you have to say."

A sadistic ageist boss felt that workers over a certain age were necessarily incompetent and too weak and brittle to be "employed," both literally (that is, hired) and figuratively (that is, used—as in, what was to become one of his favorite phrases, "If used they would break").

He equated advancing age with progressive deterioration. He spoke of those workers who were still functioning over the age of 60 with hushed amazement. He said of one, "She is 61 years old but still manages to work." To him, those over 60 were like those under 6: unable to function independently. To stereotype those over 60, he had to make his points selectively, disregarding any evidence that did not fit with his preconceived notion. He particularly had to overlook that the relationship between age and physical deterioration was in reality a variable one, and that while some of his workers felt older than their stated age, most of his older workers had the reverse problem—they looked older than they used to look but they never felt better in their lives. As for their life's work, many of them did not start with a bang, which turned into a whimper, but started with a bud, which turned into a blossom.

His negative view of his older workers was so convincing that they began to see themselves in the stereotypical way he saw them. Some became openly demoralized. Others tried to disguise what they were because they became convinced they were flawed. They did grotesque things to themselves in a misguided attempt to be admired and loved. Of course, their attempt to get love failed because they were trying to please a person who needed to dislike them, and they were trying to please him precisely in that area where he needed to dislike them the most. Any real remedies were doomed to failure because his negativity was not based on reality but was transferential—that is, it was based on his own unresolved problems with growing older, so that no amount of improved performance on their part could even begin to change his mind. All this, of course, interfered with their ability to do their work and so had the effect of fulfilling his prophecy for him.

In my opinion, corporations need fewer troubled sadistic bosses and more untroubled creative workers whose careers are not being sacrificed to benefit the whims and careers of their superiors. Yet sadistic bosses flourish, however much they are inhumane and bad for business, because in today's business world, too often abusing others is what sells.

In Chapter 8, I suggested that an effective way to deal with sadists is to become less masochistic. A danger for masochistic workers is that they seek out and/or appease those who hurt them. I have had patients who literally seek out the painful putdowns, or buy into them to justify their continued failure, which they unconsciously desire. For example, they say, "Yes, they're right. I am no good at this, and the life of the composer isn't a real life. I'll go into real estate instead and make plenty of money, and my parents, spouse, and friends will praise me for having a real job and will admire me for having a new, expensive house."

Therapists can help masochistic patients by identifying people the patients know who, for their own reasons, abuse them and sabotage their efforts. Unfortunately, instead many therapists try to convince their patients that they are imagining the abuse. The patient ends up thinking that he or she is too sensitive and even a bit paranoid. Rather than acknowledging the serious abuse and helping their patients deal with it, such therapists are contributing to the already desperate situation by denying its reality.

*Obsessive-compulsive personality disorder.*    Obsessive-compulsives are as competitive as hysterics and, like them, dislike successful people who might show them up. They are also repressed hypermoral people who are afraid to lose self-control, because that means losing control of their impulses. They are threatened by the spontaneity that is so often an integral part of creativity, because to them spontaneity looks suspiciously like dyscontrol.

Obsessive-compulsives fight not with the sword but with the pen— that is, intellectually. They use semantic weapons, so that they win by giving everyone an argument. (Ultimately, they lose because they make not points but totally gratuitous distinctions.) One boss's workers felt as if they were being marked down for their bad spelling, while what they had to say was completely disregarded because they "spelled it wrong."

A respiratory therapist with over a decade of experience in the testing laboratory advised his supervising physician that caffeine was good for children who had the same abnormal findings as a child he had just tested. His boss, overhearing this, flew into a rage, accused him of practicing medicine without a license, and warned him, "Next time say not that 'caffeine was good for' but 'could reasonably be considered to be an approach to' or 'is ordinarily helpful in' such cases." The boss had a small point—the new wording did, theoretically at least, protect all concerned from being accused of practicing medicine without a license. But it was an unnecessary criticism because the comment, in context, was merely an informal communication between two old colleagues. So the boss's criticism was less a constructive criticism than a destructive putdown, a way to establish control and dominance and an opportunity to express an anger already in place toward the technician.

As one writer, criticized by his critics for not developing his material, put it, "They think that one bad apple spoils the whole bunch. To hear them talk, you would think that Orville and Wilbur Wright's first flight was all no good because it was too short, had no development, and ended too abruptly."

Such bosses are sometimes identified with a suppressive, critical mother. They demand that people under them be unspontaneous children, neither seen nor heard, and only permit them to take baby steps, never giant steps, on their own (even those are not permitted unless they first ask, "May I?"). By condemning others as their own mother condemned them, they are unconsciously self-condemning, in effect proclaiming, "I don't like it when I do the same thing." A boss at odds with his own inability to be spontaneous condemned a worker for merely mentioning he liked a certain book on business that was popular at the time; he called the worker "opinionated." A literary critic with similar problems condemned all romanticism as gushy, by which he meant too expressive, (not repressive enough). Such bosses reveal their true colors when they turn around and do the same thing that they just condemned others for having done. One persnickety critic complained about the big words an author used; then, two paragraphs down, he condemned him for using excessively short phrases, which he dubbed "atomistic."

### Sick Society and Sick Corporations

Society and its institutions weaken people, especially those in the public eye. For example, politicians cannot win. Society parentalizes them and then makes the same impossible demands on them that children make on their parents. Just as children want their mothers to be both mothers and virgins, society wants its politicians to be both honest and dishonest, pragmatist and dreamer, sensitive to nuance and insensitive to abuse. Growth in office is invariably seen as proof of past defect, while the inability to grow in office is invariably viewed as evidence of professional stagnation. Politicians are damned for one mistake, like parents are damned for one miscalculation. A politician becomes no good because of one slip of the tongue, like a father becomes no good because he once recommended a certain profession to his son, or a mother becomes no good because she once encouraged her daughter to get married.

Sick corporations reflect the sick society in which they exist. A society that pays its plumbers more than it pays its composers spawns corporations that reward the plodder more than the poet. A society that discourages original, creative expression because it views it as defiant or perverse spawns corporations in which mediocrity sells. A society topheavy with critics who make certain that no good work goes unpunished spawns corporations in which it is the angels that mainly fear to tread. A society of fathers personally competitive with their sons spawns a company whose administration expects its male workers to hold back to avoid competing with their boss, while a society of mothers who discourage their daughters professionally spawns a corporation in which women are expected to demur in favor of men and to become passive drones to avoid being disloyal to their "assigned" role as housewife and mother.

On the one hand, the head of the department of psychiatry liked to be around creative workers. But on the other hand, while saying that he admired those talented individuals he was fortunate enough to know, he put them down every chance he got, especially when they disagreed with his theories (though they were controversial). As one of his staff said, he seems to feel that "the only good worker is the dead one, because dead men don't make brain waves."

In his hospital, to avoid being challenged by outspoken people who disagreed with him, he appointed second-in-command administrators not on the basis of their talent, ability, or training but on the basis of their inarticulateness. He hired workers who did not complain—who were, as he put it, "tongue-tied sycophants." Naturally, these were not the best individuals to attract new people to his service, which gradually sunk to the point that it was put on probation.

A speech therapist was fired from a veterans' clinic because of his outside interests in music. The rationale was that these outside interests diluted what should have been an exclusive interest in veterans' affairs. Administration could have reached just the opposite conclusion—that the veterans, many of whom were unemployed because their interests were too narrow, could have been (and actually were) inspired by someone whose talent was so broad based. But administrators did not want to admit this, because they themselves had so few outside interests and the therapist was showing them up. (Underneath it all was stern puritanism, a hypermoralism that led the top administrators to believe literally and figuratively that dancing and playing an instrument were a sin, because music was the work of the devil.)

Sick corporations minimize the importance of supporting their workers emotionally as well as financially. They award them an occasional worker-of-the-month prize, but that is no substitute for the ongoing daily approval and positive feedback they need. Most of the time, workers only hear about how they are doing when they are doing something wrong.

Sick corporations do not stop at doing little or nothing to make workers feel wanted or loved but take the next step and deliberately promote hostility toward workers as a way to beat them down, knowing that workers who feel too good about themselves are hard to tame. Such corporations specifically discourage workers' creativity. Although they are expected to keep on working and producing because that is their duty and what they were hired to do, workers are human, and they sense that the corporation finds their creativity a potentially destructive force and that they are being stifled, whereupon they respond in a predictably human way. Fearful, they lag behind to avoid a climb to the top and, with it, the dangers associated with exposure (like being noticed and criticized all the more). Or they bumble to be ineffective, to avoid becoming competitive, and to avoid getting into a confrontation with those who cannot abide talent. Most of the time, instead of just taking what is handed to them, they have their own little ways of getting back. They somatize to show the company how it is making them sick as well as to use absenteeism as their best revenge. Or they passive-aggressively drag their feet when it comes to doing their jobs. They do some work, but only the minimum—what is asked of them, no less, no more—and they do it routinely and diffidently to avoid others accusing them of trying to show them up.

Such workers naturally prefer to assure their own integrity, even if it is at the expense of the corporation's integrity. They are survivors who, to stay out of trouble, work within the system. They value most their ability to work routinely and uncreatively, keeping their profile low and not making waves, challenging the status quo, or showing others up—particularly those over them who are in (and want to remain in) their prolonged, ongoing psychic siesta.

At a government clinic where I worked, individual creativity was stifled in a number of ways. One way was to pit the patient against the doctor. Patients were allowed to read their records so that the doctors had to refrain from putting anything potentially insulting and hurtful in the record, while still being medically correct and honest. To do both was virtually impossible, especially when the patient was ill without knowing the extent of his or her illness.

Another way was to reward those who did the work expeditiously, regardless of whether or not they maintained quality. For example, one doctor working there refused to give antidepressants to patients treated for heart disease without a consultation with a cardiologist. A colleague was happy to look up the medication in the *Physician's Desk Reference* and decide, based on what he read, what was safe and what was not. The first doctor was a professional; the second was, in effect, an amateur. Management naturally preferred the second doctor because he responded immediately, did not waste precious time and money on second opinions, and was not a disruptive force to all concerned—particularly those who wanted to finish their work on time and go home at exactly 4:30 P.M.

The careful doctor got depressed because he was so unpopular. He began to think he was unpopular because he was wrong, even though he was right and even though he knew that the real reason for his unpopularity was that in being right he stepped on toes, got in the way, made more work for all concerned, and was expensive to maintain (like most careful, honest employees are). Instead of blaming others, he was now blaming himself, reasoning (being a depressive type), "If they don't love me, it must be because I am unlovable." Soon he became willing to do almost anything to be accepted by his fellow workers, be loved by the administration, and keep his job. His deterioration into a real bureaucrat had begun.

After a conference another doctor, an original thinker, was called on the carpet for what others euphemistically called "defying authority" but what he called making a proper diagnosis. At the conference, all the higher-up professors diagnosed one man's skin disease, consisting of mysterious black spots, as a rare and fatal illness. The original-thinking student saw it otherwise. He got hold of a can of ether, approached the patient with it and a sponge, and made the "diagnosis" by swiping away at the lesions. His diagnosis was the right one: "dirt."

Really sick corporations gang up on targeted workers, usually without knowing all the facts. They join in the general sadistic fun, with no concern for an individual's reputation or physical or emotional health. Often the process is started by one convincing troublemaker with a personal vendetta, and then it spreads as co-workers (most of whom can have appallingly little loyalty to even their best friends) join in the general melee and, instead of helping the person in trouble, do what gets them accepted by the group. Women and minority groups, like blacks and gays, are often the targets of this sort of group vendetta. Antiwoman, antiblack, or antigay vendettas typically erupt around something minor that becomes major because it is symbolic of the more significant underlying issue.

One gay internist was virtually driven out of his job by a gatekeeper nurse (who spoke for her administration) because he was gay. She never mentioned the real reason she fought him, instead saying that she did so because he would not indiscriminately withdraw patients who had been on maintenance diazepam from the drug, as she demanded he do. She reasoned that taking diazepam, for any reason, is immoral. He reasoned that the negative consequences of withdrawing long-term users might far outweigh the positive effects of the drug for those who needed it, because they had a long-term problem not otherwise treatable. The vendetta she started against him was both vicious and way out of proportion to what she presumed he was doing wrong. It was vicious and out of proportion because it was about something else—the morality of using and abusing drugs, which in turn symbolized the amorality presumed to be a factor in the behavior of all individuals who were gay.

In sum, sick corporations (like sick bureaucracies) want their workers depressed and inhibited. They prefer noncreative to creative workers. They encourage workers to work beneath their capacity, and if they do not yield, they encourage them to leave. In this way they are a microcosm of a society that defeats talented people, such as those likely to make changes that threaten. In the structure of such organizations (which only reflect the society that spawns them) lies the answer to a question many are asking today: "Why are there no more Beethovens?"

## TREATMENT

All workers have good days, when they feel fulfilled, and bad days, when they feel stressed. A possible goal is to change the world to eliminate all the bad days and all the stress, but usually this is not possible and workers must settle for something less. They can minimize severe stress by building a protective wall around themselves using supportive colleagues and friends as the bricks; by fighting those who are stressing them; or, when all else fails, by flight, moving on after deciding, "There are simply some things I cannot do, and some people I cannot do them with." When stress cannot be minimized, it can be handled in a healthier way—by adjusting one's reaction to stress. Emotional illness can be a way to adjust, but it should be the last choice, because it is the worst refuge. While it does deal with being abused by others, it ultimately consists of self-abuse as well.

The following are some methods therapists have used to help their patients keep what is basically a good job (although not necessarily one without any problems) without getting sick in the process. The methods range from flight—via meditation or the development of a mantra-like philosophy of self-comfort—to fight, which involves dealing with oppressors actively (verbally, not physically). No method is perfect or suitable for all, and there are risks associated with each. In particular, workers who face down their abusers can lose the relationship or the job. On the other hand, those who do not may keep their jobs and their reputations but lose their self-esteem. Two precautions must be taken before a worker chooses a way to handle stress. First, workers must be sure they are being significantly stressed and are not merely overreacting. Second, workers should never try to change what cannot be changed.

## Consider the Source

While workers have no certain way of controlling others' behavior or others' responses to them, there are certainly ways to modify their own responses to others. Considering the source (in the vernacular, recognizing where an abuser "is coming from") is the single most helpful way to do this.

Those who consider and understand the source will be less likely to accept their abuse wholesale, take it personally, and make it their own, internalizing "malignant others" and taking over their attitudes, with all the self-distortions that naturally follow. They will be less likely to see the negative things that are happening to them from the narrow perspective of "My abusers know what they are talking about. Since they are important and knowledgeable people, if they abuse me, it is because I deserve to be abused. Since they are professors they know what they profess, and they know what they profess since they are professors." They will be less likely to blame themselves and, since they understand the motives and problems of their abusers, will blame them instead. As a result, they will be able to turn the tables on and dismiss those who are dismissing them.

One technique useful for understanding where abusers are coming from involves noting their associations—the first words out of their mouths—after workers say something nice about themselves. The first response would ordinarily be congratulatory; so a worker's suspicion should be aroused when the first words are instead put-downs (a common response when self-congratulations have made others jealous).

Often critics confuse "what I like" with "what is inherently good," and they decide what they like transferentially.

One writer confided to a friend that she had a great idea for a satirical cookbook: *The Prisoners' Last Meals Cookbook*. The friend could not evaluate that idea at all. He felt it was funny, but he thought it was sadistic and a bad idea because it was cruel to use another's imminent death for one's personal benefit and disgusting to contemplate eating the same thing people ate just before they were executed. He may have been right, but his response was based not on a realistic assessment of the book's literary or commercial value but on his own unresolved childhood feelings about cooking, satire, prisoners, crime, and the death penalty. The writer, however, reacted by thinking that it was her work and its commercial potential that were being assessed. She overlooked how she had merely given a projective test, like a word-association test, and was now listening not to the literary criticism or to the business advice she thought she was getting but to "answers" to her "psychological test questions."

Often what critics say refers more to them than to the object of their scrutiny, and what they like refers to something from their childhood. A radio announcer liked sports because that allowed him to think himself a regular guy, not the one the kids used to call a sissy. An opera critic's positive feelings even about divas who could not sing reflected a personal need to forgive her mother for her indiscretions. A critic's negative feelings about heavy metal rock groups were the product of his dislike for a crude, abrasive father and his preference for identifying with his refined mother instead. Both were a way to deny his own forbidden hostile and sexual feelings.

A psychologist was upset because his supervisor refused to talk to him, which he believed was his comeuppance for a speech he gave in public that went poorly—a speech the supervisor had asked him to do and whose failure reflected on him, the supervisor. But in reality this supervisor was not criticizing the psychologist. The supervisor had just been accepted to an analytic institute and his idea of a good analyst was someone who only spoke when he or she had "something significant to say." So the supervisor was not reacting to the psychologist's speech. He was following an inner voice, the one that proclaimed his identity as "an analyst, one who never speaks, even when spoken to."

Of course, some critics are simply taking the easy way out:

A lazy teacher taught not what needed to be learned but what could be taught. A teacher of college English, he discovered that teaching creative writing was a much more difficult science, or art, than correcting spelling, so he corrected his students' misspellings and marked them down accordingly until there was not enough grade left for them to pass on the basis of what they wrote. According to his standards, not even Agatha Christie, by reputation a notoriously poor speller, would have passed her English course.

In like manner, in hospitals, utilization review committees evaluate the charts, but not the quality of the medical care that goes into making those charts. A reviewer sees if the therapy plan follows from the therapy problem, but not if the identified problem in the chart follows from the actual problem in the patient. As long as the chart is internally consistent, it passes, even though the medical care, though consistent, is consistently bad.

## Flight

Flight may involve an adjustment of one's sensitivity level. When it is not enough to know that critical authority can have feet of clay and that some critics can be hacks, it helps to make criticism less shattering by not letting it get to us.

In distancing (which is a partial flight), workers, with the exception of those who find negative feelings stimulating, keep a low profile to avoid being hurt. They do their jobs and do not look for support and congratulations at every turn. They learn that even accepting a compliment can be dangerous because, to be consistent, one has to accept criticism as well. They learn to pick their friends among co-workers carefully, and they avoid destructive relationships entirely when they cannot be mended or handled in a healthy way. They learn that seeking out and continuing to relate to sadists is both masochistic and futile. Being nice to them only encourages them further; for they think you don't mind. Being apologetic to them is misinterpreted as welcoming them and asking for more. Trying to change their minds acknowledges their presence and impact. If there is to be any involvement, being faintly nasty, when practical and safe, is the much better course. It serves notice to them that you don't appreciate what they are doing and are not going to get involved—all without requiring much energy, effort, or involvement (that is, without getting caught up in the sadomasochistic net).

## Fight

Fighting back can be done in the following ways:

- With a *tu quoque* defense, in which victims stop critics in their tracks by saying, "You are one, too" while hoping critics will overlook the presumption if they are our betters, and the manipulations if they are logisticians.
- With a passive-aggressive defense, in which the victim turns the other cheek (which, by countering hatred with love, makes the other person feel guilty) or asks a simple question, hiding the counterattack behind the innocent-appearing question.
- With false humility, in which the victim appeals for forbearance by getting there first with self-criticism.
- With facts, in which the victim counters criticism with perspective or reality. One suggested that he was not the weed his critic thought he was but a flower in the wrong garden, and for good measure he emphasized previously not-thought-of qualities of weeds. Another used the reality check of the historical perspective. For example, he

reminded his literary critics how, according to legend, André Gide mistakenly called Marcel Proust a snob and an amateur, and he re-assured himself that if Gide could recover professionally from such a significant lapse, he could recover from similar lapses too.

- With self-improvement. Self-improvement is one of the best re-sponses of them all. One works well as the best revenge and persists instead of giving up, which can be so final and irreversible.

PART THREE

## Treatment

# 12

## An Overview
## of Treatment

Even though occupational disorder is both a significant personal and social problem, devastating not only to the individual who has it but also to all others who could have benefited from the fine work never done, there is little written specifically about how to treat it. Often, the most writers on the subject say is something like, "Psychotherapy must be modified to suit the needs of individuals and their difficult situations," but they do not say how. Jeffrey Kahn (1993) states that "a psychiatrist tries to absorb what the patient is feeling as well as saying, and then chooses the most promising psychotherapeutic approach" (p. 300), but he does not say which. It seems that what Elliott P. Schuman said in 1981 about writing block still holds true and is applicable for the occupational disorders in general: "Techniques for dealing explicitly with . . . blocks are not . . . presented in the literature" (p. 115).

This is especially unfortunate because the occupational disorders can often be cured if treated correctly, but not if treated incorrectly. While bad treatment sometimes helps due to the placebo effect from the positive relationship the worker develops with the counselor or therapist (which contrasts with the negative relationship the worker has with everyone else), for the most part, bad treatment either fails and becomes just another unextended helping hand or actually does damage, bruising and battering workers once again and often in the same way and for the same reasons as the bruising and battering that created the disorder.

In the following sections I provide a partial roadmap for treating the occupational disorders. In particular, I emphasize the need to base treatment on adequate diagnosis and the advantages of using an eclectic approach.

## THE NEED TO MAKE
## AN ADEQUATE DIAGNOSIS

Some therapists diagnose the same disorder in all of their patients. Everywhere they look they see burnout or chronic fatigue. Therapists who do this overemphasize the similarities between disorders while overlooking the differences. For example, while all workers with occupational disorder are to some extent tired and fed up with their jobs, only some are burned out or suffer from chronic fatigue syndrome. Others are depressed or suffer from a paranoid personality disorder and are not fed up with their job but are overwhelmed by the persecutory behaviors they imagine exist at their workplace.

Therapists who fail to make the distinctions necessary for proper diagnosis

- Offer only superficial treatment based strictly on common sense instead of psychotherapy which begins where common sense leaves off.
- Offer only symptomatic treatment, without handling the basic problem using the time-honored methods that have evolved for treating such *DSM-IV* disorders as phobia or depression.
- Treat endogenous as if it is exogenous disorder (for example, running groups and seminars in which everyone complains about the job and no one admits to any personal contribution to their on-the-job problems). In their anxiety to help the worker deal with the problem company, such therapists overlook the company's need to deal with the problem worker and foster a state of paranoia and denial in their patients. This creates real problems, for the therapists encourage the workers to complain, and their complaints leak out and get back to the boss, who feels criticized, and to the company executives, who feel that the company has been betrayed.
- Treat exogenous as if it is endogenous disorder, focusing too much on development, dynamics, and internal and interpersonal conflict, and too little on real stress and trauma.

As I emphasize throughout, most occupational disorders are caused by an interlocking sequence of internal and external events, and so in turn disorder rarely appear unless the seeds of stress fall on the fertile ground of anxiety and conflict. By analogy, an occupational disorder is like a fall that results when an individual climbs up on a neighbor's porch and slips on an icy step. The neighbor may have been negligent in not clearing the ice, but the climber may also have been negligent in not grasping the handrail. Most workplace disorders are caused both by icy steps and by the individual's failure to use the handrail.

For example, in what is a typical scenario for depressive occupational disorder, a worker brought his personal problems to an imperfect job. First, he could not tolerate even constructive criticism, because he saw all constructive criticism as destructive and because he needed unconditional love. Second, he worked for a mean boss who believed that giving underlings positive feedback made them soft and lazy and thought that the best way to get a good day's work out of them was to show them who was in charge and, if they seemed not to see the light, to threaten them with losing their jobs.

Even the downsized patient can benefit, if only for the next job, from a study of his or her individual problems (especially when the downsizing has been long in the making). Not everyone is downsized in any given series of layoffs, and often an individual's personal problems have contributed in some way to his or her being laid off.

## THE NEED TO USE AN
## ECLECTIC TREATMENT APPROACH

The eclectic approach is a pragmatic one, but it is not a cookbook approach that offers therapists a specific roadmap for handling a specific disorder. Instead, it starts from the premise that there are many aspects to a given occupational disorder, and many equally valid therapeutic ways to handle each of them (although fortunately, not every aspect of a single occupational disorder has to be handled therapeutically). An occupational disorder can be completely disabled by disabling any one of its parts, just as a chain can be broken by cutting any of its links.

One therapist explained this by posing the problem of how to handle a vine growing on a porch, about to reach up and strangle a plant hanging above it (a good metaphor for occupational disorders). He suggested that there are three ways to deal with the problem. One can root out the vine from the bottom, saving the plant but killing the vine; prune the vine on the top and rescue the plant, though temporarily, while saving the vine; or save both, solving the problem permanently and less radically by simply moving the plant to another spot on the porch. Rooting out the vine is the rough equivalent of deep psychoanalysis; pruning it on top is roughly analogous to the more superficial cognitive therapeutic approaches, which involve altering logic without understanding the deep reasons for the illogic; and moving the plant across the porch is roughly analogous to supportive Zen therapy, in which the patient learns to coexist with a problem, observing it dispassionately, and in effect safely, from "across the room." All are valid solutions to the same problem. Which is chosen will depend as much on individual preference, time frame, and the amount of money available for treatment as on any other factor. As with the vine and the plant, a patient under job-related stress may choose to deal with the stress by psychoanalyzing its deep effects on the psyche, which is the rough equivalent of pulling up the vine. Or the patient may attempt to change his or her environment, thus trimming the vine (for example, having an open discussion or a conference with the troublesome people in his or her life). Or the patient can simply distance himself or herself from the problem by avoiding a troublemaker or asking for a transfer (moving the plant away from the vine).

Some therapists are called eclectic because they use different approaches on a case-by-case basis. They analyze some but offer support to others, tailoring their approach to the needs of the individual. Others are said to be eclectic because they treat most or all patients with a combination of well-known techniques, effecting a cure by relying on a mixture of traditional psychoanalytic, psychodynamic, interpersonal, cognitive-behavioral, and existential approaches used within a supportive framework. In this way the therapist who interprets a conflict simultaneously reassures the patient that he or she is not being criticized, or the therapist who interprets a maladaptive interpersonal reaction simultaneously reassures the patient that because any problem relationship takes two, he or she is not being singled out as a troublemaker. This group uses more than one method in the belief that "many roads lead to Rome" and "the more the merrier." For them there is strength in numbers, and they believe strength is needed if one is to overcome the strong adversary that occupational disorders represent. They feel that just as a bullfighter has to use multiple thrusts to down a bull, a therapist has to use multiple thrusts simultaneously or sequentially to overcome an occupational disorder. A classic combination approach of this sort is treating a phobia both with psychoanalysis and behaviorally—asking the phobic simultaneously to understand and face his or her fears. These eclectics emphasize the importance of avoiding an exclusive focus on insight and not overlooking the benefits to be obtained from other therapeutic modalities, which they find especially valuable in the beginning of treatment (when the disorder is in the acute stage and the patient needs to feel better immediately) and use before sitting back and understanding how things got to be the way they are. They also note the intrinsic problems with the insight method and cite the thin line between imparting insight and criticizing. They cite an expert like Peter Giovacchini, who says that some psychoanalysts use insight to reject their patients. "Disapproving of their behavior, [and of] the manifestations of [their] symptoms" (p. 39) they criticize in the guise of analyzing, often making the disorder considerably worse because, in this respect at least, they remind their patients of a rejecting mother and/or bloodying father. They forget that patients need to regain their strength and self-confidence after having been criticized enough.

The next chapters examine and explore some specific ways to treat occupational disorders. Taken together, they constitute the individual components of my treatment approach as a whole.

# 13

## Psychoanalytic/ Psychodynamic Approach

The psychoanalytic/psychodynamic approach recognizes that the occupational disorders have external as well as internal causes, but it emphasizes the latter over the former and asks patients to view their occupational disorder not merely as a passive response to stress but also as an active arrangement they make with themselves.

> A veteran needed to hold herself back, so she sabotaged her own efforts and then resisted getting help and having what help she got be effective. She developed a posttraumatic stress disorder as a way to get relief from anxiety; love and affection; and the considerable advantages associated with being ill. As for the latter, she said of her posttraumatic stress disorder, "I actually like having it. With it I don't have to work, I get veterans and social security disability benefits, and, best of all, I get a handicapped parking sticker and the great parking spaces that go with it."

The psychoanalytic approach emphasizes the central role played by instinctual conflict. For example, a patient's laziness might be the result of a fear of punishment for activity because activity is believed to be aggressivity. A central role is also assigned to the past. Workers fall ill when something from their early life carries over into their adult professional endeavors, contaminating their work with old, no longer relevant, messages. Old interpersonal experiences with parents and siblings play a crucial role, so that on-the-job problems result because patients (figuratively speaking) cannot get their parents out of their house. As a result, they work not primarily for themselves but for their mothers, or against their fathers, or to compete with a brother or sister. They view everything a boss says or does from the narrow perspective of maternal acceptance or rejection. They view every relationship with a co-worker as an extension of an old sibling rivalry. They become afraid of success, develop survivor guilt, and masochistically abdicate in favor of all rivals because of an old fixation on the guilt engendered by oedipal rivalry. They sulk in a corner, figuratively head-banging, because that is how they handled maternal rejection as children. They deal with authority passive-aggressively, because that is the only way their parents permitted them to express anger. If they were teased for being sissies or tomboys when they were children, they react now as if their masculinity or femininity is always being tested.

> A man denies his feminine side by not being compliant, which he believes is womanly. He refuses to read any memos written by women, and he even thinks it feminine to listen to what a male boss says because if he is not the one speaking, he is no longer "the man on top" but "the woman on the bottom." His counterpart, a woman, resists pursuing her work because for her that means being masculine.

> A worker saw emotional abuse in any but the most positive interactions because she was abused as a child in ways ranging from being emotionally unsupported to physically beaten. At work she avoided further abuse by hiding out, arranging (figuratively speaking) to be neither seen nor heard. In effect, she became a hack just to be safe from possible criticism and humiliation—even though this made it a virtual certainty that she would do a bad job and provoke the very criticism and humiliation she was trying to avoid in the first place.

The psychoanalytic approach favors insight-oriented methods. The analyst asks, "Why are you doing this?" and expects that the answer will help the patient get over the problem at hand. Otto Fenichel and Albert Rothenberg describe this approach to treating the occupational disorders as follows. Fenichel (1945) suggests using insight to lift repressions so that the patient is "relieved of the necessity of spending a great deal of energy on repressions and symptom formation" until "capacities that were inhibited have become accessible anew" (p. 184). Rothenberg (1990), following Fenichel, suggests that "therapists never function as work enforcers" (p. 176), but rather use "psychotherapy . . . [to help] complete a process that the creative person has already begun [because the] creative process involves attainment of partial insights . . . [and] fuller insight . . . rekindles creativity," (p. 176) "fostering personal growth . . . free of the past" (p. 179). Zachary Leader (1991) also recommends "facing and overcoming inhibiting fears [as] the way to greatness" (p. 137).

The psychoanalytic approach makes liberal use of Freudian/Jungian/existential dream analysis in the evaluation and treatment of occupational disorders. Psychoanalysts feel that dream analysis helps in revealing the childhood roots and so the unconscious basis of an occupational disorder by revealing hidden fears, such as fears of failure, and hidden wishes, such as a need for failure due to a fear of success. The fears and wishes revealed in dreams provide keys that unlock the door to understanding the current disorder. For example, the fear of success often revealed in dreams explains (as much as does the Peter Principle) why some workers get worse emotionally as their position improves realistically (say, after a promotion). (This chapter studies a variety of dreams and their meanings and provides therapists and readers advice about using dreams as they explore their patients', or their own, occupational disorder.)

> Is there any question that the following dream, which occurred to an unsuccessful writer, is meaningful and reveals something significant about the writer's lack of success—in this case an inability to succeed because of what success meant?
>
> The day of the dream, the writer watched a mystery program in which the detective Hercule Poirot agreed to shave his mustache off if he failed to solve a murder before his rival did. That night the patient dreamed he had solved the mystery, but he had to shave his own mustache off anyway, and possibly just for that reason. In the dream the results after shaving looked to him like the shaved vagina of a woman about to be delivered of a child.

Three of the topics central to psychoanalytic thinking—the role of individual contribution/responsibility, the role of the past, and the role of dreams (and the use of dream analysis)—are discussed next individually and in greater detail.

## THE ROLE OF INDIVIDUAL
## CONTRIBUTION/RESPONSIBILITY

An individual with an occupational disorder must acknowledge his or her contribution to the disorder, and not cite eternal causation exclusively. Some workers cramp their hands primarily to self-defeat, to work at cross-purposes to themselves by actively arranging not to get what they really want and deserve. Others are dealing with people criticizing, humiliating, overwhelming, or abandoning them, yet they contribute to their inhibitions by letting others get to them and get away with it. A patient with writer's block may feel that having the disorder is like having a paralyzed foot, with motivation and inspiration interfered with as if there were a kind of "nerve damage." But a psychoanalyst would point to a crucial difference and say that motivation and inspiration are being actively suppressed, so that a better model than the paralyzed foot would be a disorder called Saturday night paralysis, in which the patient gets intoxicated, comes home, carelessly drapes an arm over a chair, falls asleep in that position, and then awakens with a brachial plexus paralysis due to a disorder that is at least partly self-inflicted. The analyst would deny that the writer (or other creative worker) who runs out of inspiration is "nerve damaged." Rather the analyst sees the mind, like the heart, as something that works all the time, and believes that it is as impossible for nothing to come to mind in a living writer as it is for a heart not to beat in a living person. So if the writer cannot think of anything to write, it is because the writer needs to have nothing to say. Similarly, the analyst would say that because hands, like minds, are meant to function continuously, it is unlikely that repetitive movements can cause harm by themselves; So when RSI occurs there must be another operative factor. This factor may be an external one, due to poor design of the computer keyboard. But more likely the problem lies not with the computer keyboard but with the computer operator, who is awkward, perhaps because of a conflict about performing, and puts the hand in an uncomfortable position, which is what causes it to sustain the injury.

The less dogmatic analysts recognize that, in any given case, both internal and external factors are operative and that it is difficult to pinpoint individual contribution and distinguish it from external provocation.

> A dental hygienist complains of how her depression keeps her from cleaning teeth. She blames her depression on her anger at her boss. She is angry with him because she is supposed to start seeing patients at 9:00 A.M., but she is unable to start work until 9:15 A.M. because to increase his income her boss rents out her office to another dentist from 8:00 to 9:00 A.M., and not only does this other dentist not leave on time, but he also leaves a mess behind, and she has to clean up after him.
>
> However, by itself this is not a fatal problem, because her one-hour appointments only take 45 minutes, so she can theoretically at least get back on schedule as the day goes along. Her emotions are what make this a fatal problem, one that causes her to get depressed. Her emotions rule because she is already vulnerable—just before her depression started, her aged mother moved from an apartment she and the patient were sharing together in the city into a retirement community 60 miles away, in the country, and the patient feels lonely and is even considering leaving the city to go to live with her mother in her retirement home.

It is especially difficult to distinguish individual contribution from external provocation in angry patients. Sometimes others provoke the worker to get angry and do so in a way that would make anyone angry. At other times the provocation is minor and the reaction to it excessive. Most times it is a little of both. As described in Chapter 3, there are two kinds of anger: irrational (unprovoked) and rational (provoked). In irrational anger the patient is reacting in the absence of a stimulus, or overreacting to an actual but trivial stimulus or provocation. In contrast, in rational anger the patient is mainly reacting appropriately to a specific, actual stimulus. A supervisor gets angry with a worker for telling one of her patients that she does not like her job. Although his anger is partly excessive, because he envies her for being able to say something he cannot say, mostly it is justified. In such cases a depressive disorder results not because patients punish themselves appropriately for irrational anger, but because patients punish themselves excessively for anger that is mainly appropriate.

## THE ROLE OF THE PAST

Psychoanalytic theory views occupational disorder as primarily due to an inability to let bygones be bygones and live in the present. Patients blend the present with the past and misinterpret what is happening to them now based on what happened long ago. The job that has to be done becomes an early casualty of the emotions that have to be resolved. Early losses and parental prohibitions too often influence how a worker interprets and then reacts to present events. By implication, analytic theory goes beyond the catastrophic explanation of occupational disorder, with its emphasis on stress and trauma, to study how significant occupational disorder can arise, if not de novo, then from seemingly insignificant stress. In the psychoanalytic view, minor stress can be even more significant than major stress. Many workers can deal with the big, but not with the little, things. This is because the big things are so obvious that they stand for themselves, while the little things can be (and often are) made to stand for something else. Thus it is mostly the tremors and aftershocks of everyday life that become the destructive earthquakes of occupational disorder. Individuals who are struggling with a sensitivity to criticism because criticism means rejection will survive an entire division's being closed (although they are out of a job) better than a demotion meant for them alone (although they still have a job). In the former case there is no question of being singled out personally, with all that that usually means.

A doctor was once asked to see a patient who needed emergency medical evaluation. The patient was so sick that one glance was enough to indicate that emergency hospitalization was needed. The patient was so violent that one glance—from across the room—was all that was possible. So the doctor arranged hospitalization for the patient, delaying doing a full examination until later, after the patient was safely in the hospital. As a result, several of the patient's relatives complained to administration that the doctor did not spend enough time talking to the patient before admitting him. The doctor got upset and brooded about the matter for days. She should not have let this personal criticism (and all the letters they wrote about her to the administration) do more than ruin her day. But she got upset and brooded continuously because of her past relationship to an authoritarian father, who put her down without first, or ever, asking to hear her side of the story.

In a typical scenario, workers parentalize authority. They see the boss as a punitive father or rejecting mother, and withdraw at the first hint of being punished, criticized, or abandoned. They even use their occupational disorder as a way to hurt themselves now as their parents hurt them long ago (and often continue to hurt them in the present). In effect, they introject and identify with one or both malignant parents, so that they do the same negative things to themselves now that their parents did to them long ago.

In many men, for example, there is a history of having had a father who was unable to tolerate the competition from the son, and so put the son down for being bright, strong, and clever. There was a mother who was unable to tolerate the son's independence, and so put the son down for being a free spirit (really growing up) and humiliated him for being, and expressing himself as, an adult. In effect, for different reasons, both father and mother put the child down for "doing." Often such parental influence continues later in life as well. If the child, now an adult, is trying to go into business for himself or herself, the father, to defeat the son, calls up each night to ask, "When you are going to get a real job, one that pays a regular salary?"; and the mother, to infantilize the son, calls up to "remind you that I am ready if and when you fail, as you probably will, and I am keeping the light on for you, should you ever need to come running back to me." As a result, the man develops (1) an occupational disorder that is a way to avoid being too masculine, because it means being too effective, and being too effective in turn means threatening the father, hurting him, and being hurt in turn; and (2) an occupational disorder that is a way to avoid being too independent, because being too independent means abandoning, and in turn being abandoned by, the mother. The worker stays forever the son who plays second fiddle to avoid having to be the "concertmaster." The son avoids straying from a mother who threatens to reject him if he goes out on his own and leaves her. Instead he agrees to remain ever the infant if the mother in turn agrees to accept and love him. In general, we might say that occupational disorders in men are a way for men to protect themselves from hurting and being hurt by the father; and they are an abdication to the mother, to avoid rejecting and being rejected and abandoned by her. In each case they simultaneously represent both the taboo and the punishment for transgressing its limits.

A patient remembers being humiliated at age two when he threw dirt in a two-year-old paramour's carriage. Actually, throwing dirt was a healthy thing for him to do. It was a protest against the girl's mother's meticulousness, an excessive carefulness that was really due to a phobia of dirt, which caused her to keep her baby away from him (her child-lover) and in a "plastic bubble." Neither she nor his own mother either forgave him or let him forget it. In fact, forty years later he went to a party given by the person in the carriage and was introduced as the "man who threw dirt in my stroller."

In adolescence the patient became a talented musical improviser who anticipated such avant-garde techniques as John Cage's randomness and Henry Cowell's tone clusters. But although he improvised he never wrote anything down because of both parents' negative response to his creative efforts. While the father supported him (by helping him record his improvisations on a wire recorder; so, he later inferred, the father must have been less threatened by his musical interests and talents than the mother), he also cut him down, by dwelling on how for men music makes a better hobby than a career. He cut him down as a way to convince him to go into a field that did not suit his talents so that he did not surpass the father in fame and fortune. But the mother was so threatened by the brilliance of his piano-playing experiments that she simply dismissed them as being too noisy. For example, after a display of percussive improvisational skill, she said, "I hope you got that out of your system"—as if he had created not a thing of beauty, but excrement, that is, as if he were "throwing dirt." As a result, even today he rarely puts his improvisations down on paper, or when he does write something down and send it out, he sends it out without a return address, hoping it will be lost in the mail, or to someone unreliable, hoping it will be lost upon arrival. This is why when he finally did complete one work in score, and he performed it in public, he denied the full impact of the audience's congratulations by leaving the stage just after the audience started applauding, and he did not come back, although the members of the audience continued applauding, pleading for him to return for a curtain call.

Having a discouraging mother had another effect—he needed to be loved precisely by those incapable of loving him. Because his mother crushed him creatively, it was for this very creativity that he most wanted to be loved. This was an unfulfillable desire, first because he predictably chose people incapable of loving him, and second because even people capable of loving often do not love creative people, for three reasons. First, creativity is imperfect, and its imperfections are seen as reflecting badly on the creator; second, creativity makes people envious; and third, creators are not meant to be loved but are meant to love—to give, not to receive. Rejected by those he wanted to accept him, he spared his feelings from being hurt by withholding and blocking creatively the next time. He made it a rule never to do anything to get applause, so that he would never have to hear criticism instead, and never to do anything to impress himself, so that he would never have to be disappointed in himself. This rule had its protective aspects, but it was excessively pessimistic, assured the very rejection he feared the most, and made his mother's critical attitude into a part of him, so that he treated himself in the same rejecting way that she treated him.

In his therapy his analyst suggested that his mother was distant and critical not because of something inherently wrong with him but because she was depressed (she had lost her father the very month the patient was born). As if to confirm this theory, he replied by remembering how after her father died his mother became increasingly dependent on her mother and even brought her to live with the family. Her ostensible reason was to care for her mother because the mother was becoming senile. But the real reason, as he now saw, was for her mother to care for her. He also remembered that he thought even as a young child that both mothers viewed him with mixed feelings—that is, they basically hated him because he came between them. He recognized that his wish to fade into the woodwork as an artist now reproduced his wish to fade into the woodwork when he was a child, to avoid making trouble with both women (which could only further disrupt what little there was of his family life, and provoke the two women to extrude him as they narrowed what gap there was between them, joined forces, and removed him from their interspace like one removes a foreign body from the eye).

In summary, the patient's inability to be a successful composer was due to a combination of a fear of punishment by the father for masculinity and rejection by the mother; a silent resentment of those who were and are punishing and rejecting; an avoidance of a repetition of the punishment and rejection at all costs; a desire to maintain the relationship with the father and mother at all costs; and self-punishment and rejection based on an identification with the rejecting parents. This dynamic quintet is not confined to this patient or to composers. Rather it represents the core pathological pentad that characterizes most or all of the occupational disorders in men, especially those in which inhibition is a significant factor.

In many women, it is the father who complains about the independence and the mother who tries to squelch the competition. The father complains that the daughter is growing up and leaving him, and an occupational disorder is a way to avoid leaving daddy. The mother has problems less with the daughter's leaving than with the daughter's getting better and showing the mother up. Occupational disorder develops when a little voice inside the grown woman says, "Who are you to be the first person in this family to be an advertising executive? Instead get married to an ordinary guy, have children, and take care of the house, and be passive, compliant, and submissive to your husband, just like your mother did and wants you to do, too."

Additionally, women have a problem that men do not have: Being too effective means identifying with the father instead of the mother. Fathers often encourage their daughters to identify with them and their success. Fathers are not afraid of the competition because "daughters are not the competition." But identifying with the father raises conflicts about femininity. Some women who complain of sticky floors and glass ceilings are in part expressing disguised wishes; such women want to be held back so that they do not appear to be "queer" (i.e., to be like their father).

> A middle manager at a major company bemoaned her inability to get promoted because of the sticky floor and glass ceiling that held women back. She felt, "Nothing good ever happens to me because I am a woman." But also she wanted to fail, to appease her competitive mother, who wanted her not to grow professionally but to be fruitful and multiply. Her disorder was a statement not only of her problem, but of her solution as well.
>
> Stage fright was a main symptom and a reason for her inability to get promoted. It reproduced in part an obeisance to a mother who warned her about "life on the wicked stage" and hoped to discourage her from succeeding in any endeavor. For succeeding would have meant showing the mother up in comparison to the daughter, showing her up for the bland, untalented person the mother in fact was. The patient, however, forced herself onto the stage because she wanted to break away from and surpass her mother. But her anxiety on the stage reminded her that simultaneously she wanted, and needed, to yield to, if only to be close to, her mother—and it reminded her that she would be back in her mother's arms if only she could see her way clear to being back in her grasp.
>
> Her first memory (which, like many first memories, often reveals the developmental roots of a disorder) was of her leaving her fine-tooth comb behind at the hotel resort where she had been staying with her mother. The fine-tooth comb was the hated comb that stroked despised girlish locks, the ones her mother refused to cut off however much she pleaded with her to do so. Leaving it behind represented a wish to rebel against the mother and be like the father, with short, straight hair, and, like him, go out into the world, as she put it, "fighting like a man." It also represented a self-punishment for this wish, because she had, after all, lost something of value and of her own.
>
> Later in her professional career, a main goal became identifying with her father and being masculine. She prided herself for being a "butch" administrator—one whose manliness was apparent in her firmness and decisiveness, a position that she believed was the very opposite of the one she thought the usual woman took. Most women were, according to her, "too frilly" in their approach to supervising others to make good supervisors themselves. But her guilt over her "masculine protest" nevertheless showed. It showed in the very iron hand with which she ruled,

which was self-defeating since no one wanted to work for her, as well as in her stage fright, which held her back so that she could stay the "supervised one" rather than be the supervisor—the frightened rabbit rather than the lion, the scared, retiring housewife she felt it was her destiny, and duty, to become.

The following are some histories of workers with occupational disorders, classified according to the typical messages they report having heard and taken seriously when the workers were children. The workers took these messages along with them into adult life to become the core of their later conflicts about work.

*Get a day job, or you can be any kind of doctor you want to be.* Often creative people's parents do not want them to be creative. Every time a son or daughter so much as mentions the word *creative*, the parents make a countermove; in effect, cornering the child like a rat in a trap and keeping the child cornered and in a 9 to 5 "pain and gain" profession like accounting. To stand their firm ground and convince the child, parents often use what passes for rational argument (for example, arguing that it is hard for individuals to be artistic *and* to make money). Or they create guilt (for example, by warning the child that "not doing what I want you to do is tantamount to killing your parents").

Later in life the worker equates being creatively successful with defying a parent, who demands creative failure, and being independent of mind with abandoning, or killing, one or both parents, who demand dependency of thought. Sometimes the best the child can do is to compromise between independence (seen as a rebellion) and dependence (seen as a submission). Many continue to work at what they do best, but in a way that assures their relative failure. A man who became a professor of mathematics (although his parents wanted him to be a doctor), to assure that he would be small potatoes as a mathematician, wrote academic tracts for an obscure journal that few people read. An author in an equivalent position wrote satire because he knew that that did not sell. Others become a "renaissance man," a cook that spoils too many broths, striding each of two or more camps as a dilettante, not as a colossus.

One man spent his whole adult life alternately submitting to and defying his father, shifting between submitting to the father by being the doctor the father wanted him to be and rebelling against the father who wanted him to be a doctor by being the "artist" he always wanted to be but was forbidden to be. He either did each alternately, or compromised and did both simultaneously. When he did so alternately, one year he would "retire" from medicine to paint; another year he would give up painting to take a locum tenens job in medicine. When he did so simultaneously, as the son himself put it, "I went into medicine both because it was an inherently satisfying profession and because it was a self-sacrifice, for I was not in the field I would have chosen left to my own devices, and because it's a field full of masochists focused on others first, and willing to cow tow to non-medical administrators who rule them financially and professionally. And I specifically went into psychiatry both because it satisfied me to an extent and because it was a self-sacrifice—for I was not in the field I would have chosen left to my own devices, and it is, as I see it, an inferior medical profession, because you aren't really a doctor unless you actually work with blood." Of course, while his compromises allowed a measure of anxiety-free success, they also increased his anxiety about failure. His constant identifying and counteridentifying both slowed him down and kept him stalled, achieving nothing on the high level he could have otherwise reached.

*Nothing you do is ever right.* Parents tell their sons and daughters that nothing they do is ever right because they want them passive, or even sick, and they want this because they do not want their children to compete with or leave them. They convey this message either directly, by their own expressed criticisms, or indirectly, by siding with their children's critics and/or by withholding support when it is needed the most. Their children never develop much self-confidence, and what self-confidence they do develop diminishes as they repeatedly react to everyone in their lives as if that person were a critical parent. They get beaten down over time because eventually a mere discouraging word deflates them; and rather than fight and experience the anxiety of not being supported all over again as well as the guilt about defying their parents, they elect to stay in their comfortable corner, like the proverbial dunce. One woman in this position compared herself vis à vis her boss to a dog she knew whose owner worked in a packing store; the dog was with her but was trained to stay under a large table provided for the purpose. The training was incomplete, for the dog regularly tried to get out and "see the world." But each time she did, the woman would kick it and push it back under the table, saying to her "Don't be a bad dog—be a good one and get back under the table."

Individuals can get physically ill and become disabled to please their parents and to avoid exposing themselves to their criticism. A physical occupational disorder, like tension headaches, back pain, or writer's cramp, is often the way to be passive and submissive by being sick.

*You are what you do.* Some parents give or withhold love based not on personal attributes but on professional achievements. Later in life the child feels that any professional failure leaves them orphaned.

A musical comedy writer's mother started him off professionally by putting up the money for his first show. He repaid the favor by writing *for* her, really serenading his mother, and writing *about* her, for the major roles were all older women whose eccentricities were either derived from his mother's oddities or were the ones he wanted his mother to have so that she would be the ideal mother he always dreamed of having. He continued to write effectively until the first hint of a negative review. Then he felt both abandoned by "the symbolic good mother" and ashamed to face his real mother—who in fact did complain, "Now that you are no longer the success you once were, I notice I don't have so many friends as I used to have." He continued to write, but with less and less success, spiraling downhill as one show after another folded (partly because as the beloved "mother earth" became less of a compassionate, welcoming place in real life, his real mother simultaneously became more and more disappointed in her real son). Then she died, and for a time he stopped writing completely. There was a final burst, a show about older women that gave him the vicarious feeling that he had a whole new pool of mothers. But the substitutive effect could not be sustained. When it faded again there was nothing left but to fall completely, angrily, and sadly silent. His professed reason? "They don't like my kind of musical any more." The real reason? "What's the use; my mother is no longer around to approve of what I do."

The following are some examples of the self-destructive ways in which workers typically handle these and others unintegrated messages from the past.

*By satirizing authority.* Some workers spend their entire lives not working but getting back at authority (i.e., at the parents), often in a passive-aggressive way. Their intent is to make authority look ridiculous. They undermine the other's position instead of taking one of their own. As students, they put the professor down in sophomoric ways. One student, to humiliate a professor who plagiarized a song he wrote for a musical comedy, whistled the original song every time the professor passed by. At conferences, students make fun of the speaker in whispered asides meant to amuse and impress the people next to them; but of course, all they accomplish is that they make it impossible for everyone concerned to concentrate and take notes. Many students who do this suffer from stage fright. Unable to speak in public because that would mean exposing themselves to being humiliated and rejected, they never raise their hands to be called on or give speeches of their own (i.e., they never do anything that might count and that might advance their career). Instead they disrupt what others are trying to do. But they only make their own lives a form of "whispering in the auditorium," so that no one hears what they have to say. All we see is their annoying behavior; their talent and ability remain invisible.

*By flight or fight.* For some men the prospect of any joint endeavor arouses the feminine, submissive side they fear in themselves and causes their homosexual anxiety to flare. Such men either withdraw to avoid seeming to be submissive, or have power struggles at work as a masculine protest. Women do the equivalent thing. They shy away from being effective as individuals because it creates homosexual anxiety about being rebellious (for them being rebellious means being masculine) or they become aggressive because they have become more assertive than they planned to be.

*By displaying excessively low, or excessively high, self-esteem.* An individual's low self-esteem may be expressed at work by becoming disabled or, when low self-esteem is covered by its opposite, by becoming hypomanic. Hypomanics often have office affairs or indulge in sexual promiscuity outside of the office to undo feeling defective and unwanted. The affairs and promiscuity are meant to be restitutive, to give the illusion of personal success in the midst of what is perceived to be professional failure. But mainly the affairs create more problems than they solve (and sometimes the very problems that they were meant to solve). They leave less time for work. They cause guilt about infidelity. Those who are suspected or caught get into trouble with their spouses. Sometimes the sex itself is dangerous; and drugs, with all their problems, are part of the picture more often than most people think.

*By excessive intellectualism.* Many people cannot do their work spontaneously because each time they try to open up, they feel dangerously exposed. To avoid feeling exposed, they become too complex to be understood easily. They avoid being human to avoid being vulnerable. For some psychiatrists, a resolute psychoanalytic orientation can be a way to avoid wearing one's heart on the sleeve (where it is felt to be unprotected and easily bruised). Some writers long for a lengthy, obscure sentence each time they utter an intelligible one. Some writers change each active voice to the passive voice, so that everything that happens in their writing, or in their office, or in their lives, happens without their seeming to make it happen.

When a man's fear of exposure is due to guilt about sexual feelings (which are deemed dirty), obscurity is a way to "clean up his act." When a woman's fear of exposure involves a fear of being a success (because success means defying a mother who is "a big nobody herself" and who tells the child to keep her place, while emphasizing how all goals are pretensions and that being a housewife is the only nonpretentious thing a proper girl can do), obscurity is a way to cooperate and abdicate. However, in each case there is an element of the opposite hidden in the obscure behavior. For men, being intellectual can be a way to be seductive; and for women, it can be a way to appear to be smarter than their mother.

*By excessive fear of failure.* An excessive fear of failure may lead to retreat. Or it may lead to a defensive workaholism (in which a desperate, panicky feeling of failure is handled by trying harder and harder to succeed) that, in turn, leads to burnout. Patients work compulsively. They work too many hours a day and strain unnecessarily each hour they work. They fear that any letup will affect their reputation now and/or in posterity. Their goal is not hard work or working hard; it is shining. They have to shine to avoid the feeling that they are a big nobody, unseen because they dwell in perpetual darkness.

## Summary of the Psychoanalytic Approach

Analytic theory sees unresolved problems of infancy and childhood contaminating the ego as the chief cause of occupational disorder. In particular, work is not work but a skirmish or war with the parents. In this view, occupational disorders appear partly because of exhaustion—too much is going on at one time—and also because continuing conflicts with one's parents affect one's work, as when a worker pulls back to avoid parental retaliation. Playing the sick role itself is a way to get love, attention, and forbearance, holding sadistic parents off in the belief that "even they wouldn't kick me when I am already down."

Analytic therapy is, in effect, a process of decontamination of the ego until, paraphrasing Freud, the ego is no longer id. In simple terms, the therapist's task is twofold: (1) Workers have to be rescued from their figurative orphanage—where they feel literally abandoned by their parents; and (2) their parents have to be removed from their figurative bedroom, where they insist on still commenting on, and giving or withholding approval for, everything the worker says and does.

## THE ROLE OF DREAMS/DREAM ANALYSIS

Psychoanalysts find that Freudian, Jungian, and existential dream analysis each provide a key to unlocking the doors that hide the secret meaning of dreams. Analysis reveals the secret meaning of the occupational disorders represented in the dream.

Here are some typical dreams and nightmares of patients with an occupational disorder:

Me, winning the idea contest, or being chosen worker of the month—applause, adulation. But fade to me, in a leg trap, in the woods, and there is no one around to help me. I die.

Me, running in place without being able to move, waiting for the bus to take me to work, a bus that doesn't come. Then, when it does come, it's the wrong bus, or keeps going and passes me by. And all my co-workers are on the bus and jeering at me, from the window.

Me, driving to work, but from the back seat of my car. I pull over to the side of the road because I feel I am, and others in the car told me that I am, about to get into an accident . . . and here I am on the side of the road, and I mustn't get back into traffic. Don't touch that accelerator. Don't even move, or else.

Me, leaving my presentation for the big conference on the seat of a movie theater, trying to get back into the theater, but I don't have the money for a ticket, and they are calling the police on me, and my presentation is inside where I can't get at it, and. . . .

## The Freudian Key

Freudians believe that dreams are stimulated by an event from daily life, such as a passing comment or other personal interaction, that is often itself unimportant. What is important is the deep psychological meaning of the event, especially the childhood memories about rejection, disapproval, success, or failure that the event revives. Often a teacher sensitive to rejection cannot teach or a typist sensitive to rejection cannot word process after learning that something he or she did is not accepted. Next he or she feels inadequate and concludes, "Why bother; I cannot do this right anyway, so I might as well not do it at all" and then has a dream like the following dream, stirred up by a present rejection.

A patient dreamt he was walking down the street that led to the corner of the cross-street where his New York apartment stood. The street was dark and empty, but a lighted store beckoned at the end. Yet he could never seem to get to the light.

The man had effectively exiled himself by leaving New York City to live and work in the suburbs. The suburbs looked inviting, but the people there disliked him because he stood out from the rest, in part because he was talented, in part because he was from the city, and in part because he was gay. His being gay also caused problems at work. Over the past few months his work had deteriorated because his peer group thought him incompetent because of his sexual orientation. As he wryly interpreted it, "They must think sex, personality, intelligence, and ability to do one's work are all related, so that if you are different sexually this means you are different personally, and that means that you are incompetent professionally."

His dream occurred after an incident at work when he felt excluded from what he had hoped to be his in-group, his "family." That day, everybody took the opposite side in a theoretical debate, although his position was a moderate and reasonable one. He thought, but of course he could not prove, that they gave him an argument because of his homosexual orientation, one that everybody knew about but did not discuss openly. They did, however, "mention" it by withholding recognition, which he saw as withholding love. His first thought was that he wanted to return to liberal New York and his New York apartment, and his second was that he could not for now, because he had rented it out. So he returned to it in his dream, in which it was represented as "the light at the end of the tunnel."

His occupational disorder was handled on several levels. First the therapist identified the feelings themselves, of which the patient was previously unaware. Then the therapist asked why the patient did not recognize the feelings as justified, but instead saw them as another example of his paranoid hypersensitivity or excessive narcissistic expectations of others. Then the therapist analyzed what was keeping the patient himself from instituting the obvious remedy—moving back to New York, where he would be in contact with those he liked and admired and who liked and admired him; a place where, as the patient put it, he would not be appalled by "hearing about how last night's game was a game-and-a-half" but pleased by hearing about "whether or not I am more self- than other-directed," and a place where few cared about his sexual orientation, but instead ignored it. As he put it, "Being ignored is the closest thing that I've had to love lately."

One teacher's fears of abandonment if he asserted himself appeared in a dream:

This teacher entered therapy because of a fear of asserting himself, which appeared clinically both in his private life as sexual impotence and in his professional life as an inability to teach. The latter took the form of constantly questioning whatever he said. His students complained that each time he made a statement he took it back with the question, "Is that right?" This verbal tic drove them to distraction. They cut his classes, which took its toll on his teaching and produced so much daily tension that it affected his blood pressure and immune system, until his physician had to warn him, "If you keep this up, you will end up not only professionally blocked but also physically sick."

One night he had a dream that his lover lent the car to another person, a rival, and the lover came to pick him up at the end of the workday, but without the car. Enraged, he started to abuse the lover, pulling his head down toward his own lap, using his lover's upper lip as a handle. In the dream the lover's upper lip was a deep purple or violet from having been pulled, or was it his own lip that was that color? To his surprise, the lover did not take it, as he usually did in real life, but instead fought back, and it looked as if the relationship was about to end.

Awake, he recognized that three events from the previous day contributed to the dream. He got a letter of rejection from a school to which he had applied for a new position and became angry and desperate, feeling, "I cannot stand to beg—I hate pleading with people to give me what I need." Then he got angry because in fact his lover had had a minor accident with the car. But he was afraid to express his anger for fear he would be abandoned. And he had just had some complaints from the tenant he had rented his summer home to, a tenant whom, as he punned, "was in so many violations of the lease that her name should be violet." Although the tenant was always late with the rent check, he was afraid to demand the rent on time because he feared it would only make things worse. Either the tenant would stay and not pay the rent at all, or she would leave and the patient would not have the income he depended on.

The therapist analyzed the dream as follows: Pulling the lip represented silencing himself and his lover, and pulling the head down referred to oral sex, an expression of desired passivity. The purple lip and the head-down position also represented the tenant who, "like all tenants, complained as a way to handle feeling in the passive, abject, one-down position." In disguised, acceptable dream language, "violet lip" also stood for the violence he felt because "I've gotten so few job offers and so many letters of rejection lately that I could kill." It was partly the fear of these violent thoughts and others associated with his asserting himself professionally that kept the patient passive and constantly questioning himself, which interfered with his work, since no one could stand to listen to him and since everyone cut his classes.

Analyzing the dream did not release him, as if by magic, from his passivity and self-questioning. But it told him the direction in which he had to go to get better. He had to be able to make a statement without questioning it immediately, and to do this he had to have more confidence in himself and be able to express his thoughts openly without seeing harmful hostility in harmless self-expression and fearing that as a consequence his position with his lover, tenant, and students would deteriorate.

A CEO who feared that if he did well professionally he would lose his wife had the following dream:

A CEO dreamt that he was reading his company's prospectus to an empty hall. Then the hall was full, but the audience was turning away from him. They were doing this because he was being unfaithful to his wife.

This man needed to fail because he believed that his wife would disapprove of his being successful professionally because she would see it as his being unfaithful to her sexually. He reasoned that work was a private world from which his wife was excluded or extruded, and that his devotion to his work meant that there was "someone else" in his life. He was deliberately disrupting his work so that he could "go home to my wife and the rest of the family, and make sure that she does not find other interests in the meantime, while I am gone."

Fear of success is another common theme in dreams as well as a factor in the occupational disorders whose meaning they reveal. For successophobics, the better things get in reality, the worse they get in fantasy. In their daily lives successophobics display their fear of success as guilt about self-expression and fulfillment, which takes the form of committed withdrawal or uncommitted shifting between involvement and withdrawal (really obsessive doing and undoing, in which the patient first moves to and then away from his or her goals). At night these patients often have "examination" dreams. Sometimes these are symbolic, and they dream not of taking examinations but of busses that do not come, or of running in place but not being able to get anywhere. Or they may be actual examination dreams, in which they dream of taking an examination and, although they have studied, they do not know any of the answers and are about to fail. For some of these patients a conscious fear of failing hides an unconscious wish to fail. Although these patients have nightmares about failing, secretly they are delighted that, in the dream at least, they did not pass the test.

A successophobic physician, just before sitting for his board exams, dreamed that he was sent on an errand, whereupon he ran a red light—or did he stop in time? In the dream he reassured himself that the red light was for another lane, not his. But then he became uncertain as to whether or not he had permission to "go" or whether he would be "fined or otherwise punished" if he "went." At about this time in his life he developed a number of phobias including one of driving through *green* lights—that is, he could not "go" even when given the "go ahead."

In another related dream, one he had the next night, he dreamed that he was writing textbooks which were not selling nearly as well as a medical textbook by an author named Welch, which sold 805 books to one book of his. Dream analysis revealed that the number 805 referred to 8:05 P.M., the time a WQXR radio program called "Symphony Hall" came on the air. The program "Symphony Hall" in the dream represented the doctor's wish to leave science and go into music. The name *Welch* referred to oedipal rivalry. The author, who was Jewish, wanted to have a different name to distinguish himself from, and to successfully compete with and best, his father. Guilty, he undid his own wish by letting Welch beat him instead. In fact, he suspected that it was Welch who sent him on the "errand through that red/green light, to crash."

This last theory was given credence by a memory from the day before, a memory he reported as an association to the just-described interpretation of the dream. He recalled that *Welch* was also the name of the rival of a politician he wanted to see defeated in the next election. This politician, Reid, had put him down in the past for complaining about an eyesore in a neighbor's yard. The name *Reid* referred to something he had read in a biography of the blocked composer, Sir Edward Elgar. The author of the biography, Michael Kennedy, said, in an unintentional pun on the name Reed, that "[Elgar sitting by a pond] was trying to write down what the reeds were saying. . . . Years later, W. H. Reed recalls in his *Elgar As I Knew Him*. . . . " The pun called to mind similar intentional puns that a favorite author of his, the successful humorist S. J. Perelman, made effectively. For example, as the patient remembered it, S. J. Perelman had Groucho Marx say that he would spend not "ten days in Leavenworth" but "eleven days in Twelveworth." Perelman also wrote, again as the patient remembered it, that "a violet hush came over the city, as our heroine, Miss Violet Hush. . . ." From analyzing this part of the dream, it became clear to the doctor that he wanted to be like S. J. Perelman—if only he did not have to be as successful.

Finally, the doctor had difficulty working at home because his dog barked indiscriminately. *Welch* referred to Welsh terrier, the breed of his dog; and going through the red/green light referred to thoughts about how the dog kept him from doing two things he wanted to do: study (because of the barking) and travel (because he did not have anyone to take care of the dog when he was away). This led to associations about how his success would come at the expense of another. For example, to concentrate and do his work he would have to lock up the dog in a back room; to travel he would have to lock her up in the kennel. He also struggled with a secret and forbidden wish to hit her to stop her from barking. Some days he thought of giving up his studies completely just to keep himself from hurting the creature. In the dream he let the dog beat him to prove to himself that he was not "beating her."

After learning how much he feared success (and that his fear of success was appropriate to past concerns that no longer applied), he was able to free himself, both intellectually and emotionally, at least enough to take his boards without excessive fear and to pass them without excessive difficulty.

Successophobia must be differentiated from excessophilia, in which it appears that nothing is ever good enough.

A CEO was plagued by recurrent dreams that because of her infidelity, her lover left her and she had to look for a new one.

For this person, the dream fulfilled a secret wish (because for her nothing, and no one, was ever good enough). She was never satisfied with what she had. She always wanted the next thing that might, or actually did, come along. As she was keeping herself lonely by her infidelities, she was driving her company into bankruptcy by her constant and unwise diworseifications—acquisitions of other companies, with the acquisitions unconsciously representing a kind of infidelity to her own. Both were for a reason: Because she always felt depleted, the act of getting, more than the state of having, was the important thing for her. As she herself finally saw, "Just like my cats, I don't want food, I want to be fed. I don't want to have, I want to get, for constantly 'getting' is like constantly being loved, and I need constant love to undo the equally constant gnawing feeling that my parents detested me, and to get my daily ration of proof that they loved me instead."

For so many workers like the aforementioned CEO, the old acceptances do not count. The workers get used to these, and they lose their novelty and impact. The only ones that count are the new ones. These give them the needed illusion of being loved. That is a significant reason why they are never satisfied with anything they do, however satisfying it may be. They have to test their acceptability and, in turn, their personal viability almost on a daily basis. In effect, they are never satisfied with having graduated. They have to take, and pass, the final exam over and over again.

## The Jungian Key

Jungian analysis provides another key to the meaning of dreams and the occupational disorders they represent. Some Jungians suggest that current events, such as rejections, are significant not for themselves or because they arouse childhood conflicts, but because they arouse the primitive person in all of us—that is, because they reactivate atavistic fears that originate ancestrally. An example of such a fear might be primitive humans' fear of being eaten alive, which is revived as an adult fear of being consumed by forces beyond one's control, in situations in which one is not in control.

Many of our familiar malfunction dreams are peculiarly ancestral. Dreams (like dreams of running in place and being unable to move forward, waiting for transportation that never comes, or being in two places at once) seem almost to have been passed down to us over successive generations until they have become innate, as much a part of our basic makeup as the built-in automatic behaviors (to which they are related) of flinching and fainting. Because they are so innate and universal, they do not seem to be personally meaningful. For this reason, therapists usually do not bother analyzing them. However, they *can* be analyzed, and they are full of possibilities. But they have to be analyzed differently from the personal, Freudian dreams tailor made to an individual's life experiences. Jungian dreams cannot be traced back to that ancestral moment when an early human was about to be eaten by a dinosaur (and, in the present, the worker is about to be eaten alive once again, by an audience, an envious co-worker, or a career-busting boss). Analyzing Jungian dreams is like analyzing gooseflesh. The process of piloerection is automatic and difficult to reduce into its component parts. Yet one can learn a great deal from when the bumps arrive. Similarly, in analyzing Jungian dreams one should treat them as associations to, not as elaborations of, daily events. One of these daily events is the Freudian dreams that occur before the Jungian dreams (with the Freudian dreams, in essence, being the stimulus, and the Jungian dreams, in essence, being the response). Just as showing patients what causes gooseflesh helps them avoid what gives them gooseflesh, showing them what causes their Jungian dreams helps them learn how to identify their personal dinosaurs.

> In real life a teacher (not the one just mentioned) moved away from the city to the suburbs, only to discover that the locals did not appreciate him, or his teaching, because he was too sophisticated and he taught things that did not interest them. He began to dream on a regular basis about the city apartment he had given up to move to the suburbs. In a Freudian dream about the apartment, he saw the entrance as a "slit surrounded by high grass." The analyst interpreted the dream as representative of the castration anxiety that the dull, unexceptional suburbs created in him. Then in the Jungian dreams that followed, he felt cold and looked for his apartment, where he could warm up, but it was nowhere to be found; he finally found it, only to see it recede further and further away as he approached. The analyst thought these dreams represented his feeling of being left out in the cold in the suburbs and, as a consequence, in danger of dying from exposure.

One teacher was up for promotion to school principal. He was one of two candidates. The other candidate he and almost everyone else thought of as an undeserving clod.

As soon as he heard of his possible promotion, he began to come to school late. Then he began calling out sick on a regular basis, until his attendance became so spotty that the school threatened to fire him.

One night he dreamt of being in a bloody automobile accident. Then he began to dream on a regular basis of driving in place, never moving forward and so never arriving at his destination.

In therapy he recognized that his promotion was threatening to him because it put him into confrontation with his father. He had become a teacher in the first place as a way to remain in the shadows to avoid competing with his physician father. As he put it, he deliberately chose a field in which the most intelligent of people have to be among the most humble—where "you have to grovel to please dumb kids, who shouldn't be pleased, and incompetent school boards, who can't be pleased or, if they can, only for the wrong reasons."

Desiring the lowly position he felt teachers occupied, and fearing the almost bodily consequences of being promoted, in real life he acted out, hoping to get fired. From his Freudian dreams he learned why he feared promotion. His Jungian dreams suggested a way out: freezing in place to avoid danger, which was on both sides—not only from losing, but from winning as well.

One teacher did poorly after being promoted to an administrative position, provoking others to cite the Peter Principle. But in the main the principle that was operative here was a fear of success. This surfaced in a Freudian dream he had one night—a dream of being in the back of a cab on the highway; the cab driver was hiding and had disappeared from the front seat. When the teacher put his head over the front seat, he discovered that the cab driver had fallen asleep and they were stopped dead—or were they careening together on the road toward disaster?

This teacher was afraid of success because of a persistent childhood guilt over a pressing and ultimately forbidden wish to spy on his parents' primal scene. He wanted to join in, to be "in the driver's seat." But this was as unacceptable as a wish as it would have been as an activity. The Freudian dream revealed that he wanted to be stopped dead to avoid the disaster that would inevitably occur should he make any move at all.

The next night he had recurrent Jungian dreams of growing smaller in stature. This made him think of how animals protectively roll into a ball when in danger. He also had dreams of running in place. These made him think of how animals freeze in defensive motionlessness to fool potential enemies into believing that they are not there.

A CEO about to be promoted had recurrent dreams of being immobile—running in place—around the time that she was having recurrent dreams of being raped, which revealed a fear of success. This fear could be traced back to the time when she believed her parents sexually abused her just when she was maturing, and when she took the sexual abuse as "her punishment for developing an identity of my own."

After his first published newspaper article, a budding journalist had a Freudian dream that he was at home as a child being attacked from all sides by spies, or really as a spy. Then he had another Freudian dream that he was Belshazzar slain for "writing on the wall." (In the original story the writing on the wall told Belshazzar that he was "weighed in the balances and . . . found wanting," and then he was killed, Old Testament, Daniel 5.) He thought his Freudian dreams referred to how ashamed he was of his writing because he was exposing himself. That exposure had a special meaning for him, because it ultimately referred to two aspects of the primal scene: his wish to "peep" at his parents having sexual relations, and his fear that they would notice his masturbating while he was watching them. Clearly he was confused between his work and his sexuality, and he feared getting comeuppance for what was a completely permissible wish to create, as if it were instead a forbidden wish to spy on the primal scene.

The next night he had a Jungian dream that he was nude in public, and his genitals were on display. He felt that this Jungian dream expressed the danger that he was in, not in the personal terms of his Freudian dreams, but in more universal, human terms—that is, he was depicted not as a spy or eavesdropper, but as a helpless, cold, and naked soul, without cover or protection from the elements.

## The Existential Key

Existential analysis looks at the person's real, present plight. In existential analysis, things are just what they seem to be. The analyst offers fewer interpretations than clarifications, whose main intent is to give form, weight, and imprimatur to what the patient already suspects or knows.

One existential analyst showed a picture a patient drew of his body entering the circle of the sun. The Freudian interpretation was "sex." The existential interpretation was "wanting to shine."

A teacher dreamt that he was traveling through Europe poor, without food, transportation, or friends to help out. The wish was to educate and broaden himself. The fear was just what the dream said it was.

## Techniques of Dream Analysis

Therapists should encourage and instruct the patient (1) to have dreams, (2) not to belittle them after having them but to accept what they say, (3) to remember them and write them down, and (4) to analyze them. The analyst should prepare the patient for the actual process of dream analysis more or less as follows:

We deal with the things that concern us by repeating them in the laboratory of our minds, like a controlled experiment. Dreams are a sign that the laboratory is open and has night hours.

Dreams are like laboratory tests. They help explain and diagnose occupational disorders. They teach you that your present disorder is rooted in past events, and they point the way to getting better by living in the present without contaminating it unnecessarily with the past.

It is natural to be afraid of dreams and to suppress them because it is natural to fear what they might reveal—things like sexual and angry feelings believed base and primitive. But suppressing them does not erase them. They only seep out in other, usually destructive, ways.

To analyze your dreams, it is necessary to remember them. To remember them, it is necessary to like yourself enough to accept certain unfamiliar and even forbidden aspects of yourself.

Although this is controversial, it helps to write down dreams as they occur (say, in the middle of the night). Some therapists say that writing down dreams is a waste of time, but I think in some cases at least it keeps you from forgetting the entire dream. Writing down dreams is good practice for removing inhibitions in general. For giving yourself permission to write your dreams down, and actually doing so, is giving yourself permission to be yourself, which is the reverse of discouraging yourself (which is your problem, in a nutshell).

You should learn to use the technique of free associating to dreams to understand better what they are trying to tell you though you will not listen. You need only let your thoughts roam from and around a dream, not discounting any of these thoughts, the way that blocked writers often do with their thoughts. Soon analyzing dreams will become second nature. Connections formerly broken will be remade. Bridges will be built between the disparate parts of a dream; then between dreams, newly whole, and other dreams; and then between dreams and your occupational disorder. Next the dreams themselves will oblige. They will appear night after night, as if trying to please, and they will suggest revealing material for further analysis, as if trying to be cooperative.

Your dreams will tell you something you are trying to keep hidden, the buried feelings that take, and have, a strong hold on you. Once understood and exposed to light, these feelings will lose some of their power and relinquish some of their hold.

## SLIPS OF THE TONGUE

Slips of the tongue (or pen) differ from dreams in that they appear during the day, when the patient is awake, not at night, when the patient is asleep. Along with dreams, they reveal something of the meaning of a patient's occupational disorder. They should be analyzed as if they were dreams. As in dreams, sometimes what surfaces is a secret wish (as when a psychiatrist admonished in writing that doctors have to be very careful in how they handle their "parents"). Sometimes what emerges is a secret fear, which may be of suppressed hostile and sexual wishes or of others' reaction to those wishes. For example, in a sentence typed for this chapter the word *dream* was mistyped as *dread*, revealing my own tendency to be afraid of exposure because of a fear of criticism.

## SUMMARY

Analyzing dreams and slips of the tongue is good practice for life. Patients who do it are trying to get over their disorder, not yield to it. They are giving themselves a vote of confidence, which is the beginning of self-acceptance, which in turn is the beginning of self-respect.

Dream analysis and analysis of slips of the tongue reveal fears that contaminate the neutral act of working, making it more highly charged than it needs to or should be. Analyzing these dreams helps individuals with occupational disorders "neuter" work and return it to its native state, in which it is usually too inherently bland to cause conflict.

Analyzing dreams is hard work. At first, resistance causes patients to forget dreams or deny their significance. More difficult is making the analysis stick. Sometimes, even when patients understand their dreams, they find that their emotions swamp their intellect, and they learn about their neurotic tendencies but keep them nevertheless.

There are many connections between the individual, the individual's disorder, and the individual's dreams, and they should all be made. All the bridges should be built, so that the individual can walk over them to freedom as a whole person, without block as a constant companion.

The individual should keep at dream analysis, comforted by the recognition that occupational disorders are complex structures. As with any complex structure, to knock it all down one just has to pull one brick out from the bottom, and the whole thing collapses. Ideally a combination of Freudian, Jungian, and existential dream analysis pulls out the brick, and the patient can once again move forward after watching the barrier crumble and fall like a downed monster.

# 14

# Cognitive Therapy

Cognitive errors are illogical beliefs that can compromise occupational functioning. For example, those who think the term *similar* means "the same thing" often view their work solely from the point of view of a single, base, but not necessary representative motive for working. Women can become ashamed of and hold back their work if they think that because doing work is active, it is aggressive and masculine. Men can become equally ashamed of and hold back their work if they think that because cooperating and compromising at work is passive, it is compliant and feminine. Both sexes can become ashamed of and hold back their work if they think that being passionate about their work is the equivalent of exposing their private parts, or some other forbidden sexual activity. The same thing can happen if they believe that being spontaneous means being out of control, which means going over the edge and into madness.

Most occupational disorders are created from more than one cognitive error, so any given occupational disorder will be associated with two or more cognitive errors. For example, depression is the product of the error of some = all and the error of similar = the same thing, among others (more on this later in this chapter). In turn, because any given occupational disorder will tend to consist of more than one cognitive error, curing occupational disorder cognitively usually requires correcting more than one cognitive error therapeutically. However, while this is an oversimplification, specific cognitive errors do tend to be associated, if not with specific occupational disorders then with specific symptoms characteristic of certain occupational disorders:

---

Sections of the following chapter are adapted from Beck (1985).

One patient got depressed when he believed that if something can go wrong, it will (what I call Murphy's cognitive error), until, brooding about the hopelessness of it all, he developed delusions of world decay (or *weltuntergang*).

Another patient got depressed because she thought, "I must not be any good because I'm not all good," a some = all equivalency. She also became obsessive because she thought in absolutes. Anything less than perfect was no good at all, so that she evaluated her work and her life in an all-or-none way and made career decisions in the same way. She had two talents: art and business. She either quit doing the art and took a mundane, full-time job because there is no money at all in doing art, or she quit the mundane job to do art full time because there is no art at all in making money. Instead of searching for the perfect solution, she should have settled down to a part-time day job and integrated it with her part-time artistic activities.

A third patient became paranoid because she equated constructive criticism with a persecutory attack, a similar = the same thing equivalency.

A fourth became avoidant because she confused activity with aggression, a similar = the same thing equivalency, and stopped work to maintain a self-image of nonaggressiveness.

A fifth developed repetitive strain injury from the computer keyboard in part because she thought that writing about sex was the same thing as doing sexual things, a thinking = doing subvariety of similar = the same thing equivalency.

A sixth, confusing the symbol with what it symbolized and hoping that others would do the same (another similar = the same thing equivalency) developed a repetitive strain injury in part as a way to impress others with how hard he was straining at his work and as a way to convince others how much "strain" he was under—that is, "Look at me; one glance at my cramped hand will tell you that I take my job seriously and to heart."

A seventh developed writer's block because she equated originality with disrespect and defiance, and confused exertion with accomplishment (both similar = the same thing errors). As for confusing exertion with accomplishment, she became like the person who read many diet books rather than cutting a few calories. She thought she was writing, but in fact she never stopped researching. In confusing working hard with being effective, she thought that the result must be great because the effort was, forgetting that she could produce more by taking the easy rather than the hard way, which was merely personally exhausting. She overlooked that what people produce is more important than how much it pains them to produce it.

Her counterpart in the business world was a doctor working for a psychiatric clinic. He was told that he was working hard but hardly working, doing things right, but not doing the right things. He wrote lengthy and truly beautiful work-ups—they were much more carefully written than most. But his diagnosis was always major depression. How he managed to be lucky, or unlucky, enough to have at least 200 patients in a row all with the same diagnosis is the subject of another book. Here I merely note that while others' write-ups were short, sloppy, and illegible, they at least tried to have their diagnoses reflect more about the patient's problems than about their own, and have their treatment derive from a diagnosis that was more relevant to the patient's disorder than it was to their own.

An eighth developed an anxiety disorder because he magnified and then overread and overreacted to everything that happened to him and drew conclusions with scant information to go by. Whole cabals seemed to exist for this worker, who read, really misread, too much into the day-to-day events of his work life and then responded as if everything were a matter of life or death and as if everyone were against him. Each night he went home anxious over little or nothing. A writer with a similar problem could not use the computer without constantly worrying that he might have ruined everything he was doing. He became terrified because he was afraid that he would make a mistake and wipe out hours of work. His fear was based on a failure to distinguish between benign and malignant mistakes, a similar = the same thing equivalency. If he named a nonexistent file to copy and the computer said, "File not found, zero copies made," he felt that he destroyed his work just because he made *a* mistake, and he had to tell himself that while some mistakes are disastrous, this *particular* mistake had no practical consequences. Failing to distinguish between mistakes led to a kind of kindling, in which a big fire started from a little spark, causing him to become so anxious and paralyzed with fear that he was hardly able to drag himself to his desk to begin work each morning.

## SPECIFIC COGNITIVE ERRORS

The following is an attempt to sort and classify the cognitive errors, but this is difficult to do precisely because they overlap conceptually.

### Some = All

Those workers who think some = all (usually along with part = whole, the next error to be discussed) cannot do their work because they condemn themselves (and others) excessively for minor infractions or imperfections that are either unnoticeable or unimportant. One could do no better than to condemn a 400-page book he wrote because it contained a minor factual error. Doing this made about as much sense as condemning all of Melville's *Moby Dick* (1981, originally published 1851) because Melville said, "Be it known that, waiving all agrument [finding this typo gave the patient more ammunition for complaint], I take the good old fashioned ground that the whale is a fish." (p. 129).

## Part = Whole

Workers who confuse the part with the whole tend to be excessively perfectionistic, with a perfectionism that makes them like drivers who think they are driving safely if they constantly look back to see if something dangerous is approaching but forget that in checking for possible problems, they are virtually assuring that they will occur.

A psychobiographer, overemphasizing the necessarily second-hand quality of much psychobiography, underemphasized the real advantages of drawing conclusions about life now from studying the lives of great people. She could have viewed her work as worthy but flawed. But she chose to view it as entirely unworthy because flawed.

Burnout may result when the confusion between part = whole, along with that between some = all, engenders a sense of excessive pessimism about work and working. For example, a worker thinks, "Because some philistines are unable to appreciate what I have to offer, no one at all can appreciate what I do; therefore, I am stuck in a world full of dullards and in a job that is a waste of time." The worker feels, "Nothing is worthwhile" and retreats, feeling burned out: "What's the use; why bother?"

Paranoia can appear when individuals see only others' negative feelings toward them and overlook the positive feelings. The negative feelings may be completely imagined. They usually do exist but are not the whole story, and often those who hold them are in conflict about them and mean to keep them hidden.

## Similar = the Same Thing

An example of the cognitive error of similar = the same thing is apples = oranges. This is partly right because apples *are* like oranges (for example, they are both round). But it is also partly wrong because they are like oranges only in certain respects.

A self-employed individual took a day job because she began to feel lonely at home and thought she could get a new family at work. But she forgot how work families are unlike real families in most respects.

A critic developed a "Furor Teutonicus" (a "fetish" for things Germanic) feeling that "it's no good unless it's Germanic" because, believing that similar = the same thing, he confused intensity of sound with greatness of spirit. In his scheme of things, the composer Gustav Mahler was the greatest because he was the loudest and went on the longest. Meanwhile, the craftsmanship of reticence, suggestion, and insinuation was devalued as small potatoes, so that composers who produced subtle works were per se inferior to those who produced more grandiose ones. For example, in this critic's view Saint-Saëns was spiritually bankrupt because he implied rather than stated, leaving something to the imagination.

Another critic liked Mahler and dismissed Saint-Saëns, because he believed that because sadness was down and joy was up, sadness went deep and was therefore superior to joy, which was superficial and so frivolous.

A critic liked abstract art and abstract artists but lambasted representational art as the same thing as, and so no better than, copying (forgetting that Rembrandt "copied" faces, and Da Vinci "copied" smiles).

A graphic artist thought creativity was like madness, because both were wild things that seemed to come from nowhere. So she threw away her good works to suppress her bad instincts and to be the "eminently sane person" her self-image dictated that she be.

A clerical worker thought that because he did his work spontaneously, he did it passively—that is, it "just seemed to flow through." Next he thought that "passivity is feminine, and feminine homosexual." Then he gave up doing what he did because he wanted to be eminently straight and completely "butch."

A worker confused any disagreement with others with disrespect for them until he could do nothing but condemn himself for saying anything at all. Disrespect was not intended. The idea of disrespect was a carry-over from the time when he was supposed to listen to his parents, be seen but not heard, and agree with everything they said, because submissive = good, and speaking frankly = bad.

One worker became a workaholic when she overworked, thinking, "The more I agonize, the more worthwhile material I produce," and "Beethoven worked hard, I work hard, therefore I am Beethoven." She seemed to be saying, in effect, that "because creativity = 90 percent perspiration, 90% perspiration = creativity."

The unproductive nature of the idea that hard work is enough and will be rewarded because doing = accomplishing is further illustrated by the patient who prayed in church 6 hours a day trying to cure her husband's metastatic cancer. While I felt sorry for her and for her husband, I nevertheless thought that she prayed too much. She eventually agreed that her praying represented a kind of overscrupulosity, and that she was not praying by choice but out of a desperate need to do anything, just to do something. Also agreeing that she could better use some of her time to do something effective, she began to pray less and to spend more time working with her husband's doctors in the cancer hospital and getting close to him during his final days.

A writer, also confusing hard work with good effect, wrote a play in sonata allegro form—that is, ABCAB. The first scene was in two contrasting parts (AB). It was followed by a second scene that mingled and developed these two parts as one (C). That was followed by a third scene that was a verbatim repetition of the first scene (AB), although the mood changed from sad to happy (the equivalent of the musical key change that is sometimes part of the structure of the sonata allegro form).

This was hard to do but to no avail because, although this man had plenty to say, he did not say it. Instead he set out to impress the audience with how well he could do something difficult. But all the audience knew was that they heard the same thing over and over again and that what they heard was not very good in the first place.

This man had just broken up with a lover and was in pain. He could have tapped this experience to write with force and energy. But he was denying his feelings because he found them embarrassing. To do so he deliberately and agonizingly wrote this dull, boring, sweat-stained work.

A patient who confused exertion with accomplishment (stating, "I know what I have to do to lose weight" and then spending hours looking up and studying all the diet books, but cutting no calories) was also a methadone maintenance patient who for years looked forward to a date set for getting off methadone. Every day he counted the time he had left and thanked God that the days were getting fewer and he was getting closer to his goal. Meanwhile, he continued to take his daily dose of methadone, right up to the day he had set aside for sobriety and then right past it.

These workers, confusing effort with accomplishment, worked hard and for a cause, but not well and for a reason—that is, they worked without considering whether what they did was pertinent and useful. Instead of thinking hard work is its own reward, they should have stopped trying and started succeeding. While congratulations are in order for good intentions, having one's heart in the right place is not good enough. As one of my patient's supervisors put it, "Cadavers have their heart in the right place."

Writers in particular (but also all workers to some extent) are making similar = the same thing errors when they block because they judge and condemn their works on what is in effect an ad hominem basis. Writers think that because writing is revealing, what they do is tantamount to self-exposure—that is, it reveals too much about themselves to be acceptable. Then they hide their writings in a bottom drawer or send them for evaluation to someone they know will condemn or even lose them—the same thing, once removed, as not doing them in the first place. Yet most of what writers do reveals less about themselves than they imagine. Writers forget that writing is also obscuring. They also overlook that work and self are different, if only because creative work originates in a different part of the brain from personal behavior, sexual desire, intelligence, and madness (more on this later). According to Michael Kennedy (1987), the composer Sir Edward Elgar referred to the difference between the writer and the writings when he said that he functioned not as a composer of but as an "incubator" (p. 333) for his ideas.

A particularly dangerous aspect of the cognitive error of similar = the same thing is that it can lead to an incorrect medical diagnosis. Patients first convince themselves and then convince their therapists that they have an occupational disorder when they do not have one at all. All boredom becomes burnout, all insomnia and resultant daytime fatigue becomes Epstein-Barr, and even a temporary lapse of inspiration becomes writer's block (although it is natural to not be able to work 24 hours a day, and it is normal to need periods of rest between periods of creativity).

Artists and their critics use similar = the same thing cognitive errors to convince themselves, and their therapists, that they are mad when they are in fact sane. Some books, like Kay Redfield Jamison's *Touched with Fire* (1993), confuse creativity with madness because of the superficial similarities between the two. Some even imply that the best way to improve one's work is to lose control of oneself. However, such observers overlook that creativity comes from the supraconscious, not the unconscious. So creative people do not have to be "mad" to create, only to block.

Similarly, patients convince themselves and their therapists that they are depressed when they are not. In fact, some doctors make this cognitive error either because they do not know how to diagnose depression or to prescribe antidepressants they intended to give all along. With fluoxetine (Prozac) so popular these days, therapists often put their patients in the position of playing the nail to the doctor's new hammer (For example, writer's block is a pulling back; depression is a pulling back; therefore, all writer's block is due to depression). It is not that simple. There are many psychological disorders that produce pulling back and that produce writer's block characterized by a pulling back. Depression is only one of them.

Another potentially dangerous source of confusion is the one between emotionally and physically caused hand syndromes (discussed in Chapter 2). The patient and the doctor must make certain that actual repetitive strain is causing a repetitive strain injury/carpal tunnel syndrome before treating the patient with a new computer keyboard and certainly before an operation on the patient's hand. Some cases of repetitive strain particularly those that occur in the absence of physical findings, are not due to repetitive strain but to what is easily confused with it: continuous stress. Unnecessary surgery prescribed for an emotional disorder that might have responded to psychological methods has been known to cripple the hands, and the careers, of more than one individual.

Too often, self-help books recommend inappropriate, worthless, or harmful methods for self-improvement, and therapists use the same methods for psychotherapy (based first on similar = same incorrect diagnosis and then on similar = same methods of intervention, which in turn seem derived from similar = same fantasies like the ones found in primitive humans). Some therapists, confusing the symbol with what it symbolizes, use homeopathic methods for a reason similar to the reason that primitives let bees sting them. Primitive humans believed that because bees hit their target, getting stung by bees made them accurate archers; so primitive homeopathic doctors believe that a (dilute) hair of the dog that bit you is just the thing for a dog bite. This reminds me of the bald singer who got a hair transplant in the belief that it would help him sing like a famous pop star, who also had a hair transplant, and of those romantically inclined poets who hope to be physically compromised (and sometimes actually try to injure themselves) in the belief that having a club foot will help them write poetry like Lord Byron.

Critics who indulge in this kind of erroneous thinking can fail to distinguish "different" from superior and inferior, and then rate people and things not individually but comparatively. A typical example is from Oscar Thompson's *International Cyclopedia of Music and Musicians* (1964): "Less searching, elemental and challenging than Copland or Schuman, he, Samuel Barber, is far more adventurous in spirit than Hanson or Thompson" (p. 140). In this spirit, a well-known former drama critic of a major newspaper compared the musical *Gypsy* to *King Lear*—and then other musicals to *Gypsy*. Is it any wonder that the next modest little offering to come his way hardly impressed him?

## Personalization

Personalization blurs the distinction between the external and the internal world in two ways: by externalization/ projection, and by internalization/introjection. With externalization/projection, the world in effect has become the individual's coloring book. The result is a self-oriented view of the world, in which individuals think that external events happen with reference to them and them alone. A quiz show contestant always suspected 11 was his lucky number; then he *knew* it was when he was the 11th person picked to be a contestant on the show. Such individuals get very depressed when things do not go their way, because they take negative events, which are depressing in themselves, personally. For example, when a layoff happens at a time of personal tragedy, the painful element of "Why me?" and "Why now?" is added to the already painful experience.

With internalization, the world in effect becomes an irritating grain of sand in a worker's eye. What was outside becomes an essential and annoying part of what is inside. Negative self-views are created entirely from the stuff of what others think. With these poisonous introjects, patients do their work about as comfortably and effectively as people with sand in their eyes go about their business.

## Overgeneralization

The cognitive error of overgeneralization leads workers to form conclusions on the basis of too little and too narrow experience. Overgeneralization is the soul of hypersensitivity and paranoia. While sensitivity is a part of being an effective worker, hypersensitivity and paranoia makes individuals constantly sore. Workers read too much into everything, and no one can touch them without their feeling not touched, but poked and mauled. When combined with personalization and magnification (or overvaluing the significance of a particular event), everything assumes a degree of importance that it does not merit. In the workplace, minor professional becomes significant personal criticism, so that a fleeting negative professional evaluation becomes a significant negative personal rejection. All constructive criticism becomes destructive, until no one can tell the individual anything helpful without setting off panic and depression.

## Magnification

In magnification, panic arises when workers take things too seriously and blow them up out of proportion. Figuratively speaking, things properly measured in centimeters are instead measured in inches. Or, again figuratively speaking, an individual overestimates the pressure a phonograph needle can put on the tip of the finger as follows: After dividing the weight by the area (the right formula), the individual concludes that, because the divisor is so small, the tip of the phonograph cartridge exerts many, many pounds per square inch on the finger and then thinks, "That's enough to crush it." Or, in saving five cents on a dime purchase, an individual congratulates herself for having saved

50%—technically true, but congratulations are not necessarily in order for one who has saved just a nickel. When workers take things too seriously and blow things out of proportion in this way, they react catastrophically. At work, every day they face becomes final exam day, and anxiety and depression are simultaneously their forte, their constant companions, and their undoing.

Scrupulous morality is often the reason for this cognitive error. For example, workers take themselves too seriously because they think that to do otherwise means that they are not taking themselves seriously enough. Magnification also originates in low self-esteem, which in effect says, "I fear terrible things will happen to me because I deserve to have them happen to me, because I am a terrible person."

Stage fright, among other disorders, is a response that is irrational partly due to magnification, for nothing on the order of what one fears is warranted by the actual circumstances. Most audiences leave room for a speaker's anxiety. Most anxiety can be covered up (an attack of bronchitis can be blamed when one's voice goes). Most careers flounder but still go on if a star forgets the lyrics or a speaker makes a Freudian slip. Yet no amount of experience to the contrary seems able to convince the individual that the fears are irrational. (Individuals do not have to be on the stage to have stage fright. They can as easily have it in the privacy of their own home. Individuals who feel faint in front of an audience can feel dizzy at home and have to leave their desks to go lie down, while individuals who fear wetting their pants on stage can develop urinary burning and frequency and have to spend an inordinate amount of time traveling to and from the bathroom.)

## Absolutistic, Dichotomous Thinking

Absolutistic, dichotomous thinking divides the world into categories of "perfect" and "entirely worthless." The individual evaluates his or her work in terms of all black or white, with no gray in between. The writer either has a real job or is completely unemployed. A "real job" requires going to the office; comes with set hours, salaries, and benefits; and involves certain concrete actions, like churning the copying machine. "Not a real job," like writing, involves staying home, with irregular remuneration; produces spiritual benefits, like self-satisfaction, but not mundane benefits, like medical insurance; and involves abstract, ultimately "unproductive," activities (like thinking) more than concrete, seemingly productive, activities (like copying). Writers often have friends and family who make the same cognitive errors. Associating all work with the workplace, and all workplaces with office buildings, they suggest that what writers do is not real work because they do it at home.

They think that people who work at home must be retired, or semiretired, because they take television breaks (the similar = the same thing error in the form of, "retired people watch television; you watch television; therefore, you are retired"). Often, confusing house work with housework, and housework with drudgery, they suggest that the worker get a part-time job to get out of the house. They forget, as Michael Carter put it, "what staying home did for Emily Dickinson" (personal communication).

Real life consists not of pure whites or blacks but of shades of gray, with imperfection the norm. Imperfections always exist in anything. Software writers call them bugs (in paranoid fashion, as if they crawled in from outside instead of having been put there in a moment of inattention or incompetence). Rarely does perfection count. First, the overview is more meaningful than the up-close view, which reveals specific flaws but overlooks the big picture. Second, in real life what counts is not the imperfections but the reaction to them. People who want to like something overlook its flaws, while people who want to hate something see them, and see them exclusively. Those who want to like Wagnerian operas sleep through the dull parts, while those who do not refer to them incessantly and exclusively. One can find imperfections in a word processing or other computer program and still find it satisfactory if, instead of complaining, one looks for ways to get around the imperfections.

## Selective Inattention

Selective inattention, in which workers see one tree but not another in the forest, is the soul of crippling envy. So many people hate their jobs because they see them narrowly and in some way inferior to the jobs others have. People stuck at their desks envy writers who can take long walks (they forget that they, not writers, have a steady salary and medical benefits). People envy teachers their vacation time, without factoring in the low salary; or they envy doctors their high salary, without factoring in how little vacation time they have. Artists are envied their independence, government workers their dependence, successful people their exposure, unsuccessful people their privacy, and so on.

## Figure = Ground

Individuals who make this cognitive error become uncertain about what is cause and what is effect (i.e., whether the horse is pulling the cart, or the other way around). Depression results when they blame themselves when they are being victimized by others (as when they feel they are incompetent because they are having difficulty working on a project, when in fact they are simply having difficulty working on a project because it is a difficult one). Paranoia results when they blame others when they themselves are the problem and, if they are victims, it is because they have created their own victimization.

## CAUSE

There are two main causes for cognitive errors, each suggesting a different form of treatment. Cognitive errors can be due to self-destructive identifications with others who make the same errors. The cognitive error is not created de novo but is borrowed from friends and family. Workers who pick up and adopt as their own others' cognitive errors, and the occupational disorders that go with them, often do so because they are passive, suggestible people who look up to their parents as perfect, their friends as paragons, and their religion and society as the ultimate authority.

Cognitive errors can also be due to disordered mood (such as depression) or disordered attitude (such as narcissism). Cognitive errors change mood, as when negative cognitive errors, or "negative thinking," cause depression and work stoppage results; or positive cognitive errors, or inappropriately positive thinking, create a state of inappropriate elation that results in logorrhea or frank disorganization. In addition, bad mood generates cognitive errors to justify the mood. If a worker is down and self-esteem is low, it is human nature to explain the mood to oneself in rational terms (i.e., to find what looks like a real reason to feel worthless). One possible thought is, "Since I am not all good, then I am no good at all." Often, vicious cycling occurs between cognitive errors that are the cause of the bad moods and cognitive errors that are their effect. Breaking the cycle involves either correcting the underlying mood that is causing the cognitive errors (for example, with medication) or challenging the cognitive errors that are causing the mood (with rational counterargument and reality testing).

Here are some specific examples of how disordered moods and altered mind-sets can spawn cognitive errors.

### Depression

An individual's depression caused him to personalize all bad things, thinking they were soon to happen to him. For example, when he read in the obituaries of someone who died young, he became convinced that he was next. He magnified all potential risks in any situation and thought himself constantly vulnerable and in imminent danger.

## Hypomania

In one individual a hypomanic mood promoted the error of some = all because in a romantic high he confused a good idea with an actual accomplishment. Then, with the poor judgment that comes from suspended self-criticism, he submitted mere fragments to publishers in the belief that he had done enough for them to see the value of his work as a whole.

## (Bad) Narcissism

As mentioned in Chapter 8, good (effective) is to be distinguished from bad (ineffective) narcissism. Good narcissism is the kind that gets workers through the day by generating the high self-esteem workers must have if they are to be protected from all the negativity around them, appropriate or otherwise. It is the kind that lets workers think that they are good people even if they are not producing good things.

In contrast, bad narcissism is self-referential narcissism, which can have a disastrous effect. It causes workers to personalize. Unable to separate their works from themselves, the professional from the personal ego, they become oversensitive, too easily hurt, and feel personally wounded when professionally supervised or constructively criticized. For example, because of the personalization associated with bad narcissism, workers who are assigned menial jobs because someone has to do them see their assignment as a reflection on their professional worth in general and on their personal worth in specific.

Bad narcissism is an important component of the magnification that is the soul of stage fright. Not only is the speaker "it" in reality, the speaker also feels like "it" in a cosmic sense—watched, really illuminated, not as if merely the center of attention, but as if in God's eye. This feeling persists although the people in the audience are neither gods nor are paying that much attention to the speaker in the first place. Most are not watching the show as much as they are thinking about themselves.

Often, friends, family, and the media lancinate those in the public eye and then complain that their cries of pain are excessive and inappropriate because creative people (especially those in the public eye), ranging from artists to politicians, can be safely skewered professionally because they are being spared personally. However, separating work and person is a good idea in theory, but not in practice. Few workers have a self-view that is independent of what they produce. The psychic reality for most sincere creative workers is that they are what they do—that is, bad narcissism of this kind is neither unusual nor necessarily abnormal. Perhaps politicians and their ilk, when attacked professionally, should try to take it personally instead, if only because it helps not to expect oneself to do the impossible.

### Paranoia

Paranoid workers elaborate kernels of truth into fertile fields of grain. They magnify, often getting angrier and angrier in private, until they emerge and attack people publicly.

Their paranoia promotes a some = all worldview in which a sometimes and partly critical and unfair world is seen as always and totally critical and unfair. There is some unfairness in awarding Nobel Prizes and Oscars, but mostly individuals do not get one not because they are being slighted but because they were not properly introduced, did not earn it, or did something to antagonize the committee.

### TREATMENT

When cognitive errors are due to pathological identification, effective treatment is based on finding new people to identify with or keeping the same people but not identifying with them. When they are the result of moodiness or pathological mind-sets, therapy deals with the underlying moodiness or pathological mind-set.

Working with the depressive low self-esteem and insufficient good narcissism that spawns stage fright, a therapist informed her writers that just because they were not famous authors did not mean that they did not have anything to offer others. This made them less fearful and uncertain of themselves up there because they were more certain that others would want what they had to give. In turn, they could stop graphically fantasizing what could, and probably would, happen to worthless people who dared to get up and speak in front of such a worthwhile audience.

The same therapist asked her paranoid patients to handle their hypersensitivity by accepting their imperfections and, with that, some of the blame for their fate. She illustrated how this can help with the following humorous anecdote:

"Recently a patient of mine was at the Animal Medical Center with a pet and was subjected to a dog barking at his cap because, as the owner explained, 'he doesn't like your hat.' Did the victim complain to the management? No, he excused himself for having such a silly hat on and took it off, reassuring the dog that he was right and he would gladly get a new one, if given time. That stopped the dog's barking. It also improved the patient's appearance.

The patient concluded that instead of flying into a rage at the world, instead of exhausting oneself tilting at windmills and becoming bitter when they tilt back, when you do not get what you want or are attacked in a way you do not like, you should sometimes admit that the world is right and, instead of seeing the world as unfair, make it fairer, by changing your hat."

Whatever their origin, cognitive errors, once in place, respond to being challenged directly. This means countering the distorted illogical thinking with the therapist's ordered logical thinking (a specific instance of the general therapeutic approach of reality testing).

Cognitive distortions should be identified as they appear in the relationship to the therapist (that is, in the transference) and corrected there and then, especially when they act as resistances. For example, some patients think that if their therapist makes a mistake, then he or she is no good at all. Such patients must be disabused of that antitherapeutic fantasy.

It is not always helpful to think logically and unemotionally. Sometimes thinking illogically and emotionally serves a creative purpose. Sometimes it can be defensive, not increasing but decreasing anxiety. A simple example is denial of something one does not want to hear or know. For example, the thought "there are more fish in the ocean" is properly used to comfort oneself and get over grief after getting a rejection slip from the publisher or losing a lover. Yet it relies on the untruth that while all fish are somewhat similar, publishers and lovers are not fish and, unlike fish, are usually different in some very distinctive and important ways and so not easily interchangeable. However, this cognitive error helps patients get over their grief. It keeps them at the pier, their bait on the hook, their line in the water, still fishing.

# 15

# Supportive Therapy

The term *supportive therapy* describes a method of treatment characterized both by what it does and by what it does not do.

## WHAT IT DOES

Supportive therapy focuses on what works for an actual patient, rather than on what should work for a theoretical one. It favors a direct rather than a round-about approach. For example, a therapist deals with a patient's inhibitions about functioning not by analyzing them but by giving the patient advice on how to function better. Furthermore, it emphasizes a patient's constructive as much as a patient's destructive behavior, to avoid emphasizing weaknesses while neglecting strengths.

Supportive therapy uses aspects of the real relationship with the therapist (without crossing boundaries) to help workers overcome the feeling that they are rejected and alone. Workers with an occupational disorder invariably feel like babies abandoned in an orphanage. They have become, as Lawrence Wilson (1994) quoting Erskine Caldwell (speaking of writers with career problems) put it, "an outcast among the literary guys" (p. 10). Such patients need to do more than discuss feeling abandoned. They need a supportive holding environment within which they can feel less abandoned, one that literally props them up while they develop enough self-confidence and recover enough aplomb to hold their head up high (at least long enough to attempt to go out and function on their own).

Supportive therapy emphasizes ego therapy, a cornerstone of which is testing reality. For example, patients learn that they have to work just to work, without giving too much thought to such work contaminants as "Who am I impressing?" or "What are my critics thinking?"

## WHAT IT DOES NOT DO

Supportive therapy avoids viewing insight, whether of the cognitive or analytic variety, as an end in itself. It avoids prolonged treatment done without reference to or concern for a patient's present and immediate difficulties, especially the kind that deliberately withholds emergency assistance for a presumed greater good. Too many therapists withhold practical remedies that are available in favor of realizing such long-term goals as developing self-understanding. In effect, they believe that feeling better right now interferes with getting better in the future. They may be right. Or they may merely be keeping inhibited, blocked workers in therapy for years, telling them that their disorder will be relieved or "cured" only after all the causes of it are dealt with. To many workers with an occupational disorder, this is tantamount to receiving a death sentence.

Supportive therapy avoids persisting in methods that are not working or are making matters worse. It checks back regularly to determine how therapy is doing. It does not ask the patient to follow advice blindly or consistently without looking to see if it is more helpful than harmful and without making sure that in solving one problem, another is not being created. For example, in too many cases, blocked workers are told to remove themselves from practically all of life to focus on doing their work. They do this but at the expense of relationships with friends and family. Their occupational disorder is cured, but an interpersonal disorder is created, and the patient ends up unblocked but alone. In most cases, the worker must be helped not only to solve problems related to the disorder but also to consider the effects of the solution on others in his or her life. Writers have to work on their writer's block, but not 24 hours a day and not by neglecting their family and friends.

Supportive therapy avoids giving simplistic advice, which is often not supportive but inaccurate or dangerous.

A writer who could not work complained, "I learned from my last therapist that to get over my inability to do my work my pencils need to be sharp, I need a room of my own to work in, and I have to make my office off limits to my children and not allow anyone to interrupt me there." She continued, "This may have been good advice to get me through the Internal Revenue Service's audit of my home office, but it certainly didn't work for my creative block—at least after I got over the initial positive impact of knowing that my therapist was interested in me. In fact, it made things worse, because I still have my block and, in addition, my family is angry with me for doing the vanishing act, and I need their support if I am to be able to do any work at all. All this therapist did is make me feel even more like a failure, because not only am I sick, but I can't even respond to help that is offered to me."

Supportive therapy avoids increasing anxiety and guilt. In one common scenario a therapist recommends getting anger out only to increase the patient's guilt (and cause the patient to antagonize people the patient needs); this is a special problem for assertiveness training techniques. In another common scenario, a therapist criticizes patients with insight therapy that is little more than a form of fault finding (for example, the therapist acts the part of the editor of a book who finds one typo in 300 pages and then talks about nothing else).

Supportive therapy avoids giving support inappropriately. Psychopaths who come to grief because they have plagiarized the ideas of others need limit setting, or even criticism, but not support. Some workers, who are in fact failures, need to be told not "You are great" just so that the therapist can be nice, but how to deal with the failure that already exists and how to avoid failing again.

Supportive therapy avoids giving false hope. Patients with an occupational disorder have enough trouble with a disappointing world without having a therapist who disappoints them equally. When nothing much can be done to help the patient, at least the patient should not be set up to expect cure. Some writers are simply out of ideas; and some professionals are simply out of their element. All concerned need to know this so that they can adjust and go on from there.

## SPECIFIC SUPPORTIVE TECHNIQUES

### Assertiveness Training

Assertiveness training can help those who are excessively passive become more active without being aggressive, so that they can set limits without starting fights, get what they deserve from others without driving them away, and even get what they deserve from themselves without defeating themselves in the process.

### Nonassertiveness (Zen Removal)

Zen techniques help the worker roll with the punches. Workers who do this stay on the job rather than abandoning it because the stress is too intense.

Zen removal invokes a state of calm, which is the exact opposite of what can prevail in an anxious worker (and in anxiety-promoting therapy.) Zen calm is particularly helpful for those stuck in an unpleasant job they need when they cannot or do not want to find another. Rather than quitting their job, they learn to stay away from its stressful aspects (including people who cannot or will not give them a yes vote, if not on a daily basis, then at least occasionally).

> One patient had a job which she characterized as "three years of unspeakable bliss." She "rolled with the punches" for a while and it worked. She used the following mantra—really a way to lull herself into a state of calm. She thought of all the people who might abuse her personally and professionally, then reassured herself that they had no power over her, as follows: "Before my abusers affect me, first they have to find me; then they have to get my attention; then they have to make me understand that they intend to abuse me; then I have to stand there and let them abuse me; and then, if I stand there, I have to let their abuse get to me."

Quitting one's job is the ultimate Zen maneuver, but not the perfect solution. Mostly it is not a practical solution, and it can raise more emotional problems than it solves, because being unemployed can be worse than working under extremely stressful conditions.

Zen removal approaches are most effective when there is an external problem; while insight, not removal, is indicated when problems believed to be external are in fact imagined and/or self-created. Zen removal approaches are least effective with and can actually hurt individuals who are already too removed—especially those who have become eccentric. As we have seen, Zen can ultimately hurt the patient when removal creates real interpersonal difficulties that result in increasing isolation from friends and family.

Zen and related techniques, like meditation, must be used cautiously when doing effective work involves maintaining a degree of tension. Therapists also have to remember that in some cases the "inner voices" evoked in meditation can lead to psychotic decompensation (which can happen when those prone to detaching from reality are told to meditate, but instead turn completely inward and hallucinate).

Another problem with Zen is that it too often requires progressively upping the ante:

> One patient let herself be abused at work on a daily basis because she needed the money her job provided. Not minding and not reacting was for a while the most effective way she knew to get through the day without feeling stress. But, being human, eventually she began to take her abusers to heart and resent them. The punches began to hurt, and in spite of it all, she had to up the stakes, and quit.

### Family Therapy

Family therapy is supportive because it considers the well-being of the whole family, not just that of the patient, and because it enlists the family's assistance in helping the patient. It can avoid what happened to the writer whose case was presented previously:

> The writer working at home, who got a room of her own where no one bothered her, eventually took the next step—out the door. She bought a trailer and parked it next to her house and worked there all day long, not returning to the house until dinner time. Unfortunately, she forgot about her husband, who felt abandoned and became resentful. Finally, her husband, feeling lonely, began a therapeutic program of his own. This consisted of having an affair with a neighbor. He gradually lost interest in the marriage, and she became more and more frantic and eventually could not concentrate on her work at all. In this case the therapist should have asked how the husband was doing, found out about the husband's attitude about the treatment and any changes that were likely to occur to the patient as a result of the treatment, and possibly encouraged the husband to sit in on the therapy sessions.

Any major changes to be made should be not only worthwhile in themselves but advisable to all concerned. Family members often resent something about the patient's therapy. They always resent the intrusion of the therapist into family affairs. They believe, often correctly, that therapists think of their patients alone without considering the impact of change on everybody. And they do not always welcome improvement. Some spouses support, in a healthy way, the patient's efforts to get over an occupational disorder. Others are supportive, but for the wrong reasons. Some, for example, want to bask in the light of a writer's success for their own (not always mature) purposes. But the family members that should concern therapists the most are the ones that do not want the patient to get better, and thus undermine treatment. Some are afraid of their spouses' self-fulfillment because they do not feel fulfilled themselves and cannot stand anyone doing better than they are doing. For others it is merely the negative financial impact that bothers them (as happened when an insurance agent's salary and commissions vanished when he quit his job to become a full-time artist). In these situations spouses can, and will, defeat both the patient and the therapist in a number of ways. A common tactic is to get worse as the patient gets better, to show all concerned, "This is what you are doing to me." This is often wryly called "a complication of therapy." But in fact it is not a complication of good treatment, but a predictable result of bad treatment. The therapist, thinking only of the patient, presides over the family's demise with indifference or deliberately, and without the slightest hint of pity.

# 16

## A Step-by-Step Guide to Treating Occupational Disorders

This chapter outlines some steps for safely treating occupational disorders. In safe treatment no harm is done and the consequences of the treatment are not worse than the symptoms of the original disease. Of course, there are difficulties associated with even safe treatment. For example, it is difficult, even under the best of circumstances, for a therapist to relieve bad guilt without removing good guilt as well, making a worker who is too lackadaisical into one who is hopelessly lazy. But most complications are avoidable if the therapist is careful to do certain things, like make a diagnosis, and not to do others, like give advice without considering the personality of the patient who is getting the advice.

### STEP 1. RECOGNIZING
### THE PATIENT'S IMMEDIATE NEEDS

When patients first begin treatment, they often have pressing problems, are in acute distress and pain, and need a measure of support. A good way to give support is to convey a positive attitude. It is very reassuring for patients to hear that, although they feel alone and as if this has never happened to anyone else before, occupational disorders are very common, and probably all workers have them to an extent. It is also reassuring for patients to hear that, although it may seem at first disturbing to them that their occupational disorder is a condition that needs treatment, this is actually good news, for it means that it is something they can take responsibility for and overcome. Another reassuring message is that many occupational disorders can be at least considerably relieved, as long as the therapist pays attention to some of the do's and don'ts mentioned in this chapter. (Supportive therapy is discussed in Chapter 15.)

## STEP 2. RECOGNIZING DISORDER
## WHEN AND WHERE IT EXISTS

Often, occupational disorders are hidden and patients do not know they have them because their self-insight is compromised. Compromised insight may take several forms. Patients may not know they have problems. This may be because they are deniers who think they are functioning well when they are in fact functioning poorly and beneath capacity (doing a little and then fooling themselves into thinking they are doing a lot).

> A talented engineer had many designs in her, and that is where they stayed. She doodled but did not complete anything. She thought, "I know I'm creative; I don't actually have to prove it to the world." Then she dissipated her talent in collecting the creations of others, fussing with her computer and stereo systems and proudly displaying them to her friends, not as if she had merely put them together by following the instruction book but as if she had invented them herself. It was as if she confused having good taste with doing great things. She was too satisfied with herself for the admiration she got as a collector, and too little dissatisfied with herself for having settled for being a collector when she could have been an originator.

Some patients do not know they have problems because they are rationalizers who see their disordered behavior as normal behavior. They do not think they are withdrawn but think they are appropriately disinterested in a boring job. They do not give up art because they are afraid of being successful but because they think the world already has enough artists. They do not avoid politics because of stage fright but because of politics' effects on family life or because they cannot be honest in today's political climate. If they are women, they do not leave their jobs because they are not treated as well as men or the job makes them anxious, but to have a baby. If they are older individuals, they do not leave their jobs because they feel devalued on account of their age but to retire while they are still young enough to enjoy retirement, or to make way for a younger person who deserves the job more than they do and can do it better than they can. They are not inhibited or lazy, but have used up their talent or are slowing down because they are getting older and not better. Rationalizers think their problems are par for the course.

They expect that work makes everyone sick. They think that it is inevitable that word processors get hand pain after a few hours of work; that all actors have crippling stage fright; that all writers agonize forever and over every line; and that every one who stays on one job for any length of time eventually begins to hate it and burn out.

Some know they have problems but minimize them. Minimizers downplay the extent or implication of their difficulties and deny that their problems amount to a full-blown disorder.

Some know they have problems and know they are significant, but they do not know why they have them. Projectors blame others when they are to blame, relieving internal anxiety by blaming it on rational fear. They typically blame others for being hostile to them when they are hostile to others (incidentally, increasing their own self-esteem by lowering the self-esteem of others). In contrast, introjectors blame themselves when others are to blame. They blame themselves for being difficult people when they are in fact people working under difficult circumstances. They say they have a hard time doing an easy job when they are just having a bad time doing a hard one. Instead of denying that they are in conflict and blaming stress, they deny stress and blame conflict. They relieve fear by blaming anxiety, and lower their own self-esteem, in a self-sacrificial way, just to increase the self-esteem of others. Instead of blaming others to avoid guilt, they accept guilt to avoid blaming others.

> A patient blamed herself for being an ineffective worker when she should have blamed her job for being impossible to do. She thought she was working beneath her capacity and being a bad sport and a cry baby when in fact her company was pushing her to the breaking point. She thought she was working without realizing her potential because she did not have sufficient talent, or was hopelessly lazy, and that she as an individual had gone as far as she could go, considering her limitations. In fact, she had a job in which there were few incentives to do anything right, in which she was actively discouraged from doing anything right, and in which doing right was ultimately not even possible.

## STEP 3. MAKING A PROPER DIAGNOSIS

The next step after identifying a disorder's presence is to diagnose it precisely. While it is true that the occupational disorders are all alike in some ways (for example, all of them tend to contain elements of a fear of success), it is also true that there are as many different occupational disorders as there are different *DSM-IV* disorders—and proper treatment is that of the underlying *DSM-IV* disorder. Therapists make the worst therapeutic mistakes by not making a correct *DSM-IV* diagnosis. For example, they give advice without considering that what an individual patient can handle on the job is a function of the patient's personality or personality disorder, so that patients with a hard shell can use Zen techniques to handle an abusive environment better than those who are sensitive and take everything personally and to heart. They tell manics already too relaxed not to worry so much. They tell hypomanics already too busy to keep even busier. They encourage paranoids to face their fears when they still need to escape them by projecting. They tell schizotypal patients to meditate although they are unable to handle the introspection without decompensating. They treat brittle borderlines with insight therapy although that risks their flooding. Too often, they routinely refer patients to group therapy regardless of what bothers them, only to find that in large groups the depressives feel neglected, the paranoids feel singled out and spied on, and the hysterics cannot stand the competition from the other group members for the group leader.

Part of every diagnostic assessment is an assessment of the individual's conflict-free ego functioning—that is, his or her nonconflicted needs, desires, and goals. Therapists who do not consider these too often act like the realtor who pushes a house without asking the client about his or her life-style, or like the broker who pushes a stock without inquiring about the client's tolerance for risk. They typically give one-size-fits-all advice too freely and without thinking about the possible dangers. I make it a rule not to give advice to patients when I do not know them well, and sometimes even when I do. Usually, the best advice is, "Make up your own mind, and I will help you implement your decision." But what happened to the following patient is more typical of what actually happens in some therapists' offices:

> A psychiatrist almost ruined another psychiatrist's career with his superficial treatment of the psychiatrist-patient, giving him career advice he was not in a position to give.
>
> The psychiatrist-patient's father had in his own life abdicated in favor of an older brother, whom he put through medical school, although the father himself had really wanted to be the doctor. When the son, the psychiatrist-to-be, was born, he simply assigned him the role of "doctor" without so much as asking him what he wanted to do with his life. He then allowed the son no say in making his own career decisions. Trapping him like a rat, the father countermaneuvered his son back into the corner, with pleas, threats, and malingered illness, each time the psychiatrist-to-be tried to go his own way and not go to medical school. Unhappily for the son, he was bright enough to do many things, so that going to medical school remained an option, however undesirable.
>
> The father's persistence won, and the son went to medical school. The hour he was to begin, however, he had a mini-nervous breakdown. He cre-

ated a disturbance by screaming in public, in front of the medical school dormitory to which his father had delivered him, that he did not want to go to medical school, but instead wanted to get an advanced degree in English. In reply, the father merely clamped his iron hand on the son's soul by mentioning *sotto voce* that tuition money was available for the one thing but not for the other. As the psychiatrist-to-be later described it, "He dragged me, the helpless child, off to medical school, and I reacted like a helpless dog being dragged off to the ASPCA."

The psychiatrist-to-be described the first year in medical school as hell. He rarely slept well, or at all, partly because he was plagued throughout by urinary frequency. He thought he had mononucleosis, or Epstein-Barr, because he was constantly tired, depressed, and unable to function up to par. A few atypical lymphocytes even showed up on one blood smear.

But soon a miracle occurred. He became fascinated by dermatology. Now his "Epstein-Barr" lifted as if spontaneously. With his new fascination he felt he could conquer the world. He once again became interested in life and work. As he described it, "Like a phoenix bird, I arose again from the ashes."

"But, alas," as he continued, "the hunting season on phoenix birds had just begun. I was gay, and my father, predictably, not only wanted me to be a doctor, but also wanted me to be a straight doctor. He suspected I was gay, so to find out he entrapped me by saying the family was going on vacation, knowing I would bring home a friend for sex. But instead of going on vacation, he went to the neighbor's house to spy on me from the neighbor's window. He came roaring back when the blinds shut and the lights went off, and he caught me in the act. Then he made me go to a psychiatrist to be cured of my homosexuality." Now the threat to withdraw educational funds terrorized the son because he *wanted* to be in medical school; he *wanted* to be a dermatologist.

As the son continued, "The psychiatrist I saw was not competent. One day he asked me, 'What do you want to specialize in?' When I answered, 'dermatology,' my psychiatrist replied, 'Foolish thing to want to do. You should go into psychiatry. That's the up and coming field. Dermatologists don't make any money. And no one respects them. You know, all they do is dry it if it's wet, and wet it if it's dry. Or, if it's purple, they paint it red; and if it's red, they paint it purple.'

A few ill-considered words tossed off without thought, yet they made all the difference. I, never one to do what I wanted to do guilt free, passively complied and derailed my career, all over again."

To ice the cake, later, when he became a psychiatrist, and was working on what was the wrong job for him, his psychiatrist, instead of suggesting that he look for a new job, pushed him to work harder at the job he already had. As the patient subsequently put it, "That was in effect like fertilizing a plant that was stunted because there wasn't enough light to grow by. All that did was burn the roots and create a pale weak stalk that toppled over, collapsing under its own weight."

The story has a happy ending. When the patient's father died, the patient was in effect released. He had made enough money to retire—one of the few benefits he could name of having gone to medical school. The day the father was buried he closed his practice. He picked up his pen. He was free at last, free to do what he wanted to do, not what his father wanted him to do. He was free to write. His first work he revealingly entitled "Peace in the Land." His second he entitled, equally revealingly, "The Song of the Nightingale."

Therapists who do not make proper diagnoses will not design therapy to fit a patient's specific *DSM-IV* Axis I (clinical disorder) diagnosis, Axis II (personality disorder) diagnosis, and Axis IV (psychosocial and environmental problem) diagnosis. They will offer their patients a one-size-fits-all treatment approach that either does not help them or makes them worse.

Some of us are familiar from the media with how some job counselors deal with downsized workers as a homogenous group by telling them that their loyalty must be to their profession, not to their job—that is, "you are an accountant, not an accountant for the Water Company." Perhaps they are trying to reassure them that their fate does not depend on the vagaries of employment with a given company, and to remind them that they are and will be okay because, although they may not have their job, they still have their profession. But while this is helpful reassurance for some, it is frightening to others. There are many people out there who are chameleon-like personalities whose identity depends on their identifications. Such people feel chaotic when they are not part of a larger group. For them downsizing is disastrous not only because they are losing a job but because they are losing the group support which is the source of their identity. Such individuals need not reassurance that they will survive no matter what because they are professionals, but help to reidentify with a new group or organization, to get over the shock of being cut loose from the old one.

It is important to consider the patient's particular life circumstances and problems (*DSM-IV* Axis IV) in making a complete diagnostic assessment and instituting treatment. For example, a patient who owns a house and has a family in school is more job and location dependent, and more likely to respond negatively to losing a job, than one who has very young children and rents a home. The personalities and problems of the other people in the patient's life also must be considered. Getting anger out regardless of who is the reason for the anger and/or who will be its target may result in others respecting the patient for his or her honesty and courage, or it may destroy relationships with important people the patient needs (who may see the honesty not as courageous and constructive but as rash and foolish). Often, it is divisive to speak up and tell others how we really feel. Abreaction is a useful psychotherapeutic technique. During the session, speaking up and speaking one's mind help to discharge tension and prevent flooding. But therapy is a special situation, and what works there may not work elsewhere. Frequently, telling a stress-inducing boss what the worker thinks of the boss is offensive and creates more stress, especially for workers who are job dependent. As one worker put it, "I am right to be afraid of being honest, and so it's better to keep quiet. At work I have a great deal more to fear than fear itself. I've learned that at work, as in relationships, making peace is always better than making waves."

In summary, therapists who fail to diagnose properly and treat accordingly will view things simplistically and offer a "cure" that involves following their instincts. They will use common sense based on what feels good or is comfortable. But doing effective therapeutic work is difficult, and it is not always fun. No amount of pop psychology can change this.

### STEP 4. DETERMINING WHAT IS CAUSING THE DISORDER

Therapists who do not determine the specific cause of an occupational disorder are not finding out what is causing the problem so that they can fix it by going to the heart of the matter.

A study of causality starts with a developmental and dynamic assessment of the individual and the individual's disorder. In particular, therapists have to differentiate patients with an exogenous disorder, who are suffering because of their circumstances, from patients with an endogenous disorder, who are suffering because of themselves. In simple terms, exogenous disorders are the equivalent of what psychiatry calls the reactive, adjustment, or posttraumatic stress disorders. They are, in effect, a foreign body in the eye, a not-me affair, something experienced passively, not created actively. If patients contribute, it is modestly, for reasons ranging from a philosophical bent (in which they question their jobs because they question the meaning of life) to hypersensitivity to stress (due to a rigid inflexibility, which makes it difficult for them to adapt to any stress). In contrast to exogenous disorders, endogenous disorders are due to mental disorders in individuals who are not, at least at first, under significant stress on the job. As previously mentioned, they are the product of a worker's personality, personality disorder, or other emotional disorder. This is just another way of saying that the occupational endogenous disorders are 9 to 5 expressions of larger *DSM-IV* disorders, ranging from schizophrenia to personality disorder. As we will see, patients with an exogenous disorder need advice, support, and environmental manipulation more than insight, while it is the other way around for patients with an endogenous disorder. Patients who develop RSI because of improper posture at their computer need a new computer chair, while patients who develop RSI because of emotional conflicts about their job need not a new computer chair but the proverbial old analytic couch. While patients with an endogenous disorder need to recognize how they are partly or wholly active participants in their problem, this is not true in the exogenous disorders, and suggesting that it is is, in effect, blaming the victim.

Of course, it is not always easy to distinguish endogenous from exogenous disorder. This holds true even in what at first appear to be obviously stressful situations, such as being downsized. For example, I once worked in a well-known New York hospital that was always downsizing; there were always workers unhappy because they had been downsized. Few of them, however, tried to understand why they were downsized. Few of them admitted their own role in what happened to them. Most blamed impersonal factors, such as the economy or administrative policy, or personal ones, such as their boss's irrationality. But while this was not invariably the case, those who were downsized were often the politically inept ones—that is, they were people who knew and could handle their field better than they knew and could handle their enemies.

Bureaucracies provide us with ready-made instances of the difficulty in distinguishing exogenous from endogenous disorders. It is a cliché that bureaucrats are passive people who carve out personally defined parameters that delimit what they will, but mostly what they will not, do. Then, when asked to do something other than what they usually do, they reply, "That's not my job." However, often their individual passivity is only a reflection of their organization's incompetence. They refuse to go that extra mile because they have been asked not to, or have been stopped somewhere along the way.

A government internist/supervisor refuses to help a psychiatrist evaluate if an antihistamine can be safely given to an insomniac psychiatric patient who has severe heart damage, for which he is on multiple medications. The internist takes the easy way out and attacks not the problem but the psychiatrist. He complains, "You shouldn't have to ask me these things. How dangerous can antihistamines be? You can get them without a prescription in the drug store." But the real reason is, "I can't be bothered. I'll let you worry about psychiatric patients. I have enough of my own patients to keep me busy."

The psychiatrist under such circumstances had only a limited number of choices. He could fight; complain to the authorities; or take the easy way out and prescribe the medication anyway, pushing pills, regardless of the consequences, and then close the books on the decision and any mistakes he happened to make. He chose the latter alternative.

This psychiatrist is now a passive person. But is his passivity primarily a personal problem, or is it a justified and even a "healthy" reaction to the specific, unhealthy circumstances in which he works?

It is hard to tell, and, as in most situations in life, the truth lies somewhere in between. Most occupational disorders, like many medical disorders and like much of life itself, lie somewhere on a continuum between purely exogenous and purely endogenous causation. Most or all occupational disorders result from a combination of external difficulty and personal mishandling of the difficulty (for example, the worker cannot deal with a difficult critical boss because of the worker's own medical or psychological problems). While there are some jobs that are so bad that they are intolerable, most intolerable situations are made intolerable, or more intolerable, because of an individual's witting or unwitting contribution to what is undeniably a difficult situation. For many such workers, occupational disorder is only different from a one-two punch in that in the former, first you are down and then they hit you.

## STEP 5. TREATING THE DISORDER

The treatment methods outlined in this section are not only for counselors and psychotherapists. They are also for companies who want to develop preventive strategies for avoiding occupational disorder in their workers and methods for handling their occupational disorder once it has developed.

### Treating Exogenous Disorders

Sometimes a worker's exogenous disorder is due to bad working conditions.

Many doctors find health maintenance organizations (HMOs) stressful places to work because they focus on quantity not quality, on numbers of patients treated inexpensively, not on how well or effectively. In a government clinic (spiritually an HMO), initial diagnostic interviews—which can take up to two hours—are counted as one visit, the same as two-minute medication follow-up visits. This virtually forces physicians, who have to keep their numbers up, to treat first and make a proper diagnosis next—if ever—a difficult spot for many physicians to be in.

At other times it is merely the stress inherent in any job—what we refer to when we say, "There is a certain amount of tension that is part of working for a living; that's why they pay you."

While we often hear of how therapists blame everything on stress (that is, misdiagnose an endogenous as an exogenous disorder), therapists can just as easily misdiagnose an exogenous disorder as endogenous. They accuse a worker of being paranoid just because he or she objects to being treated badly in reality. They accuse a worker of having a low IQ although the pseudodullness is a predictable result of having been assigned a job that is outside of one's area of interest or expertise, or beneath one's capacity. They make personality disorder diagnoses when the worker is just in an impossible position. My personal experience taught me that training psychiatric residents is difficult to impossible, not because of the teacher's personal problems but because when there are discrepancies between theoretical and actual practice, it becomes difficult to teach the students what they should do, according to the textbooks, without contradicting what one's superiors are actually doing (not according to the textbooks).

The external factors may be interpersonal or situational ones that negatively affect the ability to work. I call people or situations that interfere with an individual's ability to work "blockogenic" or "depressogenic," depending on how specific an impact they have. (I have adapted both terms from the term *carcinogenic*, used in cancer research.) As we saw in Chapter 11, handling blockogenic people and situations is an important therapeutic priority and focus for all workers whose occupational disorder is mainly caused by what other people think about, say to, and do to them.

> A boss was what Joann Lublin (1994) in the *Wall Street Journal* called a career-buster (p. B1). She viewed anyone with talent, including those whom she identified as her best friends, as her rivals. She could not tolerate anyone doing better then she because that might mean their equaling her, or even taking over. She put talented people in their place by identifying and stressing the weaknesses in any of their arguments and the flaws in any of their suggestions, so that a good idea became all no good if it were not perfect. And she put talented people in their place by emphasizing the negative aspects of any of their positive behaviors, so that being cooperative was equated with being overly dependent. She particularly had it in for those with money because she was in debt, those with wives and children because she was single, those who were beautiful because she thought herself ugly, those who were publicly recognized because she was working in obscurity, and those who got promoted from their position because she had gone as far as she could go in hers.

There are four possible ways to deal with blockogenic people and situations. I call these the four A's: accepting, adapting to, avoiding, or altering the world.

A housewife was unable to cook because her husband complained of every dish she made until the only thing she felt safe and comfortable doing was chopping Chinese vegetables and letting him wok them when he came home. One therapist told her that she had an oedipal problem and that her marriage was in trouble because her husband reminded her of her father. Another emphasized not her oedipal problem but the problem of being put down—and suggested she deal with it by deciding among: accepting her husband as he is; ignoring his troublesome behavior; changing him; or changing her living arrangements.

One therapist told a worker who was depressed because others were making her depressed to study her internalized hostility. But another said that what she needed more was a plan for avoiding the people who were stirring up the hostility that she was internalizing. For example, she had to deal with an envious co-worker who, just when she was at her creative best, put her down directly and indirectly by undermining her behind her back (with her colleagues) by telling outright lies about what she had said about them, just to get her into trouble.

One therapist, who was treating an artist whose hand was cramped because her parents, instead of supporting her endeavors, were pushing her to do something with her life and "get a real job," suggested that she resolve her conflicts over exposing herself sexually, in public, in her art. Another therapist told her that what she needed was to follow the "distancing formula," which is, neurosis = 1 ÷ physical proximity to one's parents.

A performing artist with stage fright wanted to continue to perform (some do, some do not), so he had to adapt by accepting his anxiety and learning to live with the first terrifying five minutes on stage. His counterpart, a writer, adapted by accepting abuse from a world of harsh critics, who proclaimed their fairness and honesty although they were completely unfair and the only kind of honesty they knew was of the brutal kind. In contrast, a writer who wanted to continue to write but could not accept her critic's negativity about her work adapted by adjusting her methods and goals without actually changing careers. She changed how and what she wrote, and also did some work in the related field of editing. And a patient with RSI who did not want to yield to her disability adapted both by learning to live with the pain and by changing the way she worked. A dental hygienist, she came up with an ideal solution. Her hands hurt from scraping away at a patient's tartar, a process that required exerting considerable pressure, day in and day out. She needed the job, so she compromised. She stopped doing everything manually and used some of the new machines available to her, which she previously did not use because of a need to do things the hard way.

## Treating Endogenous Disorders

Endogenous occupational disorders can take many forms, ranging from marginal artistic productivity in free-lance writers excessively depressed over their first rejection to repetitive strain injury not due to a poorly designed computer keyboard but to internal factors, as when a hand syndrome is due to

- a fear of making a mistake (being a failure) (the syndrome assures that patients will not, because they cannot, make an error)
- a fear of getting ahead (being a success) (the syndrome reassuringly holds patients back from achieving anything worthwhile)
- a fear of expressing angry emotions (the syndrome is an alternative to striking out at the boss)
- a fear of expressing sexual emotions (the syndrome is a way to displease a boss to avoid getting too close).

As previously mentioned, it is common for therapists to diagnose endogenous as exogenous disorders. They attribute an endogenous depression to downsizing, bad luck, noxious fumes, a poorly designed computer keyboard, or (for those more analytically inclined) a boss acting like one's castrative father or depriving mother. Therapists who misdiagnose an endogenous as an exogenous disorder and then focus exclusively on, and respond only to, the exogenous aspects that are always to be found in any endogenous disorder will do two things wrong:

1. They will use common-sense approaches for problems that make less common sense than they think. Writers usually do not block because they do not have a room of their own to work in (Agatha Christie worked from the kitchen table), and advising them to get over block by getting a room of their own, or sharpening their pencils and going at it, usually has more to do with the therapist's fantasy than with the patient's problems.
2. They will buy into the patient's paranoia. They will join the patient in blaming the company for everything, and in general go along with patients' need to make everything that happens to them into a not-me affair: not me but company policy, the boss, my long hours, my old-style computer keyboard, or (especially) my illness.

Therapists too often forget that their patients are like the biblical Sampson, who (although truly and sorely provoked) brought the temple down on his own head. Just as workers in the wrong field should not be subjected to an inordinate amount of psychotherapy to get them to adjust (when it might be better to get them to change professions), patients in the right field who cannot adapt to a given job may need a personality change, not a job change, and not a vacation from stress but a return from the undeserved psychic vacation they are already on to work hard on themselves, on their problems, and on their work.

I once had a patient out on sick leave whose boss was so eager to fire him that he did not even wait for him to come back to work before giving him the pink slip. Instead he sent it to him at home—and not through the ordinary mail. He sent it overnight service, via Federal Express.

From my encounters with this patient, I could see why the boss was so eager to be rid of him.

The patient's official and only diagnosis was carpal tunnel syndrome. For this patient, that was an inadequate diagnosis, first because it failed to reflect his personality problems, which were severe (part of him—not the world—and at least as important in causing his work-related difficulty as any physical factor), and second because it was a not-me diagnosis that allowed him to blame outside forces for his inability to do his work, to avoid looking to himself as a significant source of his occupational problem. Naturally, he eagerly embraced the diagnosis and even accepted surgery for it, because that gave him the ammunition he needed to continue to behave badly as usual, and to do so guilt free.

I diagnosed the personality problems when they appeared in the transference. He complained to the administration about me whenever he could, and I think for no good reason. For example, when he asked me, "What is my diagnosis?" and I replied, "I'm not certain yet; let's work on it" (a true and honest assessment), he saw me as incompetent and asked for a change of doctors. One session later, before the change actually took place, he came in intoxicated from multiple unknown substances. He denied being intoxicated and, in angry response to a question, poured a can of soda first on my rug and then on me. Then, as if in a free association to what he had just done, he confessed to me that he recently disciplined one of his young children by throwing him against a wall. When I told him I would have to report this to the authorities as a case of child abuse, he told me that if I did so he would throw me against the wall too.

This patient avoided responsibility for his problems by blaming a physical cause. He entirely failed to account for the role he, as distinct from his body, played in his own occupational disorder. An operation would not make him better. To get better he had to take responsibility for himself and change his hostile and self-defeating behavior.

The following are some technical considerations in treating endogenous occupational disorders.

### Resolving Conflict

Because the endogenous disorders are, at least in the acute phase, symptoms of an underlying familiar *DSM-IV* disorder, they will, like any other symptom, arise in conflict and effect a kind of solution to the conflict. Because the symptomatic solution is always an unsatisfactory, unhealthy one, patients have to explore their conflicts so that they can either become less conflicted or find a new compromise between each side of the conflict—one better than the one they are presently using.

> For example, after a downsizing spared him, one individual developed severe chronic back pain. It was not crippling and he could continue to work, but only intermittently and always with some degree of discomfort. The symptom expressed and satisfied both sides of his conflict about staying on. In sparing his ability to work, it expressed how part of him desired to stay on; but in compromising his ability to work, it expressed how part of him was guilty about being a survivor, and remaining behind, while others had to leave. In effect, he was allowing himself to continue, but as a "downsized person." A better solution than tithing this way was simply to accept his good fortune, guilt free, and without any need to self-punish.

### *Dealing with Primary and Secondary Gain*

It is always difficult to treat occupational disorders because they are associated with considerable gain, which makes symptomatic solutions to problems as welcome as they are unwelcome. Even workers who complain about a disorder cannot live without it, so they create and maintain it. First there is the primary gain of the disorder—workers invite it in and let it stay, although it is like an unwelcome guest that eats all the food, dirties the house, takes money, and never gives thanks because it is at least some company and because, however unpleasant it may be, it serves a purpose of relieving anxiety and depression (say by providing the punishment guilty workers need). Second, there is the secondary gain of the disorder. Occupational disorders have a practical, useful side. In one case a purpose of a writer's block was to keep an artist grinding away at a lucrative job so that he could make the money his spouse wanted to spend on transitory pleasures; while in another case a chronic pain condition kept a worker from being successful to satisfy a husband who wanted to be cared for and felt a sick person who stayed at home would do a better job of caring for him than a healthy one who went to work.

Therapists often shy away from a frank discussion of the gain of illness. But they should at least attempt to deal with primary and secondary gain by helping patients rethink priorities and give up illusory or self-destructive goals.

### Dealing with Lack of Talent

Therapists should err on the side of treating apparent lack of ability as if it is disability. Seemingly untalented people who have nothing to work with, or seemingly lazy people who will not work, often turn out to be inhibited people who cannot work. Like almost everyone else, they have little Mozarts inside struggling to get out, but they do not let them out. Like most people, they could make it closer to the top if only they would put one foot over the other and climb the corporate ladder, safe in the knowledge that the ability to climb comes from actually doing the climbing, more than the other way around.

# 17

## Handling Low Self-Esteem and Guilt

### LOW SELF-ESTEEM

When we speak of low self-esteem, we are usually not speaking of warranted low self-esteem, in which one's low self-image is appropriate to one's behavior and the remedy involves changing one's behavior. We are usually speaking of unwarranted low self-esteem, in which one's low self-image is inappropriate, considering one's behavior, and the remedy involves changing not oneself but one's self-view.

Unwarranted low self-esteem (from now on called just low self-esteem) is not one but several problems with a multitude of causes to account for its different manifestations.

Low self-esteem can develop because workers too readily compare themselves to others and their achievements, regardless of the appropriateness of a specific comparison. The annals of occupational disorder are full of people who fail because of an exclusive need to go others—sometimes very talented others—one better; and professional (really jealous) rivalry, not self-fulfillment, becomes the order of the day. Workers do not accept themselves unless they think they equal or best the competition. As they work, they keep one eye open to what others who are successful can do and are doing. A writer of textbooks compares her small glory to that of a writer of popular novels, and then forms her self-view accordingly. One physician compared the sales figures of his medical books to the sales figures of the books of Dr. Norman Vincent Peale. A poet compared her remuneration from getting her poems published to a photographer's remuneration from getting his articles into the local photographic journals. In too many such cases, self-loathing and self-abuse follow, and all work stops. Reading

Donna Perlmutter's (1994) article on the pianist Van Cliburn's competitive relationship with the pianist John Browning makes me wonder if Van Cliburn's career deteriorated because, instead of practicing the piano, he preoccupied himself with comparing himself to the other pianist (as he might have been preoccupied with comparing himself to his father). Letters from Melville to Nathaniel Hawthorne (1981, originally published 1851) reveal a similar need for the first man (who believed himself unsuccessful) to compare himself to the second man, whose success he envied (p. 534). Most of us make the same counterproductive mistake (although on a lesser level) that Ravel made by wanting to be Mozart. What is wrong with being Ravel?

> A speaker who at the last minute replaced a famous psychiatrist, Doctor X, harped on how he was "no Doctor X." True. But this speaker showed up, and the audience was happy to hear him—until he reminded them of what they were missing.

In males, a fear of sexual inferiority is often at the root of the compulsive need to make comparisons.

> One male movie star's life revolved too much around his own and others' reactions to his acting. He evaluated himself constantly and worried excessively about what others were thinking. Next his work suffered, first because he was constantly distracted, and second because he constantly got depressed when he discovered, as he predictably did, that someone out there had more than he had. Feeling professionally inferior compared to a shadowy "them," he began to compete fiercely on a professional level, but because his solution was not directed to the underlying problem, it did not satisfy him. So he moved on to competing on a personal level, by displaying and hoping to be admired, literally as well as figuratively, for his genitalia.

Low self-esteem can develop because of excessively high standards. In some individuals low self-esteem is the result of their inability to accept that they are minor talents. They feel there is something wrong with being a minor talent, and they dislike themselves unless they are tops in their field—or even in the world.

> Every time one worker began to work, she blocked because she had not one but six tasks, really secret agendas:
> - First, but not foremost, she was working;
> - Second, she was constantly critiquing, really panning, her own work instead of just doing it;
> - Third, she was working to become rich and famous;

- Fourth, she was working to get approval from her co-workers, her boss, and ultimately from her parents;
- Fifth, she was contributing to posterity, taking her personal place in the ages, and writing her own entry for the time capsule; and
- Sixth, she was writing her own epitaph for the magnificent stone she planned for her cemetery plot.

In others, high standards are intended to prevent low self-esteem from developing. A perfectionist with an originality fetish expected too much of himself, tried too hard, became overwhelmed and depressed, and could not work because he discovered, each time he tried to do something, that it had been done before. He overlooked that audiences do not storm out of a room holding their ears because a composer stole a tune, but they actually have an infinite capacity for sameness and a positive desire for repetition, even something plagiarized.

Low self-esteem can develop because of shame. Shame can be a guilty overreaction to erotic and/or angry feelings and fantasies released as work progresses. It can also be a silent agreement with the social stigma society attaches to a given job, profession, or professional status. For example, the term *blue collar* has a faintly disdainful ring to it, as if artisans are somehow inferior to artists.

People who are ashamed of themselves spend an inordinate amount of time and energy trying to hide who and what they are both from themselves and others. They do things just to please other people. A writer writes (really edits her writing) to give her critics, lovers, and editors what she thinks they want from her, using a style that is not as personally meaningful as the one she would use if left to her own devices. Scientists retract their ideas if they are currently not widely accepted, thinking that there is something wrong with their observations when there is really only something wrong with current theory.

In the 1980s, for example, therapists collectively recommended that their patients get a divorce if their marriage was imperfect. They based this recommendation on the view, popular at the time, that self-realization was the most important thing, and that there were only two cries worth hearing: "If you are not all good, then you are all bad" and "Me first." They closed their eyes to how most marriages are imperfect, and their minds to how two people (the patient and the patient's spouse or lover) are involved in, and responsible for, one problem marriage. The result of the me-ism was self-ism, and the divorces that resulted were both selfish and sadistic. I remember one patient who, at her therapist's urging, gave up a perfectly good job and husband to devote her time to expressing herself by going to the disco all night every night, so that the "real me" could emerge. The therapist with low self-esteem, who thought twice about recommending inappropriate behavior like this, recommended it anyway, following not his or her instincts but the crowd. In contrast, therapists with high self-esteem not only noticed the problem but also thought, "The theory must be wrong" and shamelessly developed a new theory—namely, that an imperfect marriage, in many instances, is better than no marriage at all and is better than spending night after night at the disco.

Self-respect is an early casualty when ideals are compromised solely out of shame.

A doctor at an HMO prided herself on her caution and care in treating patients. In her clinic she always asked for consultation when she did not know enough about what she was doing to do it right. But this was politically inexpedient. It made more work for everybody. Most of the people there thought, "If she doesn't know that, what else doesn't she know?"

Another doctor, her associate, was mainly interested in impressing the management and pleasing the patients. He only cared about doing the politically and financially expedient thing, and doing what his patients wanted. In one incident, a patient with severe glaucoma needed to be given a medication for depression. Some prudent physicians in these circumstances would insist on obtaining advice from an ophthalmologist before prescribing an antidepressant. But this doctor wanted most of all to avoid looking foolish and bothering the eye doctor, who worked by the hour and believed, "The fewer patients the better." He also wanted to avoid defying an organization whose interest was mainly in sparing staff to provide care at the lowest possible cost per patient. Finally, he also wanted to avoid delaying giving the patient the quick fix the patient wanted, because that was not the way to be popular (at least with some patients). So he gave the medication without asking for an eye consultation. In short, instead of doing what was right, he did what was acceptable. He was less the doctor than the politician.

The first doctor, noticing how everyone liked her colleague better than they liked her, was ashamed of her behavior and gave up her ideals to be like the second doctor. Others liked her better, she made more money, and she kept her job. But she hated herself for what she had become, and eventually she had to leave her job just to maintain what vestige remained of her progressively deteriorating positive self-image.

Low self-esteem can develop because of real abuse. At first, low self-esteem is an appropriate response to humiliation. Eventually the problem gets worse, when individuals blame themselves for the humiliation and feel that it was deserved because provoked. One doctor felt humiliated and considered fleeing a perfectly good job because no one any longer ever asked him a question about his field. The reality was that they did not ask him a question not because *he* was defective but because *they* were defective—they were disinterested not only in his field, but also in almost everything else.

In such cases, low self-esteem appears when workers forget that the people who abuse them do so because they have their own problems. As mentioned previously, they forget to consider the source. They forget that some bosses got to be bosses because they are competitive people, and that competitive people predictably knock their employees because they see them as the competition. They forget that many bosses got where they are and do what they do because they are psychopaths, who deliberately and consciously plan to get immediate personal gain for themselves (in a hospital, all the referrals; or in an industry, a desired promotion or an employee on the cheap). They are the inspiration for what is a whole industry out there devoted to developing psychopathic gifts into techniques for lowering the self-esteem of employees to advance their own cause (or that of the corporation) in some palpable way.

A patient said her boss reminded her of her car salesman she had when she traded in her car for a new one. When the salesman first looked at her car, he said, "You made a terrible mistake by not cleaning the windows. You should have known that first impressions are what count."

This man was putting her car (and her) down for a purpose. If he put her and her car down, he did not have to pay her so much for the car. He got away with it because he knew that his customers, like most people, tended to put anyone who even remotely seemed to be in a position of power into a position of authority, a position which the salesman occupied for the moment because he was the one giving advice and holding the purse strings. This salesman was a good salesmen because he knew how his customers tended to turn a professional into a personal transaction, so that instead of a good deal they seek a gratifying relationship. He knew that some people are so desperate to be admired, praised, and loved that they will even seek love from strangers.

The patient mused, "It worked, like it works for my boss, because by the time he lowers my self-esteem I do not feel good enough about myself to expect much, or to complain about the little I actually get.

Workers often forget that some bosses are driven by neurotic needs, which are in turn based on unresolved childhood problems that reappear in their adult lives—in effect, in their transference to their employees. A boss with a lingering, unresolved childhood problem with sibling rivalry may see each of his employees as a brother or sister who is a threat to his being the number one sibling; and he may ruin their careers to keep them down so that he can be the captain of the sibship. Or he may see them as a brother or sister who is a threat to his unique status with the mother, and get rid of them so that he can be the only one left at home for mother to love.

Workers also forget that criticism goes with the territory. Workers who realize that few people ever get a note from their boss that says, "Who says that there are no more Einsteins in this world?" do not feel so cowed when they are criticized. The same holds true for writers who recognize that few (if any) of them have been spared the penultimate critical paragraph in the reviews of their works—the one in which all the flaws are pointed out so that critics can show *their* critics that they are awake and smart (or so they can promote a rival book they are writing).

Low self-esteem can develop when individuals masochistically seek out those who devastate them. (Masochism is discussed further in Chapter 8.)

Low self-esteem can be due to hypersensitivity (for example, the kind in which workers personalize what are exclusively professional issues). The boss rejects the person, not the work; the critic hates the composer, not the music. Or a hypersensitive worker may not view professional as personal criticism and rejection but see professional criticism for what it is, but take it too hard.

Finally, low self-esteem can develop simply as the result of a miscalculation. In a typical sequence, individuals confess to the world that they are lowly as a way to self-criticize before others can criticize them. They jokingly put themselves down in an attempt to gain points for being funny and/or insightful and honest. But they lose points by being self-indulgent and self-destructive. Although others disparage their negative self-view to their face, behind their back they agree with the view. Such people may be the life of the party, really the clown of the moment, but they are at the bottom of the promotion and the top of the downsizing list.

## GUILT

Guilt is a major contributing factor to occupational disorders and one that is very common among workers. Guilty workers feel that they have done, or might do, something wrong. Ashamed of themselves, they withdraw instead of working. They suffer in silence. They spend an inordinate amount of time thinking others are displeased with them, do not like them, and want to punish them. They try to repair the damage by pleasing others and asking for absolution, when instead they should be doing their work.

Most workers with conflicts due to guilt do not stop working entirely. Instead they make compromises. A degree of success is permitted as long as it falls short of the mark. This way, workers can reassure themselves that "I succeed, but not too much." They produce, but not as much as they could have produced. What they produce they contaminate or compromise. For example, Borodin plans the opera *Prince Igor* but writes a 10-movement cantata. A well-known humorist plans a saga but writes an anecdote. A CEO plans an acquisition but diworseifies. What they do comes out safe, though sorry.

There are many conscious and unconscious reasons for guilt. Conscious guilt is often appropriate—with full awareness of what was done wrong and why. Unconscious guilt is often inappropriate and originates in the following ways:

*The instincts.* That is, it originates in sexuality/homosexuality or hostility, which can flare when workers become emotionally involved in their work and in relationships with the people at work.

> I previously discussed the dental hygienist with hand cramp who was misdiagnosed as having arthritis. Her problem moving her hands when cleaning teeth arose mainly when she thought how much she hated her boss, and how he mistreated her by overworking her and not providing her with a room that she could call her own.
>
> A facet of her anger at the boss was her feeling that he was not like a mother to her. She revealed this in her associations, for each time she talked of how he mistreated her, she next spoke of her plans to retire to go to live with her aged mother in a retirement village.
>
> Consciously she believed she wanted to retire because she hated working for this man. That was true. But another reason was an unconscious one: She needed to escape not only from him but also from herself. She had to get away from her own hostility toward him, and from the consequences of that hostility: intense guilt. It was this which prompted her to consider atoning in one of two possible ways. Either she could leave her job, and go take care of her mother (causing herself professional and financial hardship and ruining her personal life); or she could stay on her job and suffer from her painful cramped hands. The cramp then simultaneously represented a wish to strangle the boss for not loving her enough, guilt about wanting to do so, and a punishment to ease the guilt—all combined in one "overdetermined" symptom.

*The conscience.* Conscience problems often originate in primitive, scrupulous morality. For example, some workers fail because they believe that making money (or all achievement and success) is an unholy thing.

*The ego.* Guilt can originate in cognitive errors. This can happen when individuals fail to make necessary distinctions, such as the ones between (1) thinking hostile thoughts and doing hostile things; (2) being active and being hostile (for example, attacking one's work and attacking the people at one's work); and (3) being active and being sexual (for example, completing and climaxing).

*Development.* Inappropriate guilt that originates earlier in life can carry over later in life into the workplace. One CEO could not buy the clothes he needed for work because whenever he did he thought, "I am doing this with the money my dead parents left me, money I feel I don't deserve to have because I hated them when I was young and they were alive." Childhood oedipal guilt and guilt over sibling rivalry are significant sources of inappropriate guilt later in life in the workplace. When oedipal guilt contributes to adult guilt, we often see survivor guilt, in which the haves think only of the have nots, and success guilt, in which every gain is forbidden. Both guilts make workers want to fail.

Specific interactions often set the stage for specific guilt-inducing adult cognitive errors (see also Chapter 13). For example, the belief that similar things = the same thing, leading to inappropriate guilt due to the belief that professional rivalry is like professional murder, can originate in excessive parental prohibition of all assertiveness because it is deemed aggressiveness. The cognitive error of some = all (a cause of guilty depression in many workers who cannot accept the slightest degree of criticism, however constructive, without seeing themselves as having been completely savaged) can originate in the parental view that run-of-the-mill childhood imperfections are serious flaws.

*Atavism.* Guilt can originate in the individual as part of a throwback to an early evolutionary stage, as when the primitive person in the worker says, "What you do has little relevance to life's important matters. You are doing nothing to promote survival of the race and food collection for the pack." It is this primitive voice that tells artists who work at home the equivalent of, "Get out and hunt instead of staying at home just painting on the walls of caves."

## TREATMENT

The following treatment methods can help patients handle low self-esteem and guilt.

*Developing superficial insight.* Workers without adequate superficial insight do not know that their self-esteem is excessively low and that they are unusually guilty. Instead they feel actually worthless and appropriately guilty, and think themselves untalented when in fact they are gifted, or think themselves bad when in fact they are no better or worse than anyone else.

*Developing deep insight.* Workers have to see how they contaminate their work with inappropriate and excessive instinctual charge and the detritus of developmental fixations.

*Not acting out a distorted self-image.* Workers who dislike themselves and feel guilty about everything they do often act accordingly and defeat themselves. Some hurt themselves by giving up a successful business to become unsuccessful artists or writers. Others give up being successful artists or writers to be successful, or unsuccessful, depending on how you look at it, in business. While many work, most do so beneath capacity. Or, viewing their works as being imperfect, they work up to par but then tear up what they do and throw it away.

*Considering the source.* As mentioned previously, workers develop low self-esteem and guilt because they are criticized *and* they think their critics are justified in criticizing them. They fail to recognize that their critics have problems of their own. In the vernacular, they fail to consider where their abusers are "coming from."

Often, negative judgments speak the most volumes about the ones doing the judging. Most judging looks rational, but it is not, because it is a self-statement projected outward to become a statement about others. In more technical terms, more often than not, abusers do their abusing in a state of narcissistic transference to their victims, as the following cases show.

A corporate boss devalued a worker and his work, but the devaluation was a transferential one, for he was merely using the other's work as a stimulus to express a personal dyspepsia already in place. He disliked this worker's formlessness, what he complained was his "weaving, indecisive, impressionistic style." His complaints were excessive, for the worker got everything done and on time; although, admittedly, he only got it done after backing and filling, but without wasting time in toto. The real reason the boss complained so much was that he himself feared becoming loose and amorphous like this man. What he really feared was that if he let down his controls and relaxed, forbidden sexual and angry feelings might come through.

Another boss disliked an admittedly too-careful clerk's "thick and ponderous" methods—that is, in the boss's opinion the worker paid too much attention to and got stuck in all the details, although the details were necessary ones. In his criticisms the boss was telling us less about the clerk than about his own relationship with his father—a man the boss disliked as a "square, peasant man, heavy, predictable, and drab—however sincere." To be the opposite of his father, the boss only approved of and fostered his relationships with people who took their work less seriously than and were not so plodding as this clerk.

A critic who hated anything American was really speaking of his own forbidden incestuous wishes, telling us in effect that the more distant anything or anyone was, the more comfortable he felt with it. Another, in telling us that the only good composer was a dead composer, was telling us of his envy and jealousy of live composers, whom he saw as potential rivals. As a result, he could only give accolades to artists who were no threat because they were underground.

A psychobiographer convinced herself that all creativity springs from madness mostly as a way to demean the great people whom she envied by calling them insane. Her official position was that the composer Robert Schumann was mad and that his creativity occurred during periods of insanity and so was likely to be a product of that madness. To sustain this view she had to forget how little madness actually existed in Schumann's brilliant accomplishments. In effect, she had to prove that B originated in A, even when there was absolutely no evidence of A in B.

A disturbing aspect of some book reviews in medical journals is that reviewers excoriate writers for overlooking an obscure corner of their field. A writer says the equivalent of, "The field of characterology pays insufficient attention to a study of borderline disorder in children," and the critic attacks by quoting some obscure author who said that "some children are borderlines too." Then the critic concludes, "This book is not of value because the writer's expertise is limited." Often, such critics are merely enhancing their own self-esteem by putting others down and being impossible to please (to give others the distinct impression that they have high standards, critical perception, and royal prerogative).

Two individuals sent letters to radio stations. One's letters demanded, "Play the Top 40." The other's letters demanded, "Play something new." Both "critics" were not merely making an aesthetic statement. They were really parentalizing the announcers transferentially, as "if they owned them." They were acting like the announcers have a responsibility to feed them and that they have certain rights to be fed. If they did not get what they liked, enough of it, and when they wanted it, they felt justified in "biting mother's breast."

Audiences often react from their state of narcissistic transference, using another's performance as an opportunity to perform themselves. To illustrate, one might think that at a recent concert of modern music, after writhing in their seats through several "tuneless modern works" (as one member of the audience put it), the audience would greet the one tonal piece on the program with relief and pleasure. But instead the audience joylessly began tracing the work's ancestry—"stolen from this, taken from that."

This audience was no different from most. It usurped the composer's thunder with the sound of its own. It was there not to improve the composer's self-esteem. It was there to elevate its own.

In like manner, audiences on live television who boo often do so not to criticize the entertainment, but to attract the TV monitor to themselves. Audiences who hover around famous people are not really interested in them as people. They just want to say "I met you"—to gratify themselves or "make their day." They are like the cat who purrs not to say hello but in anticipation of being fed, or like the dog who wags the tail less to greet than in anticipation of a pleasurable pat on the head or a food treat. Such fans are too self-centered to not let the artist down eventually. Artists who expect otherwise are just another example of someone looking for love in all the wrong places.

The ordinary worker faced with such narcissistic transferences is in the position of the analyst hearing a patient's overwrought fantasies and emotions carried over from childhood. The worker, like the analyst, becomes the boss's giving or depriving mother or castrating father, without having earned or deserved much of it (and, unlike the analyst, without really knowing what to make of it or how to handle it).

But the ordinary worker forgets this and fails to consider the source. Instead he or she becomes uncomfortable and unsuccessful at work. Hands cramp at the computer keyboard. Or individuals retire completely from active work, figuratively or literally. They do so only in part because of their neurosis. Mostly they do so because of a neurosis belonging to someone else.

To avoid feeling criticized, workers must not see criticism originating in narcissistic transference as rational formulations, on target, and personally applicable. If a boss is threatened by and looks down on and walks all over a worker who does a job that is too good, that is the occasion to pity the boss, not to abuse oneself.

*Learning how to handle one's detractors.* Understanding one's detractors, and where they are coming from, is not enough. Workers also have to learn how to handle them. Not only should they not buy into what their detractors say (for the reasons just mentioned), but they should also avoid the temptation of trying to please them no matter what the cost. Pleasing others when it goes too far can be distracting, especially when it becomes an end in itself. It often involves compromising one's ideals, and when that goes beyond a certain point, it is no longer possible to maintain self-respect. It is a waste of time, for detractors usually do not want to be pleased. They want to detract. To remain on top, they have to discourage their underlings' self-improvement programs.

When used selectively and judiciously, assertiveness training can help many workers improve their self-esteem and lessen their guilt, by confronting and setting limits on others who are lowering their self-esteem and making them guilty. There is too much heat out there for most workers. The solution is not for them to yield to the heat and get out of life's kitchen. The solution is to make it hot for others so that *they* get out of *your* kitchen. They go. The worker stays behind and, in the vernacular, "keeps on cooking."

*Accepting a certain degree of failure as inevitable.* Workers should realize that a certain amount of failure is part of work. Counselors and their therapists should do what they can to help their patients/workers avoid failure when possible. At the same time, if workers do fail, counselors should do what they can to help them make the best of things and put the failure behind them. They should not participate with their patients in denying that failure has occurred (say, by overpromoting the idea of making lemonade out of the lemon). That idea is a good one, and many advisors advocate a version of it. But it can be an even better idea just to admit that lemonade *is*, after all, something less than lemon—as one patient put it, lemonade is "dilute lemon juice, plus too much sugar, missing some of the fiber and some of the zest." Instead of participating with workers in denying the negative meaning of failure, therapists should help them admit that failure has occurred and is not a good thing. Denial will only make it difficult to integrate the failure experience, which is part of the creative life. Admitting the problem allows the individual to grieve, integrate, and get over the experience while learning from one failure how to prevent another.

In summary, failure is part of working for a living, and depression is an appropriate response to failure. Conventional advice of the "make lemonade" variety sometimes leads workers to deny the ups and downs of a job and to see failure as a good setback, part of the beneficial learning process that is life. But it is better to feel bad when the situation is a bad one, as it is with many downsizings, and then get it over with and go on from there.

*Being fueled by success.* Low self-esteem often improves when there is a real reason to feel better—a real success in the here and now, or at least a promise of one in the future.

*Psychotherapy.* Therapists treating patients with low self-esteem must recognize how deeply ingrained low self-esteem can be. Because low self-esteem is not based on reality, it resists therapeutic methods that depend on testing reality (including the counterarguments of cognitive therapy). Because it runs deep, it resists even deep psychoanalysis. Sometimes what is required is treatment that uses the classic formal techniques in the setting of a supportive holding environment, in which the therapist both explores what is wrong (to remove problems) and constructively acknowledges what is right (to give the worker a needed shot in the arm).

In psychotherapy patients need to learn how to handle excessive anger. Excessive anger that goes unexpressed and is introjected is a main cause of the low self-esteem that is at the heart of depression. But it is not true that facing and expressing this anger, no matter what, is the best way to cure depression. Expressing anger can be unwise and should always be done carefully both in, and especially out of, therapy. There is a price to pay when patients leave the theoretical world of psychotherapy and go out into the real world and get their anger out with real people. Some feel guilty; and their victims get mad, and withdraw or counterattack. This starts a damaging vicious cycle. The angrier workers behave, the more people abandon them; the lonelier they feel, the more desperate and angry they become; the more anger there is to get out, the angrier they get and behave.

Two useful distinctions are (1) the difference between facing, exploring, and actually expressing one's anger; and (2) the difference between two kinds of anger—between inappropriate and appropriate anger (also discussed in Chapters 2 and 3).

The inappropriate kind of anger is excessive and unjustified:

A petty moralist condemned himself for very little and involved himself in people's lives when it was none of his business. As an example of his pettiness, he reported standing on the express line in the supermarket counting how many items he, or another shopper in front of him, had bought, and flying into a paroxysm of rage inside himself when it turned out to be more than the maximum allowed. Regretting and becoming guilty over his pettiness, he martyred himself, and flailed his skin, by compulsively starting to recount the items, hoping to come up with less than maximum, so that he did not have to get so painfully angry. This became an obsession, for he counted once and then he had to count again, hoping that his last count was wrong so that he could feel better inside. The same niggling anger appeared at work and made it difficult for him to function and enjoy his job. For example, he flew into a silent rage when a co-worker bent paper clips out of shape, played with the wire, and then threw the twisted mess away—he said, "*Wasteful* is my judgment about that."

He did not have to get his anger out. He had to stop angrily condemning himself and others for minor transgressions and infractions. Instead of condemning all concerned roundly, he had to start giving himself a vote of confidence and letting others off the hook, even when all concerned were behaving in a way that was somewhat less than perfect.

Expressing inappropriate anger at oneself and becoming inappropriately angry with and expressing it to others is unwise because something that is by definition inappropriate or excessive should also by definition be not expressed but should be resolved or suppressed. People simmering with anger at a neighbor's noisy leaf blower that disturbs concentration, at lovers who are trying to be supportive but do not seem as supportive as hoped, or at life in general (their fate, although acceptable or unavoidable, or their mortality, although inevitable) are wasting time and energy (in reality, chopping down the whole forest of their life to get at one of the unsightly trees). They are much too mired in strong angry feelings, and are feeling too guilty and regretful about them, to concentrate fully on their work.

Instead of blowing up at the boss for blue-penciling a proposal, they should first test reality by asking themselves two questions: "What else is the boss supposed to do if he or she doesn't like something?" and "What else could I have done so that he would like it better?". Second, if they feel angry they should work the anger out or keep the anger in until it goes away (i.e., swallow their pride now to avoid having to swallow the sword later).

The appropriate kind of anger, which reflects the way we would all feel in similar situations, is a different matter entirely. This anger should, at least theoretically, be expressed. It is natural and normal, and suppressing this anger is the unnatural and abnormal thing to do (especially when it is suppressed because of excessive guilt and the fear that others will depart at the first sign of a complaint). However, although it is abnormal to do so, it is not a bad idea to suppress appropriate anger, because expressing it can be more trouble than it is worth and can even be dangerous. Most of us realize that life comes down to a choice: between keeping our anger in, and keeping our friends; and getting our anger out, and losing them—even when our friends provoked the anger in the first place. (One man compared friends who make you angry and then find your anger intolerable to the circus promoter who wanted to promote his orangutan as the Wild Ape of Borneo. To make him wild, he banged on his cage and threw water in his face. Then he got rid of the ape because he was unmanageable.)

A possible compromise is not to express the anger but to refer to it, calmly and in a controlled fashion, and never solely to get it out, but also (or mainly) to resolve the problem that has created it.

> One artist angry with his wife for putting the daily newspaper down on the pilot light of the stove—an act which he felt threatened to burn down the house (and with it his computer and the only copies of his manuscripts)— decided the best way to handle his anger with his wife was first to ask her calmly, nicely, and in a controlled manner to please be more careful and second, to get insurance and make copies of his work, which he would store away from home. His goal was not to win battles, but to prevent a fire while keeping both a needed relationship and his manuscripts intact.

Most people are reasonable. They will listen and change if the patient is both assertive without being aggressive and assertive for a purpose—to make some much needed point and changes. Under these circumstances anger can be mentioned (but not actually expressed) if done in a way that is not offensive and does not alienate people such as sympathetic friends, whom we all need for positive feedback (to support us on the way up) and for a positive relationship (to console us on the way down).

Patients in therapy also need to learn how to handle their depression. As mentioned previously, internalized anger is a chief reason for depression, and internalized anger can be either of the inappropriate or appropriate kind—excessive or justified. In the first case, the anger is the problem; while in the second it is not the anger but either the circumstance creating the anger or the guilt about the anger that is the problem. Depressives suffer because of both kinds of anger. They get too angry unjustifiably, and they get too guilty about justified anger. Then they fail to distinguish the two and become more assertive when they are already too aggressive, or try not to make trouble when they are already too passive. Whether depressives are getting inappropriately angry when criticized constructively, or appropriately angry (and too guilty about it) when attacked gratuitously, they should usually deal with their anger—not by internalizing or abreacting it, but by negotiating with the individual who is perceived as being antagonistic. Depressives need people more than most people need people; so they have to be especially careful to clear the air, without ruining the relationship.

A depressive individual constantly complained of insomnia because her cat was annoying her by caterwauling in the middle of the night. She recognized that she could either continue to suffer from the noise and the resultant insomnia, work out her reactions to her cat in psychoanalysis, or take a moment to solve the problem by finding out what the cat wanted, and then give it to her, so that they could both get some rest. Instead of waking and staying up mad or taking her problems to her therapist, the patient, by simply pouring the cat a bowl of milk, was able to quiet the cat and go back to sleep.

# Bibliography

Abse, D. Wilfred. (1959). Hysteria. In Silvano Arieti (Ed.), *American handbook of psychiatry*, (pp. 272–292). New York: Basic Books.

American Psychiatric Association. (1994). *Diagnostic and statistical manual of mental disorders (DSM-IV)* (4th ed.). Washington, DC: American Psychiatric Association.

Atchity, Kenneth. (1986). *A writer's time: A guide to the creative process from vision through revision.* New York: Norton.

Beck, Aaron. (1985). Cognitive therapy. In Harold I. Kaplan & Benjamin J. Sadock (Eds.), *Comprehensive textbook of psychiatry/IV* (pp. 1432–1438). Baltimore, MD: Williams & Wilkins.

Bergler, Edmund. (1959). *100 homosexuals: Conspiracy of silence, or curing and deglamorizing homosexuals?* Paterson, NJ: Pageant

Berne, Eric. (1965). *Games people play.* New York: Grove Press.

Blakeslee, Sandra. (1995, September 26). Traffic jams in brain networks may result in verbal stumbles. *New York Times*, pp. C1, C9.

Blom, Eric. (1954). *Grove's dictionary of music and musicians.* New York: St. Martin's Press.

Christie, Agatha. (1977). *An autobiography.* New York: Berkley Books.

Condrau, Gion. (1988). Daseinsanalytic therapy with a patient suffering from compulsion neurosis and writer's cramp. *The American Journal of Psychoanalysis, 48*(3),211–220

Crouch, Tammy, & Madden, Michael. (1992). *Carpal tunnel syndrome and overuse injuries.* Berkeley, CA: North Atlantic Books.

Deutsch, Felix. (1959). *On the mysterious leap from the mind to the body.* New York: International Universities Press.

Eliot, George. (1964). *Middlemarch.* Reprint. New York: New American Library. (Original work published 1872.)

Fenichel, Otto. (1945). *The psychoanalytic theory of neurosis.* New York: Norton.

Freud, Sigmund. (1955). Analysis of a phobia in a five-year-old boy. In Collected papers (Vol. III) (Alix & James Strachey Trans.). London: Hogarth Press.

Freud, Sigmund. (1957). Some character-types met with in psycho-analytic work. In *Collected papers* (Vol. IV) (Alix & James Strachey, Trans.). (pp. 318–344). London: Hogarth Press.

Freudenberger, Herbert J. (with Geraldine Richelson). (1980). *Burn-out: The high cost of high achievement.* Garden City, NY: Anchor Press.

Gardner, Howard. (1993). *Creating minds.* New York: Basic Books.

Gedo, John E. (1989). *Portraits of the artist.* Hillsdale, NJ: The Analytic Press.

Gibbon, Edward. (1980). *The decline and fall of the Roman empire.* London: Viking Press. (Original work published 1776–1788).

Giovacchini, Peter. 1978. "Treatment of the Alienated Patient." In *New Perspective on Psychotherapy of the Borderline Adult.* Ed. James Masterson. New York: Brunner/Mazel.

Goldberg, Natalie. (1986). *Writing down the bones: Freeing the writer within.* Boston: Shambhala.

Goldberg, Natalie. (1990). *Wild mind: Living the writer's life.* New York: Bantam.

Haymen, Ronald. (1993). *Tennessee Williams. Everyone Else is an Audience.* New Haven: Yale University Press.

Hirschfeld, Robert M. A., & Shea, M. Tracie. Affective disorders: Psychosocial treatment. In Harold I. Kaplan & Benjamin J. Sadock (Eds.), *Comprehensive textbook of psychiatry/IV* Baltimore, MD: Williams & Wilkins.

Hugo, Victor. (1982). *Les miserables.* London: Penguin Classics. (Original work published 1862.)

Jamison, Kay Redfield. (1993). *Touched with Fire.* New York: The Free Press.

Jaynes, Gregory. (1995, September 25). Meet Mister Wizard. *Time* pp. 60–67.

Kahn, Jeffrey, P. (1993.) *Mental health in the workplace: A practical psychiatric guide.* New York: Van Nostrand Reinhold.

Kantor, Martin. (1988). *Determining mental status.* Chicago: Charles C. Thomas.

Kantor, Martin. (1990). *Problems and solutions.* New York: Praeger.

Kantor, Martin. (1992). *Diagnosis and treatment of the personality disorders.* St. Louis: Ishiyaku EuroAmerica.

Kantor, Martin. (1995). *Understanding writer's block.* Westport, CT: Praeger.

Kaplan, Betty. (1995, November 1). Dear Diary: Metropolitan Diary. *New York Times*, p. C2.

Kennedy, Michael. (1987). *Portrait of Elgar.* New York: Oxford University Press.

Kishlansky, Mark. (1996, January–February). *Serendipity and skepticism: The craft of writing history, from scholarship to potboilers. Harvard Magazine,* pp. 31–35.

Leader, Zachary. (1991). *Writer's block.* Baltimore, MD: The Johns Hopkins University Press.

Lee, Mathew H. M. (Ed.). (1989). *Rehabilitation, music, and human well-being.* St. Louis: MMB Music.

Lublin, Joann S. (1994, August 24). Managing your career: How to get around a boss who blocks your career path. *Wall Street Journal,* p. B1.

Lynch, Peter, & Rothchild, John. (1989). *One up on Wall Street: How to use what you know to make money in the market.* New York: Simon & Schuster.

McEvoy, Vicky. (1994, summer). The Crichton syndrome: From physician to writer (and back). *The Harvard Medical Alumni Bulletin.*

Melville, Herman. (1981). *Moby Dick.* New York: Bantam Books. (Original work published 1851.)

Minninger, Joan. (1980). *Free yourself to write*. San Francisco: Workshops for Innovative Teaching.

Nelson, Victoria. (1986). *Writer's block and how to use it*. Cincinnati: Writer's Digest Books.

Nemiah, John C. (1985). Phobic disorders (phobic neuroses). In Harold I. Kaplan & Benjamin J. Sadock (Eds.), *Comprehensive textbook of psychiatry/IV* (pp. 894–904). Baltimore, MD: Williams & Wilkins.

Orenstein, Arbie. (1991). *Ravel: Man and musician*. New York: Dover Publications.

Pascarelli, Emil, & Quilter, Deborah. (1994). *Repetitive strain injury: A computer user's guide*. New York: Wiley.

Perlmutter, Donna. (1994). "A Little Night Music" *New York Times*, pp. C1, C8.

Peter, Laurence J. & Hull, Raymond. (1969). *The Peter Principle: Why things always go wrong*. New York: William Morrow.

Rank, Otto. (1959). "The myth of the birth of the hero." In Philip Freund (Ed.), *The Myth of the birth of the hero and other writings*. (pp. 3–96). New York: Vintage Books.

Reich, Wilhelm. (1949). *Character-analysis*. New York: Orgone Institute Press.

Rothenberg, Albert. (1990). *Creativity and madness: New findings and old stereotypes*. Baltimore, MD: The Johns Hopkins University Press.

Schuman, Elliott P. (1981). A writing block treated with modern psychoanalytic interventions. *Psychoanalytic Review*, *68*(1), 113–134.

Stoudemire, G. Alan. (1988). Somatoform disorders, factitious disorders, and malingering. In John A. Talbott, Robert A. Hales, & Stuart C. Yudofsky (Eds.), *The American Psychiatric Press textbook of psychiatry*. (pp. 533–556). Washington, DC: American Psychiatric Press.

Thompson, Oscar. (1964). *The international cyclopedia of music and musicians*. New York: Dodd, Mead & Co.

Wilson, Lawrence. (1994). Erskine Caldwell: A Biography. Review. *The Key Reporter*, p. 10.

Winston, Arnold, Pinsker, Henry, & McCullough, Leigh. (1986). A review of supportive psychotherapy. *Hospital and Community Psychiatry*, *37*(11), 1105–1114.

# Index

Abreaction, complications of, 218–219

Abse, Wilfred, 17, 18

Absolutistic, dichotomous thinking, 192, 200–201

Abuse, as source of low self-esteem, 232

Acting out, of one's distorted self-image, 236–237

Adjustment Disorder, 5, 129, 134

Advice: giving, considerations in, 216; simplistic, 208

Affairs (promiscuity), defensive, 177

Affect: depressive, 47–49; in conversion disorder, 17–18

Ageism, 146; and depression, 45

Alarmists, 63–64

Alcoholic polyneuropathy, 27

Ancestral (Jungian) dreams, 184–185

Anger: appropriate, 19, 241, 242; dealing with, in depression, 52; and depression, vicious cycling between, 48–49; in depression, 48–49; excessive, handling of, 240–241; as a factor in somatoform disorder, 16; fear of expressing, 224; getting out, complications of, 218–219; handling anxiety over, 60; handling, in obsessive-compulsives, 97; inappropriate, 19, 241–242; irrational (unprovoked), 168–169; rational (provoked), 168–169

Anhedonia: in Schizoid Personality Disorder, 108; in Schizophrenia, 106

Antibodies (emotional, reacting to emotional antigens), 64

Antigens (emotional, making one's job antigenic), 64

Anxiety: equivalents, in anxiety disorder, 14; syndrome, physical manifestations of, 34–35; treatment of, 68–69

Anxiety occupational disorder, 59–69, 193

Appropriate anger. *See* Anger, appropriate

Arthritis, 29, 33

As-if (chameleon-like) personality disorder, 218

Assertiveness training, 209, 239

Associations, with new people, as way to treat phobia, 78

Asthma, as manifestation of psychosomatic disorder, 13

Atavistic origin of guilt, 236. *See also* Guilt

Attention Deficit Disorder, pseudoneurological, 27–28

Attitudinal disturbance, as cause of cognitive error, 202–204

Authority: diminishing, as way to handle stage fright, 82; parentalizing of, 170–171

Autism, in schizophrenia, 106

Autosuggestion, 24; and regression of conversion symptoms, 20

Avoidance, defense of, against anxiety, 61

Avoidant Personality Disorder, 67, 108, 192

Avoidant workers, 62

Back pain, 29, 175; and downsizing, 226

Barber, Samuel, 48

Beethoven, Ludwig van, 113, 195

Behavior, depressive withdrawal, 50

Bergler, Edmund, 49

Berne, Eric, 96

Blakeslee, Sandra, 91

Blindness, conversion, 20

Blockogenic: people (people who cause block), 222

Borderline Personality Disorder, in workplace, 1, 4, 19, 110, 216

Borodin, Alexander, 235

Borodin Block, in obsessive-compulsives, 95

Boss: career-busting, 118, 134, 222; humiliating, 19; incompetent, 56; passive-aggressive, 143–144

Brahms, Johannes, 113

Bridge phobia, 72, 85

Browning, John, 230

Bruckner, Anton, 48

Bureaucracies, effect of on workers, 220

Bureaucrat, 140, 151; creation of, by bureaucracies, 220

Burnout, 58, 128–129, 160, 178, 194, 197; conversion, 28–29; exhaustion as symptom of, 28–29; fatigue as symptom of, 29; and Inadequate Personality Disorder, 2; sexual interest, decreased, as symptom of, 29; versus depletion, 127; versus depression, 2, 129

Caldwell, Erskine, 207

Carpal Tunnel Syndrome, 15, 114, 197–198, 225; description of, 26; imitative, 25; physical versus emotional, 27; in Schizophrenia, 35

Carter, Michael, 201

Cause and effect, confusing. See Figure = ground, cognitive error of

Causes of anxiety, 62–66; external causes, 62–63; internal causes, 63–66

Changing profession, as way to handle phobia, 80

Chemical imbalance, and depression, 52

Christie, Agatha, 76, 224

Chronic fatigue, 28–29

Chronic Fatigue Syndrome, 5, 51, 160; questionable case of, 18

Chronic pain, and secondary gain, 226

Classification of Personality Disorders Occupational Disorder, 105

Claustrophobia, 72

Cliburn, Van, 230

Clumsiness, in Repetitive Strain Injury/Carpal Tunnel Syndrome, 26

Cognitive errors, 68, 191–205; in depression, 49–50; in obsessives, 93; as source of guilt, 235. See also individual cognitive errors

Cognitive therapy, 191–205

Comparisons with others, as source of low self-esteem, 229–230

Competitiveness, hysterical, 136, 137–140

Computer, fear of, 61, 67, 72, 193

Condreau, Gion, 20

Conflict-free ego, 216

Conscience, as source of guilt, 235

Controlling obsessives, 91. See also Tyrannical obsessives

Conversion disorder, 2, 23–29; conversion Attention Deficit Disorder, 13; conversion Carpal Tunnel Syndrome, 13; conversion Repetitive Strain Injury, 13, 16; conversion Writer's Cramp, 13; diagnosis of, 15–20; differential diagnosis of, 20; dynamic/developmental features of, 18; ontogenetic explanation of, 25; phylogenetic explanation of, 25; versus depression, 51, 55

Corporations, sick, 148–152
Counterphobic mechanisms, healthy, developing, as treatment of phobia, 79
Countertransference diagnosis, making a, 19–20
Co-workers, hostile, 6
Cramp: of hand, 239; occupational, 24–25
Creative block. *See* Writer's Block
Criticism, as a cause of depression, 40–41
Critics: similar = the same thing, aesthetics of, 198
Crouch, Tammy, 26

DaCosta's syndrome (cardiac palpitations), 62
Delusions, in Schizophrenia, 106
Denial: compromised insight and, 214; defense against anxiety, 60
De novo, development of conversions, 24
Depletion, 127–128; false, due to inhibition, 128
Depression, 37–58, 160, 191, 201–202; anger and, 60, 169; burnout and, 5, 28; as cause of back pain, 18–19; as cause of being downsized, 3; as cause of cognitive error, 202; as cause of headaches, 18–19; cognitive error causing, 192; equivalents, 18–19; exogenous factors in, 38–47; low self-esteem and guilt, dealing with in, 243; making the diagnosis of, 37; misdiagnosis of, 197; and pain, 30, 35; physical manifestations of, 51; somatic delusions in, 35; treatment of, 51–55
Depressive symptoms: differential diagnosis of, 37; versus depressive disorder, 37
Depressives, 67, 122; countertransference reaction to, 20; in group therapy, 216

Depressogenic individuals, 222
Dereism, in schizophrenia, 106
Detractors, handling one's, 239
Deutsch, Felix, 12, 24
Diabetic polyneuropathy, 27
Diagnosis, need to make an adequate, 160–161
Dickinson, Emily, 201
Disorientation, as symptom of burnout, 28, 29
Displacement: defense against anxiety, 61; and Obsessive-Compulsive Disorder, 92
Diurnal variation, in depression, 50
Diworseification, of Lynch and Rothchild, 2, 50
Doing and undoing: defense against anxiety, 60; in obsessive-compulsives, 94
Double-bind, as a cause of depression, 40
Downsizing, 6, 72, 133, 161, 240; and back pain, 226; as endogenous problem, 224; handling, 218; provoking one's own, 220;
Dream analysis, 178–188; technique of, 187–188
*DSM-IV,* 13, 23, 32, 134, 160; generative disorders, 5, 226; making proper *DSM-IV* diagnosis, 215–216; nonsomatoform *DSM-IV* disorders included with somatoform, 13; overlooks work disorders, 1
Dystonia, 20, 26

Eclectic: therapists, definition of, 162; treatment approach, 7, 161
Ego, guilt formation in, 235. *See also* Cognitive errors
Ego therapy, 207
Elgar, Sir Edward, 182–183; 197
Eliot, George, 45
Endogenous depression, 47–51
Envy, 201. *See also* Hysterical personality disorder

Epidemic hysteria, 24
Epstein-Barr (Chronic Fatigue Syndrome), 2, 197, 217. *See also* Chronic Fatigue Syndrome
Ergonomic (nonergonomic) computer keyboard, 15
Errors, of therapy, in depression, 52–53
Evolutionary reasons for phobia, 76
Excessophilia, 183
Exhaustion. *See* Burnout
Exhibitionism, and overconcern with others' reactions, 102–103
Existential dream analysis, 166, 178, 187
Exogenous and endogenous depression, importance of distinguishing, 56
Exogenous and endogenous disorder, different therapy for, 6, 219–221
Exogenous factors contributing to depression, 38–47
Exogenous (reactive) occupational disorders, 133–156
Externalization (projection), as part of personalization, 198–199

Facts, fighting back with, 155–156
Factitious disorders: 30–32; *DSM-IV* definition of, 13
Failure: accepting, 240; desirable, 182, 236; fear of, 66, 177–178, 224; in obsessives, 93
Family therapy, 210–211
Father, competitive, 170–171
Fatigue. *See* Burnout
Fatigue, depressive, 51
Fenichel, Otto, 166
Fetish, occupational, 102
Fight, as a treatment method, 155–156; self-destructive, 176–177
Figure = ground, cognitive error of, 201–202
Fired, being, 60, 72
Flashbacks, 14, 35
Flight, as a treatment method, 155; self-destructive, 176–177

Flooded, fear of being, 66
Flooding, 129; as complication of insight therapy, 216; in schizophrenia, 106–107
Fluoxetine, 197; causing paranoia, 54
Four A's (in dealing with blockogenics), 223–224
Freud, Sigmund, 92, 178
Freudenberger, Herbert J., 28–29
Freudian Dream Analysis, 166–167, 178, 179
Freudian slip, 64, 200

Garlic personality disorder, 105, 136
Gastric reflux, 13
Gastritis, 11
Gibbon, Edward, 7
Gide, Andre, 156
Giovacchini, Peter, 162
Gould, Glenn, 142
Grandiosity: in obsessives, 88–89; protective, as defense in phobia, 80; in Schizophrenia, 107
Grief, 43–44
Group therapy, 216
Grown-up, fear of being, 75
Guilt, 64–66, 75, 209, 234–236; creation by parents, 174; about defying parents, 175; developmental origin of, 236; about hostility, 66, 84; instinctual, 64; leading to masochism, 121–122; oedipal, 236; originating in sibling rivalry, 236; sexual, 66, 177; about success, 64, 236; survivor, 64, 75, 236; treatment of, 236–243; unconscious (inappropriate) versus conscious (appropriate), 235; zero-sum, 64

Haley, Jay, 81
Hallucinations, in schizophrenia, 106
Hand cramp, due to guilt, 235
Hand pain, as the result of being criticized by boss, 25

Hand syndrome: conversion, 19; depressive, 51; difference between emotional and physical, 197–198; emotional causes for, 5, 224; as part of dependency, 22

Hans, Little, case of Freud, 92

Harm, fear of bodily, as reason for phobia, 73

Hawthorne, Nathaniel, 111, 230

Hayman, Ronald, 96

Headaches, 2; depressive, 51; as manifestation of psychosomatic disorder, 13; provoked by others, 19–20; as symptom of burnout, 28, 29; tension, 175

Herd phenomenon, 33

"Hiatus hernia," as psychophysiological conversion, 29

High standards, excessiveness of, 230–231. See also Perfectionism

Hirschfeld, Robert M. A., 50

Home life, as source of stress, 135

Horowitz, Vladimir, 25

Hugo, Victor, 6, 137

Hull, Raymond, 56

Humility, false, fighting back with, 155

Humor, as a way to deal with perfectionism, 89

Hypersensitivity, 199; as source of low self-esteem, 234

Hypesthesia, conversion, 20

Hypochondriasis, 13, 22, 33–34

Hypomania, 177, 216; as cause of cognitive error, 203

Hysterical (Histrionic) Personality Disorder, 105, 110–111, 137–140

Hysterics: in group therapy, 216; countertransference reaction to, 20

Identification: as cause of cognitive error, 202; as cause of Conversion Disorder, 24–25

Identification figures, therapists serving as positive, 81

Identifying, with the aggressor, as cure of depression, 46

Imperfection: normal, 201; learning to accept, 204

Impotence, 180–181

Impulsiveness, in Schizophrenia, 107

Inadequate Personality Disorder, 2

Inappropriate anger, 241–242. See also Anger

Increasing self-esteem, mechanism of, as treatment of phobia, 80–82

Indecisiveness, as a defense against anxiety, 65

Indecisive obsessives, 87. See also Perfectionistic obsessives

Individual contribution to occupational disorder, 167–169

Infantilism, in schizophrenia, 107

Injustice collecting, 67

Insight: criticizing patients with, 162–163, 209; deep, developing, 236; excessive use of in psychotherapy, 162–163, 208; insight-oriented treatment, 166; superficial, developing, 236

Instincts, as a source of guilt, 235

Instinctual conflict, 165

Internalization (introjection), as part of personalization, 199

Introjection: compromised insight and, 215; as a way to deal with reality in depressives, 67

Introjects, poisonous, 68

Job dissatisfaction, 119–123; as a cause of emotional disorder, 16; reactive, versus endogenous, 121–123

Jungian Dream Analysis, 166–167, 184–187

Kahn, Jeffrey, 159

Karasek, Robert, 17

La belle indifference, in Conversion Disorder, 17–18

Lack of talent, dealing with, 227

Laziness, and burnout, 28

Leader, Zachary, 48, 166
Learning disability, emotional, 28
Lists, making, and using, for obses-
    sive-compulsives, 98–99
Loss, as a cause of depression, 41–44
Loss of self-esteem, 66
Low back pain, 13
Low IQ, as a factor in the Somatoform
    Disorders, 14
Low self-esteem, 177; depressive,
    204; handling, 229–243; in
    phobias, 83; treatment of,
    236–243
Lublin, Joann S., 222
Lucire, Yolande, 16
Lynch, Peter, 2, 50

Madden, Michael, 26
Magnification: cognitive error of, 193,
    199–200, 203; originating in low
    self-esteem, 200
Mahler, Gustav, 194, 195
Maladaptive defenses, dealing with, 67
Malingering, 32–33; as accusation
    rather than diagnosis, 20; as
    DSM-IV V-code, 13
Mania, 50
Mantra, 210; defensive, for obsessives,
    89
Masochism, 5, 115–118, 127; as part of
    hypochondriasis, 34; as source
    of low self-esteem, 234
Masochists, 115–117
Medical diagnosis, incorrect, based on
    cognitive error, 197–198
Meditation, 210. See also Zen
Melville, Herman, 48, 230; comparing
    self to Hawthorne, 111; factual
    error in Moby Dick, 193
Mental manifestations of endogenous
    depression, 47–50
Mental status evaluation, diagnostic,
    17–18
Meticulousness, 171
Minimization, compromised insight
    and, 215

Miscalculation, as source of low self-
    esteem, 234
Moby Dick, error in, 193
Mood disorder, as cause of cognitive
    error, 202–203
Morality, scrupulous, 200
Mother, smothering, 170–174
Mozart, Wolfgang, 111
Murphy's cognitive error, 192
Myths, in treating depression, 57–58

Narcissism, 122; bad (self-referen-
    tial), 203–204; as cause of cog-
    nitive error, 202–204; effective,
    111–112; excessive, in stage
    fright, 83–84; good, 203; inef-
    fective, 111; lack of, in stage
    fright, 83
Narcissistic entitlement, and malin-
    gering, 33
Narcissistic Personality Disorder,
    111–112, 140
Negative stressors, 135–148
Nonassertiveness (Zen removal),
    209–210
Non-DSM-IV occupational disorders,
    125–129
Nonverbal expression, somatoform
    symptoms and, 14
Numbness, 23; due to pressure on the
    nerve, 27; in Carpal Tunnel Syn-
    drome/Repetitive Strain Injury,
    26; in Conversion Disorder, 27

Obsessive-Compulsive Occupational
    Disorder, 60, 87–99
Obsessive-Compulsive Personality
    Disorder, 147–148
Obscurity, defensive, 177
Obsessiveness due to absolutistic
    thinking, 192
Oedipal fantasies, and conflicts, in
    conversions, 24
Oedipus, problems with analyzing,
    118
Old age, 77–78; and depression, 44–45

Older workers, 61–62
Onion personality disorder, 105
Originality, fetishistic, 231
Out of date, feeling, as a symptom of depression, 46–47
Overgeneralization, 199
Overload, 125–127

Pain: as depressive equivalent, 35; as psychophysiological conversion, 29; organic versus psychological, 30; syndrome, 19, 33
Paradoxical inertia. See Stubborn mind
Parameter, in treatment of phobia, 78
Paranoia, 109, 192, 194, 216; causing cognitive error of magnification, 204; causing cognitive error of some = all, 204; and computer bugs, 201; due to blaming others for one's problems, 202; and hypersensitivity, 199; and not-me, 224–225; in Schizophrenia, 107; treating hypersensitivity in, 204–205
Paranoid Personality Disorder, 107–108, 136, 160
Paranoid workers, 62; in group therapy, 216
Parents, introjection of, and identification with, 170, 173
Paresthesias, 23, 24; in Carpal Tunnel Syndrome, 26, 27; in Repetitive Strain Injury, 26
Part = whole, cognitive error of, 194
Pascarelli, Emil, 2, 16–17
Passive-aggressive: defense, fighting back and, 155; getting back at authority by workers, 176
Passive-Aggressive Personality Disorder, 114–115, 141–144
Passive-Dependent Personality Disorder, 112–114, 140
Passivity, as possible cause of "malingering," 33
Perfect, need to be, as part of stage fright, 83

Perfectionism, 127, 194, 201, 231
Perfectionistic obsessives, 87–89, 94
Performance anxiety, tricks in getting over, 84
Personality Disorders, 5, 105–118, 216
Personalization, cognitive error of, 198–199
Peter, Laurence J., 56
Peter Principle, 56, 134–135, 167, 186
Pharmacotherapy (medication): for stage fright, 85; in depression, 53–55
Phobia of driving, 182
Phobic hump, getting over, in relieving Writer's Block, 79
Phobic Occupational Disorder, 71–85
Physical manifestations of nonsomatoform DSM-IV disorders, 34–35
Placental Characters, 112
Positive stressors, 134–135
Posttraumatic Stress Disorder: 31, 32–33, 129, 134; and burnout, 5; flashbacks in, 14; malingered, 33; and physical symptoms, 35
Praise, as a way to relieve occupational inhibition, 103
Primal scene observation, 186
Primary gain, dealing with, 226–227
Projection, 67; compromised insight and, 215; defense against anxiety, 60–61; in Paranoid Personality Disorder, 107–108
Psoriatic arthritis without the psoriasis, 12
Psychodynamic (psychoanalytic) treatment approach, 165–189
Psychopathy (Psychopathic/Antisocial Personality Disorder), 105, 109–110, 136–137, 209; as possible cause of malingering, 33
Psychophysiological conversions, 29
Psychosomatic disorder, 13, 29
Psychotherapy, for guilt and low-self esteem, 240–243
Put-down, parental, 170

Quilter, Deborah, 2–3, 16–17
Quintet, dynamic, 172

Racism, 145
Rationalization: compromised insight
    and, 214–215; and defenses
    against anxiety, 61–62
Ravel, Maurice, 111
Reality, and real fears, 75
Reality check, fighting back with,
    155–156
Reality testing, 205, 207
Red pepper personality disorder,
    105–106
Reich, Wilhelm, 3, 116
Rejection: as a cause of depression,
    41; fear of, 66, 74–76; in writers,
    224
Repetitive Strain Injury, 15–17, 18, 58,
    116, 224; anger, due to, 3; cogni-
    tive error and, 192; computer
    keyboard, and, 2; conflict and,
    168; conversion disorder and, 2,
    5; description of, 26; diagnostic
    descriptive characteristics of,
    27; differential diagnosis of, 27,
    197–198; emotionally-induced,
    115; imitative, 25; pain in, as
    manifestation of pain disorder,
    13; physical, 12; physical versus
    emotional, 27; pianist's cramp
    and, 26; Quilter's discussion of,
    16–17; treatment of, based on
    cause, 220; Writer's Cramp and,
    1. See also Hand syndrome
Repression, defense against anxiety, 60
Resistances, transference, in obses-
    sive-compulsives, 95
Resistant obsessives, 89–91
Resolving conflict, as way to treat en-
    dogenous disorder, 226
Restitutive behaviors, antitherapeutic,
    in depression, 46
Retirement, arguments against, 46
Rolfing, 116
Rothenberg, Albert, 166

Sadism: as part of hypochondriasis,
    34; toward older people, 44–45
Sadists, 115; dealing with, 117–118, 147
Sadomasochistic Personality Disorder,
    115–117, 144–147; treatment of,
    117–118
Saint-Saëns, (Charles) Camille, 195
Schadenfreude, 144
Schizoid Personality Disorder, 108
Schizophrenia, 106–108; avoiding
    antidepressants in, 54; as cause
    of physical symptoms, 35; as
    possible cause of "malinger-
    ing," 33
Schizotypal Personality Disorder, 105,
    108–109, 216
Schuman, Elliott P., 159
Schumann, Robert, 116, 142, 238
Secondary gain, dealing with, 226–227
Selective inattention, cognitive error
    of, 201
Self-acceptance, as cure of depres-
    sion, 46
Self-esteem, low, 75; in depression, 48;
    in Schizophrenia, 106;
Self-help books, simplistic, based on
    cognitive error, 198
Self-improvement, fighting back with,
    156
Sexual and occupational inhibitions,
    matching, 101–102
Sexual disorders, 101–103
Sexual harassment, as counterphobic
    mechanism, 79–80
Sexual promiscuity, 177
Sexuality, fear of expressing, 224
Shame, as source of low self-esteem,
    231–232
Shyness, as a cause of occupational
    disorder, 16
Sick role, 14, 15
Similar = the same thing (cognitive er-
    ror of), 191–193, 194–198, 201,
    236; diagnosis based on cogni-
    tive error of, 197–198; treatment,
    based on cognitive error of, 198

Slips of the tongue, 188
Society, sick, 148–152
Somatic: delusion, in Depression, 13, 35; delusion, in Schizophrenia, 13; equivalents, in Dysthymic Disorder, 13; manifestations of nonsomatoform disorders, 13
Somatization disorder, 13, 20–23, 29
Somatoform Disorder, 11–35; classification of, 13–14
Somatoform scenario, 11–12
Some = all, cognitive error of, 68, 193, 203, 236; and burnout, 194; and depression, 191; and self-condemnation, 193
Stage fright, 173, 176, 200, 203, 223; anxiety and, 59; description of, 83; displacement and, 61; due to insufficient good narcissism, 204; external cause of, 62; negative self-attitude and, 82; physical hold of on speaker, 76; rationalization of, 61; and relationship to mother, 173; and superstition, 76; treating, 82–85; treating with pharmacotherapy, 85
Stocking (sock) and glove anesthesia, 27
Stoudemire, G. Alan, 11, 14–15, 17, 18
Stress, 198; creating imaginary, 68; dealing with, on-the-job, 152
Stubborn mind, 90–91
Stubbornness, 28; in obsessive-compulsives, 89–91, 94
Stubborn obsessives, 89–91
Substitution, defense against anxiety, 61
Success, fear of, 110–111, 135, 136, 181–182, 224; and masochism, 2; suffering and, 5. See also Successophobia
Success, fueling success, 240
Success guilt, 122. See also Success, fear of; Successophobia
Successophobia, 73, 75, 234–235. See also Success, fear of

Suggestion: as a characteristic of conversion hysteria, 16; as cause of conversion symptoms, 20
Superstitiousness, 76
Supportive therapy, 207–211; of depression, 41–42
Supraconscious, 197

Tooth pain, 29
Tendonitis, 5, 12; Quilter's discussion of, 16
Tennis elbow, 12
Theorell, Torres, 17
Thesis block, 66
Thinking = doing, cognitive error of, 192
Thompson, Oscar, 198
Thought, disordered in depression, 49–50
Traffic jams in brain networks, 91
Transference: cognitive errors in, as resistances, 205; cure of phobia, 81; diagnosis, making a, 19–20; narcissistic, as source of criticism, 237–239; problems, in treatment of obsessive-compulsives, 93–97
Transferential aesthetics, of critics, 153
Treatment: of cognitive errors, 204–205; of endogenous disorder, 224–227; of exogenous disorder, 221–224; overview of, 159–163
Treatment, safe, 213
Treatment techniques: dealing with abuse and, 153–154; and psychopaths, 233; source, considering the, 45, 51, 56, 77, 237–239
Tu quoque defense, fighting back and, 155
Typist's cramp, 115, 145
Tyrannical (controlling) obsessives, 91–92

Underlings, hostile, 6
Undifferentiated somatoform disorder, 23

Undoing, as a defense against anxiety, 65
Unwarranted low self-esteem versus warranted low self-esteem, 229

V-Codes, 134
Vicious cycling, in depression, 50
Violence, 181

Wagman, Richard, Dr., 54
Wall Street Journal, 222
Weltuntergang (delusions of world decay), 192
Whiplash, 26, 32
Why Don't You—Yes But, Obsessive-Compulsive game of, 96

Williams, Tennessee, 96
Withdrawal, as symptom of depression, 50
Workaholism, 28, 125, 143; confused with creativity, 195; and fear of failure, 177–178
Writer's Block, 60, 120, 192, 224, 226; books on, 2; and cognitive error, 196–197; in obsessives, 95; overdiagnosis of, 197; that is not depressive, 197
Writer's Cramp, 18, 23, 60, 175; conversion, 1, 26; differential diagnosis of, 15; trick for overcoming, 20

Zen, 209–210

## About the Author

MARTIN KANTOR is Clinical Assistant Professor of Psychiatry at the University of Medicine and Dentistry of New Jersey. He is the author of a half dozen books, including *The Human Dimension of Depression* (Praeger, 1992), and *Understanding Writer's Block* (Praeger, 1995).

ISBN 0-275-95529-X

90000>

EAN

9 780275 955298

HARDCOVER BAR CODE